Lower-limb Tendinopathy

(Achilles, Patellar, Hamstring and Gluteal)

by Daniel Lawrence

First published in 2018 by Physio Books Ltd

Lower-limb Tendinopathy/Daniel Lawrence. 1st ed.
ISBN: 9781980872559

To my sons, Oliver and Lucas. You provided the motivation and support for me to write this book, even though you were largely unaware of the project. I wanted to show you what you can achieve in life with a little passion, belief, and dedication.

Contents

Preface

Lower-limb Tendinopathy provides a comprehensive guide to lower-limb tendon problems using a blend of clinical experience and the latest research from over 300 individual scientific studies. After the introductory chapter on *Tendon Anatomy*, and chapters on *Evolutionary Biology* (Chapter 2) and *Tendon Pathology* (Chapter 3), the four main tendinopathies of the lower limb (Chapters 4–7) have been given dedicated chapters, along with chapters focusing on *Biomechanics* (Chapter 8), *Strength and Conditioning Principles* (Chapter 9) and Gait Manipulation (Chapter 10). With a total of 16 chapters, the book covers a wide range of subjects. If fast facts and clinical tips are needed, these can be found in the assessment and rehabilitation guidelines in *Appendix 1*. These guidelines and other clinical resources are available to download from the website supporting the book (www.PhysioBooks.com).

The book begins by detailing tendon structure from a macroscopic to a cellular level. The structural continuity between tendon and muscle units is also discussed, highlighting the fact that the tendon forms part of a unit and should not be isolated by the scientific tendency to deconstruct and "zoom in" on problem areas.

Before diving into the detailed pathology of tendinopathy, the book invites the reader to take a moment to think about human evolution, bipedalism, tendons, and why we are shaped the way we are. This short chapter raises some interesting questions before we get started.

Many well-known tendinopathy experts have written about tendon pathology over the last 10 years. The main processes are fundamentally non-inflammatory, but there is still an undertone of pro-inflammatory research available.

Loading programmes are considered the gold standard of management. Since Alfredson published his groundbreaking protocol for Achilles tendinitis, experts and researchers have battled with eccentric versus concentric exercise. Once again, this comparative emphasis has distracted researchers and practitioners, and negated the need to consider simple, time-tested exercise principles, needs analysis, and the real-life problem of exercise adherence. Chapter 9 on *Strength and Conditioning Principles* discusses how the tendon forms part of the connective tissue network, why heavy resistance training is important for endurance athletes, and how to individually programme for and progress your patients without following a rigid one-size-fits-all protocol.

While research does not provide a clear correlation between running style and tendinopathy, it is fast becoming an area of increasing interest for therapists who specialise in treating runners. Once again, zooming out from problem areas, we can appreciate that the way we move is a key factor for injury risk. We often explain to patients the notion of "overuse", but perhaps in many cases it may be an issue of "wrong use". Poor movement patterns, bad landing mechanics, and running form all play a part in the balanced, non-injurious absorption of force. Chapter 10 on *Gait Manipulation* frames the argument for a potential missing link in the treatment of tendinopathy against the backdrop of recent research and advances some clear methods for putting theory into practice. Even without a treadmill and a camera, the practitioner can offer some simple advice to patients based on sensible movement principles. The research for this chapter was both fascinating and entertaining. Minimalist running is also discussed.

Among the new trends and treatments, the simple effective power of hands-on massage should not be overlooked.

The therapy profession has a habit of constantly needing to progress even without reason or, alternatively, to rebrand and repackage old modalities and techniques and give them new names. For example, massage became soft tissue release and now perhaps fascial manipulation. Whatever the name and however it is delivered, the fact remains that massage is one of the oldest treatment modalities. Chapter 11 (*Massage for Tendon Pain*) details some great techniques for reducing tendon pain.

Taping, as discussed in Chapter 12, offers a fast and simple way to modulate pain for many soft tissue conditions. The chapter highlights some simple and effective techniques specifically for tendon pain.

The chapters on *Extracorporeal Shockwave Therapy* (Chapter 13) and *Regenerative Biomedicine* (Chapter 14) may have futuristic-sounding titles but they ask the simple question "Are these treatments really advancing the medical management of tendinopathy?" Some unusual tendinopathy treatments are also reviewed in these chapters.

This book and supporting resources bring together the current research and best practice for managing lower-limb tendinopathy in a clear and clinically useful way. The book contains information and guidance for therapists less familiar with current research. It also offers a concise summary for more experienced clinicians.

I sincerely hope you enjoy this book and find it interesting. Most importantly, I hope your patients benefit as a result.

Daniel Lawrence MCSP

Acknowledgements

Thank you to my wife for maintaining her interest in my imaginary book for almost seven years. If you are reading this now, it means I have actually finished! ☺

Judy Lawrence being one of the illustrators was not a coincidence. Thank you mum, for your unwavering support and patience when drawing strange pictures for me!

Unfortunately, my father passed away in 2010 but I know he would be very proud; he taught me how to work hard by example.

Sonia Cutler, medical copy-editor. Sonia was the first professional to assist me with bringing this book to publication. I learnt a lot from working with her and was amazed by her attention to detail and the volume of grammatical corrections she was able to highlight. A very important member of my publishing team. I will work with Sonia again in the future.

Judy Lawrence & Abdul Mannan, illustrators.

David Redondo, typesetter and designer.

Tomis Kalmar and Kim Lawrence, models. Tom and Kim star in most of the photographs throughout the book.

CHAPTER 1

TENDON ANATOMY

INTRODUCTION

Tendons are found throughout the body in different forms. Some are flat, some are round, and some are both because their shape changes throughout the length of the tendon. The small tendons of the hands and feet are often separated into thin slips, with sheets of pearly white fibrous tissue (aponeurosis) taking the place of tendons and connecting muscles with the parts they move. Most tendons connect muscle to bone, but intramuscular tendons connecting muscle to muscle also exist throughout the body. Although there is much variation among tendons, the internal components are much more consistent. This chapter outlines the important anatomical features that make up a tendon.

The Achilles tendons are the largest tendons in the body and their shape changes from a flat aponeurosis proximally to a cord-like structure distally. They are important tendons in the field of anatomy, injury prevention, and rehabilitation and much of the literature has focused on them. This chapter provides a general anatomical overview.

TENDON MICROANATOMY

Tendons that wrap around bones and joints have a synovial sheath to maintain their position and reduce friction. An example of this in the lower limbs are the fibularis tendons that are sheathed as they bend around the lateral malleolus. In the larger tendons, fatty areolar tissue typically fills the space between the tendon and its sheath; the paratenon, which is often termed a false tendon sheath, allows free movement against the surrounding structures. Tendon microanatomy is shown in **Figure 1.1** below.

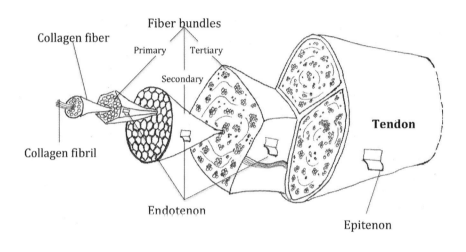

FIGURE 1.1   Tendon microanatomy. The structural contents of a typical tendon, from outermost layer to individual collagen fibril.

The Achilles paratenon is a continuation of the muscle fascia that covers the tendon and blends with the periosteum of the calcaneus. The internal paratenon is lined with synovial cells that communicate with the outer surface of the tendon, the epitenon. The paratenon and the epitenon are often referred to as the peritenon. Adhesions or swelling within the peritenon space is a likely cause of the morning stiffness and crepitus commonly associated with many tendinopathies. Within the tendon, collagen fibres are arranged into fibre bundles (fascicles), enveloped and separated by a thin network of connective tissue called the endotenon. Blood vessels, nerves, and lymphatic vessels are present within the endotenon network. The fascicles can slide independently within the tendon; this helps to transmit tension when joint angles change (Fallon et al., 2002). Fascicles and fibrils also slide under tension to allow a degree of tendon lengthening under the control of the proteoglycans (PGs) that bind them together (Puxkandl et al., 2002) and allow the elastic properties of tendon deformation and recoil.

COLLAGEN

Tendons consist of collagen and elastin embedded in a proteoglycan water matrix known as the ground substance of the extracellular matrix (ECM). The ground substance is an amorphous, gel-like intercellular material in which fibril-forming collagen, PGs, and glycoproteins are embedded. Collagen accounts for between 65 and 80% of tendon dry mass (Kannus, 2000). Tendon collagen is mainly type I collagen with a small amount of type III found mainly in the endotenon network. The presence of type III collagen increases with chronic tendinopathy. The function of elastin is not well understood, but it may assist in the recoil of the wavy collagen configuration (Butler et al., 1978), thereby promoting recovery of the wavy collagen configuration after tendon stretch.

Each collagen fiber (**Figures 1.2 a-e**) is formed from a coalescence of striated collagen fibrils (e). These fibrils are constructed from collagen molecules linking together with a quarter overlap into striated microfibrils (d). The collagen molecules are constructed from the amino acid glycine and surrounded by a thin layer of proteoglycans and glycosaminoglycans (c) that bind together to provide stability to the triple-helix structure (b,a).

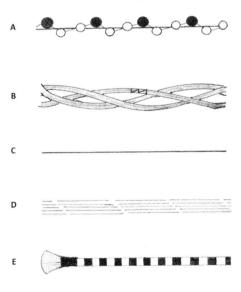

FIGURE 1.2   The constructs of collagen at a molecular level.

TENDON CELLS

Tendon cells, or tenocytes, are important but sparse spindle-shaped cells that produce the important components of the ECM. Tenocytes comprise about 90–95% of the cellular elements of the tendon. The other 5–10% include chondrocytes at the pressure and insertion sites, the synovial cells surrounding the tendon, and vascular cells (Khan et al., 1999).

Tenocytes also communicate with each other via "gap junctions" that link the cells processes and essentially couple cells together metabolically, chemically, and electrically. These gap junctions are very active and can remodel themselves in a matter of hours following mechanical stimulus; they respond to load via a mechanism of mechanotransduction (Banes et al., 1995; Maeda et al., 2012).[1]

PROTEOGLYCANS

PGs are found in-between collagen fibres and aid the fibrils in resisting tensile and compressive forces. Their negative electrical charge helps them repel each other and their carbohydrate content helps them soak up multiple times their weight in water. Their ability to imbibe water makes PGs hydrophilic.

PGs are found within the ECM and consist of a protein core and one or more covalently attached GAG chains; this provides elasticity and allows gliding between collagen fibrils in the ECM. Thus, the tensile strength of the tendon is the product of many thousands of connected strands and not simply a collection of long fibrils. To appreciate this, if you pick the microfibres out of wool or rope, you can see that they are short strands; yet, they collectively make up a long strand with significant tensile strength.

The PG content of the ECM is predominantly made up of a small PG called decorin (approximately 90%). A more even distribution of small and larger (fibrocartilage-producing) PGs has been reported in the tendon pressure zones where they are compressed against bone, usually within the insertional region. In a pathological tendon, the number of larger PGs like aggrecan (also known as chondroitin sulfate proteoglycan 1) also increases. Aggrecan's higher molecular weight means that it can imbibe more water; thus, aggrecan is responsible for some of the signs of tendinopathy, including swelling and collagen fibre separation. This is discussed in greater depth in Chapter 3.

---

[1] Mechanotransduction refers to the process of a cell responding to a mechanical stimulus by altering its biochemical make-up.

VASCULAR SUPPLY

The relative vascularity of a tendon compared to muscle is easy to appreciate by noting the colour of tendon (white) compared to muscle (red). In general, tendons have relatively low vascularity compared to muscle, but tendons are still sufficiently vascularised for their metabolic demands. For longer tendons, like the Achilles tendon, the mid-substance is not non-vascular; it is only less vascular. The blood supply to tendons typically comes from the musculotendinous and the osteotendinous junctions via the para-, epi- and endotenon networks that surround and infiltrate the tendon. The tendon blood supply has been shown to decrease with age, particularly after the third decade of life (Åström and Westlin, 1994). The tendon is reported to have a microlymphatic system that runs near the venous system. Lymphatic failure within the tendon has not been recognised and fluid drainage requirements are mostly met by the venous system (Józsa and Kannus, 1997).

NERVE SUPPLY

Tendon innervation primarily consists of sensory nerves with a vascular regulatory function (Ackermann et al., 2001). Free nerve endings are also present and can generate a noxious stimulus. Neural influence on tendon pain is reviewed in Chapter 3.

TENDON TO BONE

Tendons connect to bone at specialist sites called enthesis, the connective tissue between tendon or ligament and bone. These specialised regions have four transition zones: tendinous area; uncalcified fibrocartilaginous region where structurally cells change to chondrocytes; calcified fibrocartilage; and bone (**Figure 1.3**). This is a typical arrangement for most teno-osseus junctions (Apostolakos et al., 2014)

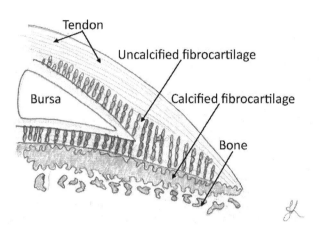

FIGURE 1.3   The differentiated zones of a typical enthesis organ: tendinous area; uncalcified fibrocartilaginous region; calcified fibrocartilage; and bone.

FASCIA: DO TENDONS ACTUALLY EXIST?

Tendons, like all parts of our anatomy, were identified and labelled by anatomists whose dissections were often interpreted by artists and brought forth through time to present-day anatomy books awaiting their opportunity to educate the next generation of students. Often, these images are not a true reflection of the structure and functional reality of the human architecture found under the skin. Do tendons exist? Or are they simply a component of connective tissue? Arguably, there is enough that is different about tendon structure to warrant its own label, but we must be cautious not to view the tendon as an isolated structure when assessing and treating patients.

STRUCTURAL CONTINUITY

The continuation from muscle to tendon allows us to appreciate the anatomical flow of the connective tissue. The paratenon is a continuation of the muscle fascia that then continues to envelope the tendon. The epimysium, a sheath of fibrous elastic tissue surrounding a muscle, has continuity with the epitenon of the tendon; the endomysium, a layer of areolar connective tissue that ensheathes each individual muscle fibre, has continuity with the endotenon. Tissue continuity between muscle and tendon, is presented in **Figure 1.4.**

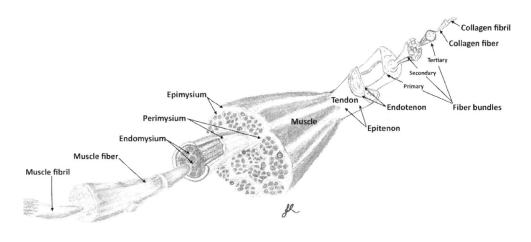

FIGURE 1.4   Representation of tissue continuity between muscle and tendon.

The fascial connections of tendons can be highly variable between individuals, but specific tendons often show unique patterns and arrangements.

At the patella, the deeper fibres of the patellar tendon connect to the patella from the quadriceps, and then from the patella to the tibial tuberosity, while some superficial fibres directly attach the quadriceps to the tibial tuberosity. It is common to find this pattern of functionally discrete, deep and superficial fibre arrangements in both ligaments and tendons.

At the hip, the gluteal muscles (gluteus maximus and minimus) have large areas of non-bony attachment to fascial connective tissue, including: the gluteus maximus non-bony attachment points to the lumbar fascia, sacrotuberous ligament, and iliotibial band; and the gluteus minimus connection to the superior hip joint capsule.

These often-expansive fascial attachments help to dissipate forces and give muscles a chance to dynamically control more passive structures like joint capsules and ligaments. These connections enhance the importance of healthy muscle function. This is good news for therapists and coaches, because muscles are one of the easiest and quickest structures to strengthen.

The progression of this continuity theme sees us step away from regional examination to appreciate the bigger picture of myofascial lines, fascial slings, kinetic chains, and anatomy trains. Some of these are introduced here and serve as a helpful reminder of the tissues directly influencing tendons.

THE KINETIC CHAIN

One of the oldest theories that views tendons and muscles as part of functional units rather than isolated structures is the kinetic chain theory (**Figure 1.5**). The concept of the kinetic chain originated in 1875, when Franz Reuleaux, a mechanical engineer proposed that if a series of overlapping segments were connected via pin joints, these interlocking joints would create a system that would allow the movement of one joint to affect the movement of another joint within the kinetic link. In 1955, Dr Arthur Steindler adapted this theory and included an analysis of human movement. Kinetic chain movements are often categorised as either "open" or "closed chain" depending on whether the distal segment, that is, the foot or hand is fixed (closed chain) or free (open chain). Using the basic premise of kinetic chain theory, we can appreciate how forces can be shared or shifted between the joints of the lower limb for assessment and rehabilitation purposes.

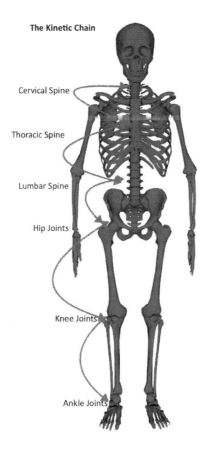

The Kinetic Chain

Cervical Spine

Thoracic Spine

Lumbar Spine

Hip Joints

Knee Joints

Ankle Joints

FIGURE 1.5   An example of the kinetic chain system through the human body.

THE MYOFASCIAL SLING SYSTEMS

In Diane Lee's book *The Pelvic Girdle: an Integration of Clinical Expertise and Research* (2011), four important myofascial slings hinging around the pelvic region are identified (**Figure 1.6**):

- *anterior oblique sling*: the external and internal oblique muscles sling with the opposite leg adductors and anterior abdominal fascia;
- *posterior oblique sling*: the latissimus dorsi muscle, thoracolumbar fascia, and opposing gluteus maximus;
- *deep longitudinal sling*: spinal erectors, thoracolumbar fascia, and biceps femoris muscle;
- *lateral sling*: gluteus medius and minimus and the opposite adductors of the thigh.

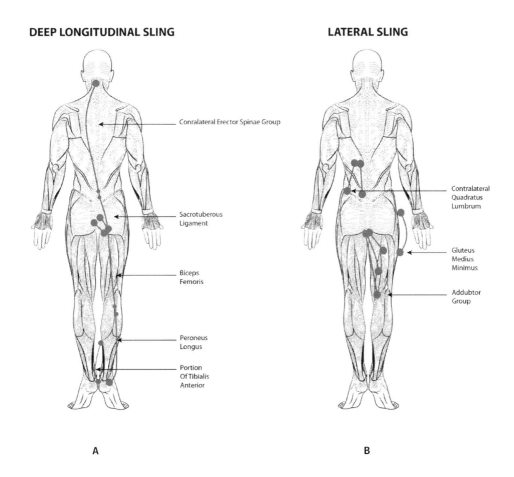

DEEP LONGITUDINAL SLING

Conralateral Erector Spinae Group

Sacrotuberous Ligament

Biceps Femoris

Peroneus Longus

Portion Of Tibialis Anterior

A

LATERAL SLING

Contralateral Quadratus Lumbrum

Gluteus Medius Minimus

Addubtor Group

B

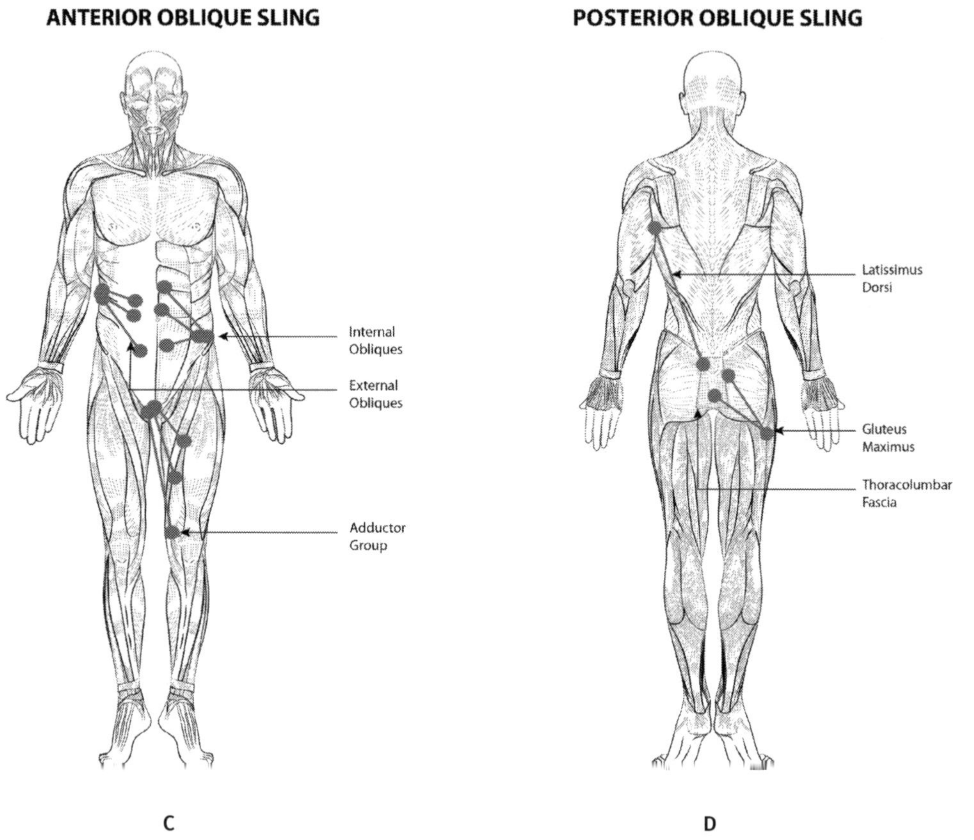

ANTERIOR OBLIQUE SLING

POSTERIOR OBLIQUE SLING

Internal
Obliques

External
Obliques

Adductor
Group

Latissimus
Dorsi

Gluteus
Maximus

Thoracolumbar
Fascia

C

D

FIGURE 1.6   Myofascial slings, (a) Deep longitudinal Sling, (b) Lateral sling, (c) Anterior oblique sling, (d) Posterior oblique sling (as originally described by Lee, 2011).

ANATOMY TRAINS

In his book *Anatomy Trains: Myofascial Meridians for Manual and Movement Therapists* (2001), Thomas Myers presents his concept of myofascial continuity and compares it to a train with tracks and stations representing the myofascial lines of tissue with their various attachment points. As a therapist or coach, these lines are very easy to visualise and use for assessment purposes. In addition, each of the tendons described in the book features as part of an identified "track" of tissue.

The superficial back, superficial front, and lateral lines as described by Myers (2001) are shown in **Figure 1.7**.

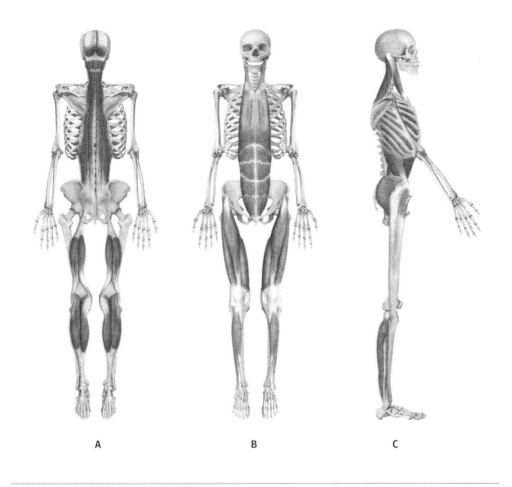

FIGURE 1.7　Anatomy trains, as described by Myers (2001). (a) Superficial back line. (b) Superficial front line. (c) Lateral line.

CONCLUSION

This chapter has presented the key components of tendons from a macro to micro, and then cellular level. The anatomy of individual tendons will be discussed in their respective chapters. One of the key messages from this chapter is the structural continuity of tendons with muscle and surrounding tissues. Tendons are not isolated structures.

REFERENCES

Ackermann PW, Li J, Finn A, et al. (2001). Autonomic innervation of tendons, ligaments and joint capsules. A morphologic and quantitative study in the rat. *J Orthop Res.* **19**:372–378.

Apostolakos J, Durant TJ, Dwyer CR, et al. (2014). The enthesis: a review of the tendon-to-bone insertion. *Muscles Ligaments Tendons J.* **4**:333–342.

Åström M, Westlin N (1994). Blood flow in chronic Achilles tendinopathy. *Clin Orthop Relat Res.* **308**:166–172.

Banes AJ, Tsuzaki M, Yamamoto J, et al. (1995). Mechanoreception at the cellular level: the detection, interpretation, and diversity of responses to mechanical signals. *Biochem Cell Biol.* **73**:349–365.

Butler D, Grood E, Noyes F, et al. (1978) Biomechanics of ligaments and tendons. *Exerc Sport Sci Rev.* **6**:125–181.

Fallon J, Blevins FT, Vogel K, et al. (2002). Functional morphology of the supraspinatus tendon. *J Orthop Res.* **20**:920–926.

Józsa L, Kannus P (1997). Histopathological findings in spontaneous tendon ruptures. *Scand J Med Sci Sports.* **7**:113–118.

Kannus P (2000). Structure of the tendon connective tissue. *Scand J Med Sci Sports.* **10**:312–320.

Khan KM, Cook JL, Bonar F, et al. (1999). Histopathology of common tendinopathies. Update and implications for clinical management. *Sports Med.* **27**:393–408.

Lee D (2011). *The Pelvic Girdle: an Integration of Clinical Expertise and Research.* 4th ed. Churchill Livingstone: Edinburgh.

Maeda E, Ye S, Wang W, et al. (2012). Gap junction permeability between tenocytes within tendon fascicles is suppressed by tensile loading. *Biomech Model Mechanobiol.* **11**:439–447.

Myers TW (2001). *Anatomy Trains: Myofascial Meridians for Manual and Movement Therapists.* Edinburgh: Churchill Livingstone.

Puxkandl R, Zizak I, Paris O, et al. (2002). Viscoelastic properties of collagen: synchrotron radiation investigations and structural model. *Philos Trans R Soc Lond B Biol Sci.* **357**:191–197.

FURTHER READING

Barkhausen T, van Griensven M, Zeichen J, et al. (2003). Modulation of cell functions of human tendon fibroblasts by different repetitive cyclic mechanical stress patterns. *Exp Toxicol Pathol.* **55**:153–158.

Benjamin M, Kaiser E, Milz S (2008). Structure-function relationships in tendons: a review. *J Anat.* **212**:211–228.

CHAPTER 2

EVOLUTIONARY BIOLOGY

INTRODUCTION

The study of tendinopathy, tendons, and our musculoskeletal system should arguably begin from a historical and evolutionary perspective. This chapter asks the question: Why have our bodies evolved in a certain way and for what purpose? This allows us to tackle the problem of tendinopathy against the backdrop of a basic knowledge of tendon-related evolutionary biology throughout the remaining chapters.

The continued discovery of early hominoid fossils provides new fragments of physical evidence about our ancestral features, with some likening these discoveries to the ability to time travel.

One of the features that show our differentiation from the great apes and more recent humanoid linages most distinctly, is the ability to give birth to infants with large brains. Our pelvis has evolved to allow the passing of larger heads, even in males.[2] The second feature is our default use of bipedalism for locomotion and how this has shaped the evolution of our spine, pelvis, and lower limbs. In fact, bipedalism came before larger brains and wider pelvic openings, the evolution of which may have slowed us

---

[2] The default mammalian genotype is female, so the alteration of the female pelvis through evolution has also altered the male pelvis. The differences seen in adults today are caused by different hormone expression during adolescence (Lovejoy, 2005a).

down compared to our smaller-hipped (wide but less circular pelvis) bipedal ancestors, such as *Australopithecus afarensis,* an extinct hominin that lived between 3.9 and 2.9 million years ago. The most famous fossil remains is the partial skeleton named Lucy (3.2 million years old; **Figure 2.1**) discovered in Ethiopia in 1974.

Anthropologists often refer to *A. afarensis* as Lucy because their theories are based on the research using her skeletal remains. The discovery of Lucy strengthened the notion that bipedalism was a key feature in the survival of our lineage, bearing in mind increased brain capacity appears to have developed much later.

FIGURE 2.1   Artist's impression of *Australopithecus afarensis* an early hominin who predominantly moved about on two legs. Trainers raise the philosophical question of our commonality with our ancestors and the progress we have, or have not, made in our ability to walk and run efficiently and without injury. Please do not misinterpret this as a suggestion that we should all be barefoot; it is not that simple.

Some of the most fascinating evolutionary musculoskeletal changes occurred at the pelvis to facilitate an erect trunk and to stabilise the body on one leg during the stance phase of locomotion.

Key adaptations of the hominin pelvis to an upright posture include: a widening of the pelvic bowl to support the viscera; an anterior tilt of the sacrum to facilitate the natural curvature of the spine; bringing the centre of gravity over the hips; and an increased lower-limb extension during gait (**Figure 2.2**).

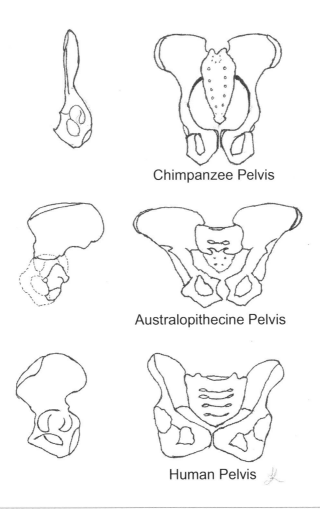

Chimpanzee Pelvis

Australopithecine Pelvis

Human Pelvis

FIGURE 2.2   Key adaptations of the pelvis. Although the anterior view of the chimpanzee pelvis looks like an early human ancestor (australopithecine) pelvis and a present-day human pelvis, the lateral view demonstrates more anterior ilia that wrap around from the sacrum to provide gluteal attachments superior to the hip joint; this allows the lateral gluteal musculature to function as hip stabilisers during single-leg stance.

Key adaptations of the hominin pelvis to single-limb stance are the more anterior ilia that wrap around from the sacrum to provide gluteal attachments superior to the hip joint; this allows the lateral gluteal muscles to function as hip stabilisers and prevent the pelvic drop commonly known as the Trendelenburg's sign. Our glutei maximi still function as powerful hip-and-trunk extensors, but the musculature of this region has more of a dual role of extension and stabilisation than in quadrupeds, where the gluteal muscles predominantly contract to extend the hip joint. This is examined further in Chapter 7.

Significant changes also happened at the knees, to straighten our legs. The hallux moved from an abducted, opposable, thumb-like structure to its alignment with the metatarsals resulting in increased rigidity for weight-bearing (**Figure 2.3**). Humans still have the structural ability to oppose the big toe; people who have lost their upper limbs, or were born without them, often develop the ability to write, pick things up, and manipulate objects with their toes.

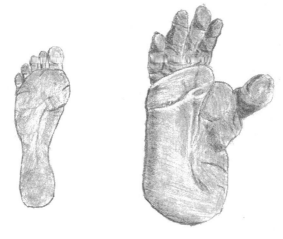

FIGURE 2.3   Human and a gorilla foot. Our feet have evolved into adaptable and weight-bearing structures, but they still contain the joints and muscles that allow prehensile function.

Once hominins became habitual terrestrial bipeds, adaptations had to occur in the musculotendinous units of the lower limbs. The most examined of these was the development of a large elastic tendon at the back of the foot – the Achilles tendon.

THE ACHILLES TENDON

Many evolutionary biologists believe that the Achilles tendon adapted over time to support efficient running. The energy storage capacity of tendons is one of the important mechanisms that allowed hominins to rise from the flexed posture of apes to walk and later run on two legs for long periods of time. Evolutionary biologists Bramble and Lieberman (2004) suggested that our unique running endurance is provided through efficiency and thermoregulation and has allowed us to run down much faster animals with persistence rather than speed.

If we expand our review of the Achilles tendon to the equivalency in the animal world, we can further appreciate its function in running. Primates have a much smaller Achilles tendon equivalent that does not share the same strength or properties of the human Achilles tendon. As we evolved, this tendon strengthened first in response to walking and then further in response to running. One reason for this may have been a change in climate that may have affected the hunting environment and our hunting methods (Malvankar and Khan, 2011).

Once we were up and running with an increased efficiency, we were still at a considerable disadvantage in terms of speed. If we were to chase a gazelle on the African planes, we would soon lose the chase. But a knowledge of the gazelle's cooling mechanisms and respiratory patterns in motion would lead us to stay in pursuit of the animal and wait for it to overheat and collapse with exhaustion (**Figure 2.4**).

FIGURE 2.4   Human cooling mechanisms and a respiratory pattern that is independent from our ribcage movement, in addition to the efficient anatomy of our myofascial systems, allow us to run with superior efficiency.

While it is unlikely that you will be chasing a gazelle this weekend, the next time you try to chase something faster than you, try patient persistence to see if you can catch them. Caution, though; this is highly dependent on your personal fitness.

Another way of thinking about the comparison between human bipedalism and quadrupedalism is that running on two feet is more efficient than running on all four in the same way that a four-wheel drive car will outperform a two-wheel drive car, but it is generally far less fuel efficient.

COOLING

Our bodies can cool and maintain a safe internal temperature during exercise. No other species sweats as much as we do, and our predominantly hairless bodies allow the cooling effect of air to pass over our skin when running. In contrast, many quadrupedal animals rely on a respiratory cooling mechanism (panting) to thermoregulate. While this mechanism provides some advantages over sweating, the animals' inability to breathe independently from their stride pattern leads to overheating and eventual exhaustion.

Humans can maintain an independent breathing pattern because the movement of the ribcage is independent from their gait. In contrast, galloping animals are restricted to one breath per stride because their ribcage expands and contracts with anterior limb motion.

So, perhaps now we can see why evolution has favoured humans. We have been able to adapt and use the efficiency of our bipedalism to both preserve energy and catch or gather food, while maintaining our core body temperature and having the brain capacity to adapt, learn, and communicate this learning to the next generation. "Survival of the fittest" perhaps does not entirely reflect the influences of our evolutionary trail. "Efficiency and adaptability" appear the more determining factors.[3] Based on pure physical fitness being the deciding virtue, we may well have ended up as less cerebral Neanderthals struggling even more to understand why our tendons hurt!

A recommended read is "Endurance running and the evolution of *Homo*" by Dennis Bramble and Daniel Lieberman (2004). Daniel Lieberman also has some excellent

---

[3] Although one could argue that to do this, one also needs to be fit and certainly fitter than other animals or even members of your own species.

evolutionary biology lectures on YouTube. Owen Lovejoy is another recommended author and speaker on the topic of evolution and bipedalism (Lovejoy, 2005a,b).

Finally, I will leave you with this question: If we evolved to be on two feet and run, then why do so many runners get injured?

What are we doing wrong?

REFERENCES

Bramble DM, Lieberman DE (2004). Endurance running and the evolution of *Homo*. *Nature*. **432**:345–352.

Lovejoy CO (2005a). The natural history of human gait and posture. Part 1. Spine and pelvis. *Gait Posture*. **21**:95–112.

Lovejoy CO (2005b). The natural history of human gait and posture. Part 2. Hip and thigh. *Gait Posture*. **21**:113–124.

CHAPTER 3

TENDON PATHOLOGY

INTRODUCTION

The pathogenesis of tendinopathy and the cause of the associated pain continue to challenge both researchers and clinicians alike. The flow of new information can take many years to go from hypothesis to everyday clinical use; this is highlighted by the slow uptake of the non-inflammatory tendon treatment approach. This chapter describes the continuum theory, explains the idea of tendon stress shielding, discusses the potential role of inflammation, and highlights some of the pain mechanisms likely to be involved.

This is a complex chapter. It outlines the pathology of tendinopathy, but it remains clinically useful and accessible to clinicians and practitioners alike.

THE TENDINOPATHY CONTINUUM

The tendinopathy continuum proposed by Cook and Purdam (2009) has gained the most acceptance when compared with other, often inflammation-based, theories. This is due to its pooling of current knowledge and clinical efficacy. The first part of this chapter explains this continuum.

TENDON PATHOLOGY

Tendon damage was previously thought to be like muscle damage; that is, fibres would tear in varying degrees thereby triggering an inflammatory response. The swelling of the tendon and pain were previously assumed to be of inflammatory origin and the term tendinitis has been widely used historically. More recently, the terms tendinosis, tendinopathy, and paratenonitis have become prevalent (see **Table 3.1**). Tendinopathy is a clinical diagnosis of pain, stiffness, and impaired tendon function. Paratenonitis refers to the presence of inflammatory cells between the tendon and its sheath-like outer layers. It is not uncommon to have a mix of pathologies.

TABLE 3.1   Common tendon terminology

TERM	DEFINITION
TENDONITIS	A once popular, now lesser-used term to describe inflammation within the tendon. The suffix "itis" denotes inflammation.
TENDINOSIS	First used to describe a failed healing response, it is now a term used to describe tendon degeneration, usually in the absence of inflammation.
TENDINOPATHY	The most commonly used term that denotes a clinical diagnosis of pain, impaired function, and possible swelling.
PARATENONITIS	Refers to the presence of inflammation in the paratenon. This commonly causes the tendon to creak, a process known as crepitus.
ACHILLODYNIA	A lesser-used term that describes pain in the Achilles tendon.

THE THREE-STAGE CONTINUUM

Cook and Purdam (2009) proposed that the pathology of tendinopathy could be described as a three-stage continuum with an increasingly limited scope for reversal (**Figure 3.1**).

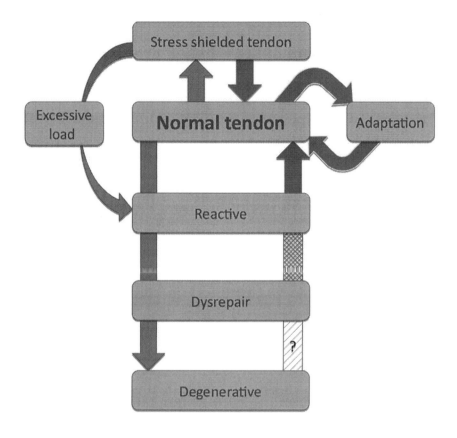

FIGURE 3.1 The three-stage continuum. The tendinopathy continuum as described by Cook and Purdam (2009).

The following explanation of the continuum theory is supported by the diagrams from an animation freely available from the Physio Channel on YouTube.[4] **Figure 3.2** is a useful way to familiarise yourself with some of the key components of a normal tendon before comparing it to the pathology diagrams in Figures 3.3–3.5.

[4] Lawrence D (2014). *The Tendinopathy Continuum.* Available from www.youtube.com/watch?v=6MRPE9_vwYk (accessed 11 December 2017).

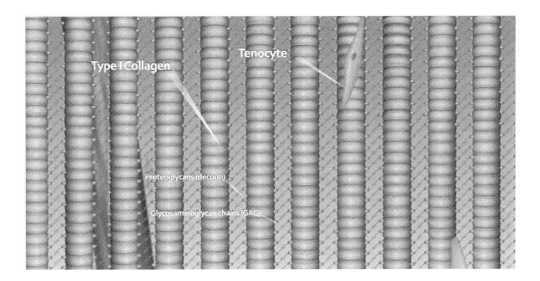

FIGURE 3.2   Representation of normal tendon structure at a cellular level. The vertical tubes represent collagen fibrils at the cellular level. The small cells represent a specific proteoglycan called decorin, which consists of a protein core and a glycosaminoglycan chain that provide a connection, tensile strength, and viscoelasticity between fibrils. The larger, spindle-shaped cells are the specialist tendon cells known as tenocytes. These cells maintain the health of the tendon by synthesising new collagen fibres and proteoglycans in the correct quantities. In the healthy tendon, they are spindle-shaped but they change shape when the tendon is stressed.

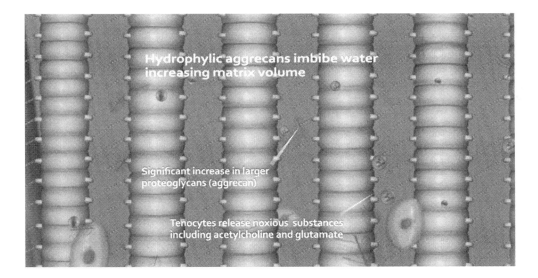

FIGURE 3.3   Reactive tendinopathy. The tenocytes have changed from a spindle shape to more rounded structures. The small circles labelled "P" represent the release of noxious substances into the extracellular matrix. The feather-like structures represent the aggrecan proteoglycans that bring more water into the tendon and expand the distance between collagen fibrils, as represented by the increased space between collagen columns in the image.

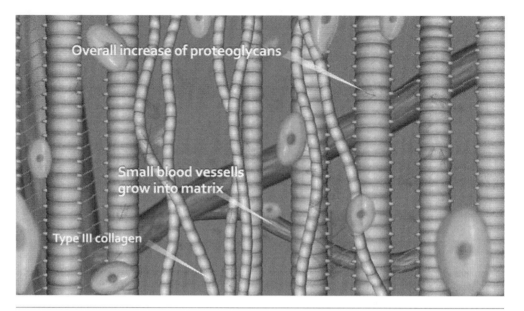

FIGURE 3.4   Tendon in the disrepair phase. Key features of this stage are the deposition of thinner, type 3 collagen fibres and the growth of neovessels into the matrix.

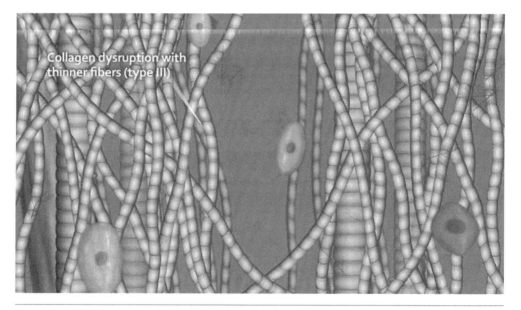

FIGURE 3.5   Tendon in the degenerative phase. Key features are an increased replacement of type 1 collagen fibres with thinner, more irregular type 3 collagen fibres.

The three stages of the tendinopathy continuum as described by Cook and Purdam (2009) are as follows.

Reactive tendinopathy

Tendons react to acute overload with a short-term, load-adaptive thickening caused by increased cellular activity and proliferation (Parkinson et al., 2010). This hypercellularity brings about an increase in the synthesis of large, water-imbibing aggrecan and versican proteoglycans (PGs). These push the collagen fibres apart and fatten the overall tendon because of increased water volume. (Aggrecan molecules are depicted as feather-like structures in **Figure 3.3**.) This presents clinically as a thickening of the tendon body, which is often mistaken for an inflammatory reaction. Tenocytes change shape from a spindle to a rounded structure possibly because of mechanical stress, chemical influence, or both. The change in shape causes a change in behaviour and altered substance production. The process of cells responding to a mechanical stimulus by altering their biochemical make-up is known as mechanotransduction. Mechanotransduction is thought to be a key mechanism in both the aetiology and rehabilitation of tendons via load management and is discussed further in Chapter 9. The release of noxious substances, represented as the "P" cells in **Figure 3.3**, is also an important component of the reactive stage and potential pain generation. Importantly, **Figure 3.3** shows that collagen fibre integrity is maintained, which reflects the positive reversibility of this stage. Reactive tendinopathy is commonly, but not exclusively, seen in younger athletic patients. It can be very painful, but can be resolved completely. The reactive tendon is thought to respond to acute overload by increasing its stiffness and reducing stress; it does so by increasing its overall volume within a short period. Reactive tendinopathy can also be superseded by a chronic degenerative tendon, as seen more commonly in older patients. These are general principles; we rarely see textbook presentations in the clinical setting.

Disrepair

If reactive tendinopathy endures because of persistent overload, then increased protein production continues and a failed healing response is seen within the structure. In the later stages of disrepair, neovessels start to show up on Doppler ultrasound (US) and increased production of the weaker, irregular type III collagen begins. The importance and relevance of neovessels that develop within tendinopathic tissue remains in question (Danielson, Alfredson and Forsgren, 2006). Some authors report that their presence correlates with pain, while others do not agree. The infiltrating vessels are thick-walled, have a small lumen, and are of inferior quality to have much influence on tendon pathology. The accompanying vasculo-neural ingrowth, once thought to be a source of tendon pain, consists mainly of sympathetic nerves that regulate neovessels and do not contain any sensory fibres.[5] While the full clinical relevance of vasculo-neural ingrowth is yet unknown, it is used as a marker of whether the tendinopathy stage has progressed from a "reactive/early disrepair" with no neovessel ingrowth, to "late disrepair/degeneration" with evident ingrowth. The potential reversal between the two can also be monitored. Patients with tendons in the early disrepair phase often present clinically with ongoing intermittent symptoms. A reduced capacity for full structural repair has been reported, but the function of the tendon and muscle tissue surrounding the pathological tendon zone can still be positively influenced. At this point in the continuum, we need to think about how we explain things to the patient; the language we use should receive the same attention we pay to our communications with chronic pain patients. Mentioning theorised permanent changes and irreversibility is likely to increase patient anxiety about their condition and outcome. However, for patients who refuse to heed our rehabilitation advice, such information may influence their decision to listen and cooperate. As the tendon enters the disrepair phase, noticeable structural changes occur (**Figure 3.4**), including neovessel ingrowth around the collagen fibres and breakdown of the glycosaminoglycan chains. The rounder tenocytes also begin to synthesise weaker, irregular type III collagen. In time, cellular changes lead to structural changes that are essentially more permanent and less reversible.

Degenerative

This differs from the reactive and disrepair stages and is characterised by large changes to the matrix, with areas of reduced cellularity among an otherwise hypercellular matrix. Type I collagen content reduces and is replaced by type III collagen and debris. These patients do not usually report much pain and may not present clinically unless an acute reactive tendinopathy is overlaid on a chronic pathology following acute unaccustomed overload (Cook and Purdam, 2009). This tendon state has a poor prognosis for structural reversal back through the stages. While a structural reversal is unlikely, the tendon should still be able to adapt with a correct loading stimulus and tolerate functional loading. **Figures 3.2–3.5** do not show a full tendon rupture because this is not part of the tendinopathy continuum, although a tendon having reached the degenerative phase will not tolerate loading as well as a healthy tendon; the poor structure without associated and somewhat protective pain greatly increases the risk of apparently spontaneous rupture. In one study of 891 patients, 97% of ruptured tendons

[5] Cook J (2012). Tendinopathies Masterclass Lecture. London, November 2012.

showed degenerative changes that were undoubtedly present before rupturing (Kannus and Józsa, 1991).

These proposed stages of tendinopathy tend to occur with some heterogeneity throughout a single tendon by displaying microscopic zones of differing pathology throughout the tendon. This tendon heterogeneity may be the cause of stress shielding. Put another way, the changes we have been discussing occur within small pockets of the tendon, leaving much of the tendon intact so that even the most tendinopathic tendon is still very strong; this is an important point to relay to patients when prescribing a loading programme.

STRESS SHIELDING THEORY

The damaged fibre zone within the tendon receives some stress shielding from the surrounding intact fibres. This theory highlights two potential causes of further degeneration: understimulation of the damaged zone leading to a degenerative process; and further degeneration resulting from the altered mechanics and loading of the remaining tendon tissue, which may be stressed beyond its standard capability threshold. While research tells us a lot about tendons adapting to loading, less is known about responses to chronic unloading (Shin et al., 2008). Space flight research indicates that chronic unloading causes myofibril protein loss, reduction in the size of muscle fibres, and altered neuronal recruitment patterns and fibre type conversion (Steffen and Musacchia, 1986; Edgerton et al., 1995; Edgerton and Roy, 2011). Overall, this chronic unloading leads to reduced tendon stiffness (Magnusson et al., 2003) and resting tendons is generally agreed to be a poor long-term rehabilitation plan.

REVISITING THE INFLAMMATORY MODEL

The inflammatory theory of tendon pathology has been questioned in the literature since the 1970s. In 1976, a published report titled "A classification of Achilles tendon disease" (Puddu, Ippolito and Postacchini, 1976) highlighted the irregularities between histological findings and current terminology. Only in the late 1990s did the more clinical and less definitive term "tendinopathy"[6] start to become more widely used. Even today, the term tendinitis is still used. The question remains. Is tendon pathology a non-inflammatory condition?

---

[6] Tendinitis refers to a defined inflammatory pathology. Tendinosis is confirmed with histology, but tendinopathy is a clinical diagnosis of tendon pain and dysfunction; it does not define the pathology.

Although the inflammatory model has been largely overshadowed by a more degenerative paradigm, a few researchers supporting the inflammatory model have consistently and increasingly identified inflammatory mediators as potential components of the tendinopathy aetiology (Millar et al., 2010; Dean et al., 2016). Put another way, a type of hidden inflammation may be involved in causing a tendinopathy.

There are three key reasons why we may have been potentially misled by the notion of a non-inflammatory pathology.

First, the definition of inflammation is not clear and can be subcategorised into acute, chronic, symptomatic, and asymptomatic. Tendinopathy may have an asymptomatic chronic inflammatory component, which is involved in the asymptomatic buildup to a symptomatic tendon (Dean et al., 2016).

Second, many studies have demonstrated a histological absence of inflammatory cells in tendinosis; however, most of these studies would have involved symptomatic tendons. If an inflammatory precursor was involved, it would not be detected in the later symptomatic stage. In support of this idea, animal studies have shown regulation of inflammatory cells with induced tendon stress (Archambault, Wiley and Bray, 1995; Molloy et al., 2006).

Finally, many histological studies have only used basic techniques without specific cell markers to detect specific inflammatory cells. There are many markers of inflammation and the absence of a few key cells does not guarantee the absence of inflammation in its entirety.

TENDON PAIN

Tendinopathic tendons often generate a sensation of pain from previously non-painful actions, such as walking or direct touch. This pain reaction to a non-noxious stimulus is termed allodynia. An increased sensitivity to a graded nociceptive stimulus, is referred to as primary hyperalgesia. Secondary hyperalgesia refers to changes within or mediated by the central nervous system (CNS); this is often referred to as central sensitisation and has become the focus of recent tendon pain research (Tompra, van Dieën and Coppieters, 2016).

One of the most important points to highlight early on in this discussion of tendon pain is that a reduction in tendon pain does not reflect the underlying pathology. So, reduced pain after a short-term treatment like massage is not a marker of any structural changes. Perhaps more surprisingly, reduced pain after a long-term loading programme has been shown to occur faster than structural adaptations. This should encourage and justify continued rehabilitation beyond the point of simple pain reduction.

The basic physiology of tendon pain, as described by Rio and colleagues (2014), can be explained using **Figure 3.6.** The peripheral ends of nociceptors, or free nerve endings, on thin, unmyelinated (C group) or thinly myelinated (A delta) nerve fibres situated in the peritendon and peripheral portions of the tendon tissue contain thermal, heat, and mechanically activated ion channels. In the nociceptor, changes in the chemical, thermal, or mechanical environment are transduced into electrical signals or action potentials. The signal travels through nerves to the dorsal horn of the spinal cord where the nerve synapses connect with second-order neurons or spinal nociceptors. Spinal nociceptors send a signal to the thalamus via the lateral spinothalamic tract and then the brain. A complex evaluation process occurs across multiple brain areas and protective outputs are activated. One such output is pain. Others include motor output and immune activation. In addition, descending projections (shown as thin lines in **Figure 3.6**) modulate nuclei in the brainstem, which in turn send signals down the spinal cord to modulate the same synapse in the dorsal horn. These neurons are activated to either facilitate or inhibit the spinal synapse, thereby turning nociception up or down, like a volume control. The manner of modulation depends on how the brain evaluates the need for pain and protection. As such, the spinal cord represents the first stage of integration and processing of the nociceptive signal (Rio et al., 2014). Within this basic description of tendon pain physiology, we can pick out the many opportunities to influence tendon pain from both the peripheral starting point and during CNS processing.

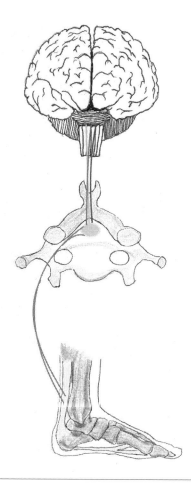

FIGURE 3.6   Schematic representation of the physiology of tendon pain.

Structurally, we know that tenocytes and the gap junctions between them are more metabolically active (25 times that of normal tendons) (Parkinson et al., 2010) and that they respond to load in very short time frames. While tenocytes are predominantly seen as the collagen- and extracellular matrix-producing cells, they have also been shown to produce other substances that may play a role in tendon pain. One of these is the neuropeptide substance P, a noxious substance.

In addition to tenocytes, the tendon contains lesser-researched cells, which may have an integral role in nociception. These include mast cells, which are associated with immunity and can produce cytokines that could trigger a noxious pathway. Glial cells may also be implicated in ongoing pain (Cao et al., 2009).

PAIN BEHAVIOUR

The initial loading of a tendinopathic tendon appears to rapidly increase tendon pain, which then reduces after a "warm-up" and, in many cases, is not painful during activity (although not always); pain is then reported to increase after a short rest period; that is, the next day the pain is significantly increased, a bit like a "pain hangover". This delayed response, perhaps like delayed muscle soreness, is characteristic of tendinopathy. One theory that may explain the reduced pain/increased pain pattern involves acid-sensing ion channels (ASICs).

ACID-SENSING ION CHANNELS AND LACTATE LEVELS

Tendinopathic tissue has shown resting lactate levels of double those typically seen in healthy tendon tissue (Alfredson et al., 2002). Increased lactate levels are due to the dominant anaerobic metabolism seen in older tendons as well as tendinopathic ones. The presence of increased lactate levels upsets the pH balance, which negatively influences the gap junctions (**Figure 3.7**) between tenocytes by allowing the free flow of metabolites between tenocyte rows, thus potentially increasing the response and spread of mechanical load influence through to neighbouring tenocytes. Perhaps this could be explained by suggesting that the tendon becomes more "reactive" as a result, in line with the reactive stage in the continuum.

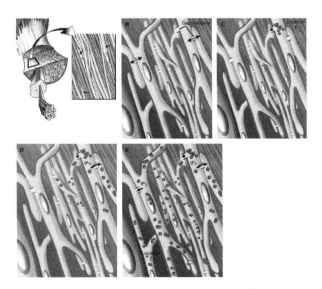

FIGURE 3.7   Gap junctions within the extracellular matrix provide a cellular communication system between tenocytes. These gap junctions are influenced by pH balance.

This increase in lactate and resultant acidic environment increases the activity in ASICs (Kellenberger and Schild, 2002). This may help explain the unusual pain behaviour experienced with tendinopathy. Desensitisation of ASICs occurs after approximately 3 minutes of persistent stimulation (Jones et al., 2004), which may explain the clinical feature of tendon pain reducing with activity. In addition, the resensitisation of ASICs occurs over a longer period, which fits with the pain and stiffness experienced after a rest period following activity, that is, morning pain and stiffness.

THE CENTRAL NERVOUS SYSTEM

Just as the increase in tendon pain is influenced by the CNS, then a decrease in pain is also modulated by the CNS via descending inhibition and altered pressure pain thresholds (Kosek and Lundberg, 2003). This is the main proposed mechanism behind pain reduction following isometric fatiguing of muscle tissue adjoining the tendon.

In addition to the analgesic benefits of tendon loading, the correct conditioning stimulus has also been shown to positively influence tendon structure at a cellular level. Sustained submaximal, non-ballistic loading mechanically stimulates the tenocytes to produce more of the smaller PGs (e.g. decorin) and less of the large water imbibing ones (e.g. aggrecan). Sustained tensile force is also thought to squeeze out some of the excess water content within the tendon. For a higher load and possibly more ballistic loading there is a possible need for substantial time between high loading activities, to allow for structural adaptation but also to reduce the sensitisation of the pathway (Rio et al., 2014).

The response to loading is discussed in more depth in Chapter 9.

SUDDEN PAIN

Sudden pain can indicate a partial tear, which often occurs in the pathological zone and should be treated in a similar manner to tendinopathy but with an understanding that it may take longer to heal. A more severe sudden pain from the Achilles region with marked dysfunction is suggestive of a complete rupture; patients often report a loud "shot"-type noise or the feeling of being kicked in the back of the heel when a rupture occurs.

OTHER ANATOMICAL CAUSES

With all tendinopathies, it is possible for pain to arise from tissue damage to any of the surrounding structures, which may form part of or all the nociceptive input. Irritation of bursal tissue and fat pads is the most commonly proposed source of tendon-related pain. These will be discussed in the individual tendon chapters.

ASSESSING THE PAIN

If pain reduces after a massage or the application of tape, this is clearly a good outcome; however, neither of these modalities will solve the underlying issues of structure and strength.

Clinicians and therapists should not overassess pain (i.e. too frequently) and discourage patients from doing so because it can be demotivating to monitor micro-changes when rehabilitation requires a sustained personal effort from the patient.

With knowledge of a tendon's typical delayed response to loading, I suggest using two subjective assessment tools.

A simple symptom diary (consciously avoiding calling it a pain diary). This diary should be used as an assessment of how tendons react to the previous days' loading, whether from intentional rehabilitation or incidental functional activities of daily living. Ask your patient to record pain intensity and time-to-pain-free each morning for Achilles tendon patients, and pain intensity with known exacerbating tasks for other lower-limb tendinopathies. An example of the type of information needed is shown in **Table 3.2**. A sudden increase or any increase in pain over a 2–3-day period should indicate a necessary reduction in daily tendon loading with the techniques and principles of treatment discussed in this book. Pain, of a tolerable nature, during exercise may have little to do with the pathological state or outcome.[7]

---

[7] Cook J (2012). Tendinopathies Masterclass Lecture. London, November 2012.

TENDON TYPE	DATE	TIME	FUNCTIONAL TASK	PAIN SCALE AND TIMING	PREVIOUS DAYS' ACTIVITIES	MEDICATION CHANGES
Achilles	–	7 a.m.	Walking first few steps in the morning	6/10 pain, reducing by 50% after 5 minutes	Normal walk to work	No medications as usual
Patellar	–	6 p.m.	Walking down steps at train station after work	3/10 pain, onset only during last few steps	Minimal only isometrics a.m./p.m.	Paracetamol at 11 a.m. for headache not tendon pain
Hamstring	–	1 p.m.	Lunchtime run	7/10 after 5 minutes running	Half marathon	Ibuprofen 400 mg three times daily
Gluteal	–	10 p.m.	Sit to stand from sofa	9/10	Christmas shopping trip, lots of walking and heavy bags	No change

TABLE 3.2   Example of diary entries from different patients covering the four common lower limb tendinopathies

A more detailed and comprehensive assessment can be achieved with the Victorian Institute of Sport Assessment (VISA) for Achilles, patellar, hamstring, and gluteal tendinopathy; the assessment can be used to monitor the success of the rehabilitation programme by converting subjective information into a numerical score out of 100. A patient who has fully recovered should achieve a VISA score of 100, which logically represents 100% recovery. The sensitivity of the assessment allows the often-slow recovery to be tracked effectively and provides the patient with helpful feedback. To avoid overtesting, a VISA assessment should be performed approximately once per month.

CONCLUSION

Despite the consensus of a non-inflammatory model, there is now convincing evidence that an early asymptomatic inflammation may provide a cellular driver that contributes to tendinopathy. If this is a consistent occurrence, then it may have clinical relevance if it can be more easily detected and used to monitor training volume responses for athletes and help avoid the onset of tendinopathy. It is also being considered in the development of more targeted anti-inflammatory medications, has implications for dietary factors, and throws new light on the efficacy of anti-inflammatory treatments.

The continuum theory provides a clinically useful model of a complex pathology. The stage of tendinopathy on the continuum significantly influences treatment choices. No specialist testing equipment is required to determine a patient's tendinopathy stage, but the use of Doppler US or US tissue characterisation may increase diagnostic accuracy.

This chapter discussed a few different tendon pain concepts. The increased sensitivity of ASICs provides a compelling mechanism to explain the unusual pain behaviour. One of the most important things to remember in clinical practice is that increased tendon pain does not equal increased tendon damage; tendons specifically show a poor pain/pathology correlation. This provides a further management challenge that begins with patient education.

It is perhaps rational to conclude that tendon pain may be triggered by multiple mechanisms – chemical, structural, cellular, neurological – with a primary driver that differs between clinical presentations.

This chapter provides the underpinning theory that supports and justifies much of the assessment and management advice outlined throughout the remaining chapters of this book.

REFERENCES

Alfredson H, Bjur D, Thorsen K, et al. (2002). High intratendinous lactate levels in painful chronic Achilles tendinosis. An investigation using microdialysis technique. *J Orthop Res.* **20**:934–938.

Archambault JM, Wiley JP, Bray RC (1995). Exercise loading of tendons and the development of overuse injuries. A review of current literature. *Sports Med.* **20**:77–89.

Cao L, Palma CD, Malon JT, et al. (2009). Critical role of microglial CD40 in the maintenance of mechanical hypersensitivity in a murine model of neuropathic pain. *Eur J Immunol.* **39**:3562–3569.

Cook JL, Purdam CR (2009). Is tendon pathology a continuum? A pathology model to explain the clinical presentation of load-induced tendinopathy. *Br J Sports Med.* **43**:409–416.

Danielson P, Alfredson HK, Forsgren S (2006). Distribution of general (PGP 9.5) and sensory (substance P/CGRP) innervations in the human patellar tendon. *Knee Surg Sports Traumatol Arthrosc.* **14**:125–132.

Dean BJ, Gettings P, Dakin SG, et al. (2016). Are inflammatory cells increased in painful human tendinopathy? A systematic review. *Br J Sports Med.* **50**:216–220.

Edgerton VR, Roy RR (2011). Neuromuscular adaptations to actual and simulated spaceflight. Supplement 14: Handbook of Physiology, Environmental Physiology. *Compr Physiol.* 721–763.

Edgerton VR, Zhou MY, Ohira Y, et al. (1995). Human fiber size and enzymatic properties after 5 and 11 days of spaceflight. *J Appl Physiol.* **78**:1733–1739.

Jones NG, Slater R, Cadiou H, et al. (2004). Acid-induced pain and its modulation in humans. *J Neurosci.* **24**:10974–10979.

Kannus P, Józsa L (1991). Histopathological changes preceding spontaneous rupture of a tendon. A controlled study of 891 patients. *J Bone Joint Surg Am.* **73**:1507–1525.

Kellenberger S, Schild L (2002). Epithelial sodium channel/degenerin family of ion channels: a variety of functions for a shared structure. *Physiol Rev.* **82**:735–767.

Kosek E, Lundberg L (2003). Segmental and plurisegmental modulation of pressure pain thresholds during static muscle contractions in healthy individuals. *Eur J Pain* **7**:251–258.

Magnusson SP, Hansen P, Aagaard P, et al. (2003). Differential strain patterns of the human gastrocnemius aponeurosis and free tendon, in vivo. *Acta Physiol Scand.* **177**:185–195.

Millar NL, Hueber AJ, Reilly JH, et al. (2010). Inflammation is present in early human tendinopathy. *Am J Sports Med.* **38**:2085–2091.

Molloy TJ, Kemp MW, Wang Y, et al. (2006). Microarray analysis of the tendinopathic rat supraspinatus tendon: glutamate signaling and its potential role in tendon degeneration. *J Appl Physiol.* **101**:1702–1709.

Parkinson J, Samiric T, Ilic MZ, et al. (2010). Change in proteoglycan metabolism is a characteristic of human patellar tendinopathy. *Arthritis Rheum.* **62**:3028–3035.

Puddu G, Ippolito E, Postacchini F (1976). A classification of Achilles tendon disease. *Am J Sports Med.* **4**:145–150.

Rio E, Moseley L, Purdam C, et al. (2014). The pain of tendinopathy: physiological or pathophysiological? *Sports Med.* **44**:9–23.

Shin D, Finni T, Ahn S, et al. (2008). In vivo estimation and repeatability of force–length relationship and stiffness of the human Achilles tendon using phase contrast MRI. *J Magn Reson Imaging.* **28**:1039–1045.

Steffen JM, Musacchia XJ (1986). Spaceflight effects on adult rat muscle protein, nucleic acids, and amino acids. *Am J Physiol.* **251(6 Pt 2)**:R1059–1063.

Tompra N, van Dieën JH, Coppieters MW (2016). Central pain processing is altered in people with Achilles tendinopathy. *Br J Sports Med.* **50**:1004–1007.

FURTHER READING

Easley ME, Le ILD (2008). Noninsertional Achilles tendinopathy: an overview. In: Nunley JA ed. *The Achilles tendon: treatment and rehabilitation.* New York: Springer. pp. 144–167.

Hoeger Bement MK, Rasiarmos RL, DiCapo JM, et al. (2009). The role of the menstrual cycle phase in pain perception before and after isometric fatiguing contraction. *Eur J Appl Physiol.* **106**:105–112.

Jósza LG, Kannus P (1997). *Human Tendons: Anatomy, Physiology, and Pathology.* Champaign, IL: Human Kinetics.

Kosek E, Ekholm J, Hansson P (1996). Modulation of pressure pain thresholds during and following isometric contraction in patients with fibromyalgia and in healthy controls. *Pain.* **64**:415–423.

Lawrence D (2014). The tendinopathy continuum explained. *SportEx Medicine & Dynamics.* **60**:21–26.

Millar NL, Wei AQ, Molloy TJ, et al. (2009). Cytokines and apoptosis in supraspinatus tendinopathy. *J Bone Joint Surg Br.* **91**:417–424.

CHAPTER 4

ACHILLES TENDINOPATHY

INTRODUCTION

Because it is such a large and prominent anatomical structure, the Achilles tendon has been well documented ever since it was first described by Andreas Vesalius (1514–1564) in his seminal work *De Humani Corporis Fabrica* (1543/1998).

 Several sources claim that Philip Verheyen (1648–1710), a Flemish surgeon and anatomist, was the first to create the eponym "Achilles tendon" in his book *Corporis Humani Anatomia* (1693/2011). The eponym describes the common tendon for the gastrocnemius and soleus muscles, although, at the time, Verheyen named it the "chorda Achillis". Verheyen reportedly conducted most of his dissection work on his own leg following its amputation. A thought-provoking image of this is shown in **Figure 4.1.**

FIGURE 4.1   Illustration showing Philip Verheyen dissecting his leg. This image is reported to be an artist's philosophical depiction and not based on fact, thus questioning the authenticity of the story.

Finally, we must consider the work of Leonardo da Vinci, who reported on the Achilles tendon's spiral arrangement as part of his anatomical studies in the 16th century. Much of his work remained unpublished at the time, but was rediscovered several centuries later.

GREEK MYTHOLOGY

According to Greek mythology, Achilles was the son of the Nereid Thetis and Peleus, the king of the Myrmidons. Following the birth of her son, Thetis dipped Achilles in the river Styx, a river flowing from the earth to the underworld (**Figure 4.2**).

FIGURE 4.2   Thetis dipping Achilles in the river Styx. Thetis is holding Achilles by his, not yet named, Achilles heel (an artists impression of the said event).

This made Achilles invincible, except for the heel by which his mother held him. During the Trojan War, the death of Achilles was brought about by Paris with an arrow to the heel (according to Statius). We still use the term "Achilles heel" to describe a weakness or vulnerable point.

EVOLUTIONARY THEORY

The Achilles tendon is believed to have first evolved from an existing weaker tendon over 2 million years ago when we transitioned from herbivorous apes to fast-running and efficient hunters capable of endurance bipedalism by means of the strength and elasticity of our tendons (see Chapter 2).

ANATOMY

The Achilles tendon forms an integral part of a long line of soft tissue running down the back of the body (**Figure 4.3**). This myofascial continuity has been described as the *superficial back line* by Thomas Myers (2001).

The interlinking structures of the superficial back line are as follows:

- plantar surface of toe flexors;
- plantar fascia and short toe flexors;
- calcaneus/Achilles tendon;
- gastrocnemius/soleus muscles;
- condyles of the femur;
- hamstrings;
- ischial tuberosity;
- sacrotuberous ligament;
- sacrum/sacrotuberous fascia;
- erector spinae muscles;
- occipital ridge;
- galea aponeurotica (epicranial aponeurosis).

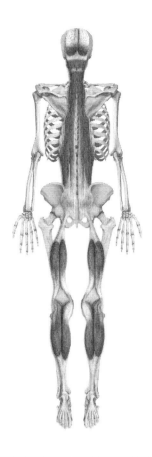

FIGURE 4.3   Representation of the continuity of the posterior myofascial tissue that houses the Achilles tendon and is referred to as the superficial back line by Myers (2001).

The gastrocnemius-soleus complex

Two adjoining muscles, the gastrocnemius and the soleus are often referred to as the triceps surae (three-headed [muscle] of the calf). The two distinct heads of the gastrocnemius muscle and the single muscle belly of the deeper soleus muscle form the triceps surae. Both muscles are found in the superficial posterior compartment of the lower leg along with the plantaris muscle. The compartment separates these muscles from the other lower-leg musculature located in the remaining three compartments: anterior; lateral; and deep posterior (**Figure 4.4**).

The gastrocnemius (**Figures 4.5** and **4.6**) originates from the posterior femoral condyles via strong tendons that extend over the upper muscle bellies to form a flat, tendinous aponeurotic covering. This significant tendinous anchoring hints at a lack of functional contractile range from the muscle while increasing its ability to withstand high load during isometric muscle contraction.

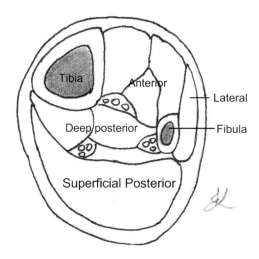

FIGURE 4.4   Cross-sectional diagram of the lower-limb compartments.

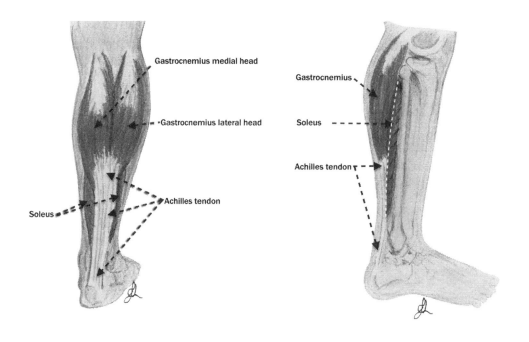

FIGURE 4.5-4.6   Posterior lower-limb musculature (left). Lateral view of the gastrocnemius-soleus muscle complex (right).

Both heads of the gastrocnemius also attach to the back of the knee joint capsule and the oblique popliteal ligament.

The belly of the medial gastrocnemius muscle is both longer and larger than the lateral belly; a higher incidence of muscle tears occurs at the musculotendinous junction (MTJ).

Two bursae are located under the heads of the gastrocnemius muscle; the medial bursa often communicates with the posterior knee joint. A small sesamoid bone, the fabella, is present under the lateral head in about 10–30% of the population (Duncan and Dahm, 2003); a medial fabella is also present in some people.

From each head of the gastrocnemius, muscle fibres run diagonally and unite into a central raphe. This broadens into an aponeurosis then narrows distally to unite with the tendon of the soleus to form the Achilles tendon. Fascicular geometry is a determinant of muscle function. The shorter fascicles with high insertion (pennation) angles seen in the gastrocnemius allow a high contractile force potential over a relatively short range, thereby favouring isometric action.

The gastrocnemius-soleus unit crosses three joints: knee; ankle; and the subtalar joint. The opposing movements of ankle dorsiflexion and knee extension can stretch the gastrocnemius excessively and cause muscle fibre rupture via a variety of proposed mechanisms, as seen with other multi-articular muscles, such as the hamstring group or the rectus femoris. The subtalar joint does not directly compete with the talocrural joint in the same plane of movement, but studies have suggested that it can impart a detrimental shearing force on the Achilles tendon (Clement, Taunton and Smart, 1984).

The gastrocnemius provides a large proportion of the power required for propulsion during activities such as walking, running, and jumping.

The gastrocnemius is innervated by a branch of the tibial nerve (sacral nerves S1, S2), with dermatomes L4, L5, and S2.

The soleus

The soleus originates from the posterior surface of the fibula head, and extends down the proximal quarter of the posterior fibula and the middle third of the posteromedial border of the tibia.

The muscle fibres are arranged in a multi-pennate (feather-like) fashion, which, like the gastrocnemius, contributes to a higher contractile force potential offset by a reduced range of movement. The soleus is wider than the gastrocnemius and resides between two aponeuroses, which eventually unite with the tendon of the gastrocnemius to form the Achilles tendon. Most clinicians consider the gastrocnemius to be the dominant calf muscle; however, research indicates that the soleus makes up over half the volume of the posterior compartment (Albracht, Arampatzis and Baltzopoulos, 2008), provides approximately half of the plantarflexor contribution required for vertical support during running (Dorn, Schache and Pandy, 2012), and produces forces superior to those of the gastrocnemius. Despite the continuity and shared tendon, the soleus also has contractile independence from the gastrocnemius, having a more dynamic function compared to the usual isometric activity of the gastrocnemius (Cronin, Avela and Finni, 2013).

The soleus assists with the maintenance of posture when standing and consists of mainly slow-twitch (type I) fibres, indicating its importance in endurance running. Regular contraction of the soleus also assists venous return.

Innervation comes from two branches of the tibial nerve (sacral nerves S1, S2), with a dermatomal supply from S2.

Do they have an "accessory soleus"?

The prevalence of a unilateral accessory soleus is about 0.7–10% (Brodie et al., 1997; Kouvalchouk et al., 2005). If present, this muscle is located below the soleus, is usually enclosed in its own fascia, and has its own blood supply. The presence of this muscle is often asymptomatic, but may cause compartment syndrome with pain and swelling around the posterolateral ankle. Clinically, accessory soleus muscles are more common in athletic men who have reached musculoskeletal maturity (Brodie et al., 1997). Magnetic resonance imaging (MRI) is the most suitable diagnostic technique to detect and differentiate this accessory muscle. If surgery is needed, resection is considered safer than a fasciotomy (Kouvalchouk et al., 2005).

Plantaris muscle

The plantaris is a thin muscle that arises from the posterior distal femur, just above the lateral supracondylar ridge, passes posterior to the knee joint capsule, and becomes tendinous distally to insert into the Achilles tendon. The muscle has a 7–10 cm belly at the top and a long, thin tendon that crosses between the gastrocnemius and the soleus muscles. The tendon inserts into the posteromedial part of the calcaneal tuberosity with or separate from the Achilles tendon.

The plantaris is absent in about 7–20% of people (Simpson, Hertzog and Barja, 1991). The plantaris is innervated from the tibial nerve root (sacral nerves S1, S2). It has earned the name of "freshman nerve"; its very thin, nerve-like appearance means that new medical students often mistaken it for a nerve.

The plantaris has an unusually high number of sensory nerve fibres suggesting a role as a sensory organ for the lower leg (Moore, Agur and Daily, 2008).

The Achilles tendon

The Achilles tendon begins as a tendinous continuation of the gastrocnemius muscle; its broad, flat origin narrows and rounds distally, and then flattens at the calcaneal insertion.

The tendon receives fibres from the soleus, which often continue to insert near the calcaneal insertion. The number of fibres from the gastrocnemius and the soleus vary considerably. In most individuals, the soleus contributes most of its fibres to the tendon. Distally, the tendon attaches to the mid-posterior calcaneus through a stiff, fibrocartilaginous expansion, shaped liked an upside-down triangle or delta. Some of the distal tendon fibres are continuous with the plantar fascia.

The collagen fibres of the tendon have a spiral arrangement that twists the tendon by around 50–90 degrees. The degree of rotation is dependent on the position of tendon fusion between the respective gastrocnemius and soleus tendon fibres.

Figure 4.7 shows a common distribution of Achilles tendon fibres from the superior musculature. This distribution varies, as shown in **Figure 4.8.**

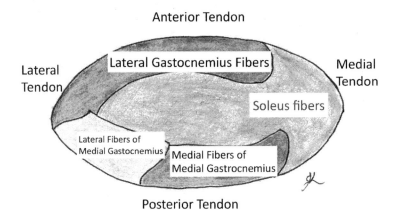

FIGURE 4.7 Cross-sectional representation of the Achilles tendon fibre contribution from the superior musculature.

The contribution of tendon fibres to the Achilles tendon was shown to vary in a study of 60 Japanese cadavers (Edama et al., 2015). The three classifications, which refer to the degree of torsion, from least to extreme, are shown in **Figure 4.8.**

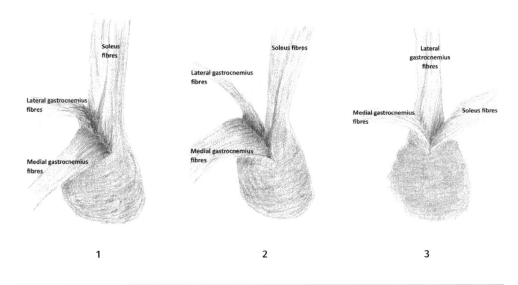

FIGURE 4.8 (1,2,3) The different contributions to the Achilles tendon, based on a study of 60 Japanese cadavers (Edama et al., 2014).

Fibre rotation reaches a maximum approximately 2–5 cm proximal to the tendon insertion. This high-stress area has a lower blood supply than the surrounding tendon and the lowest cross-sectional area; it is termed the mid-portion or mid-substance and is a common area of tendon pathology.

Neighbouring anatomical structures

The retrocalcaneal bursa (**Figure 4.9**) lies between the Achilles tendon and the posterior calcaneus (heel bone). This synovial, fluid-filled sac acts as a cushion between the two structures. Inflammation of this bursa is a common cause of localised heel pain.

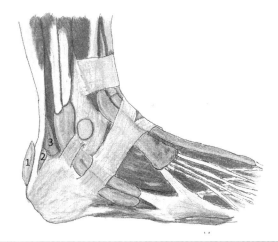

FIGURE 4.9   Diagram of the non-contractile structures around the Achilles tendon: (1) the subcutaneous Achilles bursa; (2) the retrocalcaneal bursa; (3) the Kager's fat pad triangle.

The subcutaneous Achilles bursa lies between the skin and the tendon. This bursa is less commonly irritated than the retrocalcaneal bursa, but it can become inflamed from excessive friction of a shoe heel cup. A non-defined inflammatory soft tissue condition called "pump bumps" can develop from irritation of this bursa. This differs from a bony growth in this region, which is termed a Haglund's deformity.

Kager's triangle is a mass of adipose tissue, commonly referred to as a fat pad; it is bordered anteriorly by the flexor hallucis longus (FHL) muscle, posteriorly by the Achilles tendon, and inferiorly by the calcaneus. The fat pad has three distinct regions with unique functions, as described by Theobald and colleagues (2006) (**Figure 4.10**).

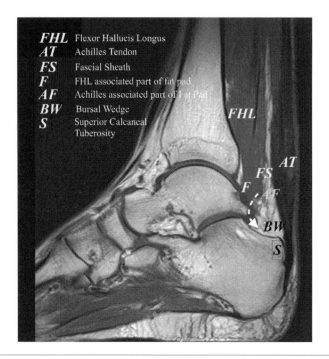

FIGURE 4.10 MRI of Kager's fat pad in a dorsiflexed foot in the sagittal plane showing the three regions of the fat pad: the Achilles-associated part lies immediately anterior to the Achilles tendon; the flexor hallucis longus (FHL)-associated part is enclosed within the fascial sheath, which extends from below the muscle belly of the FHL; and the calcaneal bursal wedge. The arrow indicates how the FHL-associated fat passes beneath the Achilles-associated fat in a J-shaped curve to fuse with it and form the bursal wedge.

Achilles fat pad

The Achilles tendon part of the fat pad is the most superficial. It lies anterior to the tendon and is surrounded by the paratenon, which holds the fat against the tendon, thus protecting the integrity of the small blood vessels from the posterior tibial and fibular arteries. Clinically, oedema can occur within the fat pad; this has been associated with inflammation that could temporarily diminish blood flow to the tendon. The use of corticosteroids in this area may cause fat pad atrophy (Cole and Schumacher, 2005), and could influence the other parts of the fat pad.

The flexor hallucis longus fat pad

The FHL-associated part of the fat pad lies anterior, or deeper, than the Achilles part and is enclosed within the FHL sheath. On MRI, the FHL fat pad is seen to extend down towards the calcaneus and under the Achilles fat pad, with which it then fuses and forms the third part of the fat pad, the calcaneal bursal wedge. It has been suggested that the FHL influences the bursal wedge by assisting its movement superiorly during plantarflexion. FHL pathology may be linked to posterior heel pain through fat pad dysfunction.

The calcaneal bursal wedge

The lower part of the fat pad is afforded some independence through loose folds of connective tissue that allow it to move into the retrocalcaneal bursa during dorsiflexion and away from it during plantarflexion. This maintains a balanced pressure within the triangle. Following any periods of immobilisation, the risk and effect of adhesions around the bursal wedge need to be considered.

The calcaneus and enthesis

The calcaneus is the largest tarsal bone and a weight-bearing anchor point for the Achilles tendon. The superficial tubercle of the posterior calcaneus can compress against the tendon during dorsiflexion; this potential source of pain is discussed later in this chapter. When deformed, as with a retrocalcaneal exostosis (Achilles heel bone spur), which is also known as a Haglund's deformity, it is unknown whether the bony deformity irritates the tendon or whether long-term tendon irritation causes the bony exostosis, or perhaps a mix of the two.

As mentioned in Chapter 1, the calcaneal enthesis is a specialised region with four zones: tendon; fibrocartilage; mineralised fibrocartilage; and bone (**Figure 4.11**). This is a typical arrangement for most teno-osseus junctions. Some of the tendon collagen fibres continue directly to the subcortical bone; these are often referred to as Sharpey's fibres.

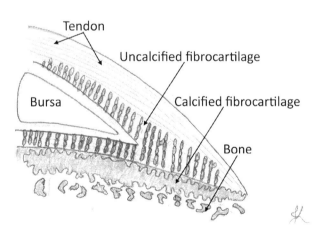

FIGURE 4.1   Diagram of a typical enthesis region with its differentiated zones.

TENDON MICROANATOMY

The Achilles tendon does not have a synovial sheath. Instead, it is enveloped in a loose elastic sleeve called the paratenon. This fibrillar covering allows free movement against the surrounding structures. The Achilles tendon shares many of the typical features of the other large lower-limb tendons (**Figure 4.12**). Chapter 1 provides more specific details on general tendon anatomy.

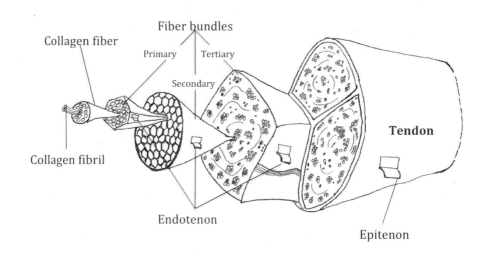

FIGURE 4.12   Microanatomy of a tendon.

The fascia cruris

One unique anatomical feature within the Achilles region is the fascia cruris (**Figure 4.13**). This mass of connective tissue surrounds the posterior structures of the calf and connects to the Achilles tendon via a confluence with the paratenon, a few centimetres above the calcaneal insertion.

The fascia cruris allows some gliding between the surrounding tissues and becomes tensioned with loading of the gastrocnemius-soleus musculature. A tear in the fascia cruris is a suggested cause of sudden-onset mid-tendon pain, with a presentation like a paratendinitis (Webborn et al., 2015).

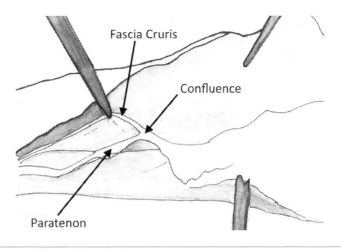

Fascia Cruris

Confluence

Paratenon

FIGURE 4.13   The fascia cruris and its connection to the paratenon.

VASCULAR AND NEURAL SUPPLY

This is covered in more detail in Chapter 1, but the Achilles tendon is sufficiently vascularised for its metabolic demands.[8] Blood supply to the tendon appears higher in women and is generally shown to decrease after the third decade of life (Åström and Westlin, 1994).

KEY BIOMECHANICAL PROPERTIES

The Achilles tendon is reported to stretch and recoil 1700–3500 times per day on average (Stevenson et al., 2009). A conditioning response or "transient lengthening" occurs within the first few steps (Maganaris, Narici and Maffulli, 2008).

Strains or deformations as high as 10% with hopping, 7% with running, and 5% with walking have been recorded (Lichtwark et al., 2009), but the most important biomechanical feature of the Achilles tendon is its energy-saving elasticity that saves approximately 90% of the force absorbed through the tendon and releases it on propulsion, thus saving a huge amount of muscular effort and energy when walking, running, and jumping. This allows the gastrocnemius-soleus muscle complex to predominantly function as isometric tensioners; as previously mentioned, this is aided by the high pennation angles of the muscle fibres that surround the tendon.

[8] Cook J (2012). Tendinopathies Masterclass Lecture. London, November 2012.

Each cycle of this energy-saving elasticity loses approximately 10% of the stored energy (Maganaris, Narici and Maffulli, 2008). This energy loss is termed hysteresis and causes a buildup of heat above that of fibroblast cell viability (Wilson and Goodship, 1994). This may account for the degeneration of healthy tendon with repetitive use. Heat and cell viability has not been discussed in recent research.

VISCOELASTICITY

Viscoelasticity refers to an interesting combination of properties that allows a stretch and recoil if a load is applied rapidly, but a more semi-permanent deformation in response to a longer loading time.

WALKING WITH YOUR ACHILLES TENDON

While it was previously thought that the energy storage capacity of the Achilles tendon was not used during walking because of the long stance times, research has demonstrated that this may not be correct. The plantarflexor muscles tension the tendon, which acts like a catapult as it slowly stores energy during the stance phase and then releases it during push-off (Ishikawa et al., 2005). This allows the ankle joint to be far more energy-efficient than the knee and hip joints. This mechanism supplies the ankle joint with efficiency that is 2–6 times greater than that afforded by muscle contraction alone (Sawicki, Lewis and Ferris, 2009).

RUNNING

As running speed increases, more power is generated by the hip and knee musculature. This power generation and energy storage is reflected in the anatomy of the lower limbs. As previously described, the lower-limb plantarflexors have short muscle fibres and higher pennation angles with a long, elastic Achilles tendon. This is contrasted by the larger and longer musculature and shorter tendons found around the hip joint. One of the most notable differences between a sprinter and a distance runner is the size of their gluteus maximus muscle as opposed to their gastrocnemius muscle. The hind limb of a horse is another example of proximal muscle bulk and more distal tendon tissue (**Figure 4.14**), an arrangement that favours running.

FIGURE 4.14   The hind limb of a horse showing the arrangement of the powerful proximal muscle bulk and the lighter, slenderer tendinous distal anatomy lending itself to the development of speed, endurance, and efficiency. We can appreciate how the human leg follows this pattern to a lesser degree.

BIOMECHANICAL CAUSES OF ACHILLES TENDINOPATHY

Little has been written about the potential biomechanical causes of Achilles tendinopathy. Overpronation of the foot is an unlikely cause as suggested by the twisting and wringing theory (Clement, Taunton and Smart, 1984). Overpronation could have an influence on childhood development of the tendon, but this has not been researched. It is also possible that supination may keep the foot locked and increase tensile force through the tendon.

Research has also identified a correlation between poor gluteus medius and maximus function and Achilles tendon pain (Franettovich Smith et al., 2014). The cause of this link is unclear, but it supports the need to consider the full kinetic chain and overall movement control during assessment and rehabilitation.

ALTERED MUSCLE ACTIVATION

Within tendinopathic limbs, an increased force and total time of activation has been observed in the gastrocnemius and soleus muscles (Azevedo et al., 2009). This indicates that the muscles might be working harder and for longer to dissipate forces and reduce the stress on the tendon, thus also reducing the strain.

PATHOLOGY

Pathology theories and pain mechanisms are covered in Chapter 3. Some specific Achilles tendon-related pathology issues are covered in this section.

TRUE TENDINOPATHY

A true tendinopathy is one that occurs purely in the mid-substance. Other tendinopathies often involve the enthesis and should be correctly termed enthesopathies. However, they are most commonly referred to as insertional tendinopathy or just tendinopathy.

INSERTIONAL ACHILLES TENDINOPATHY (ENTHESOPATHY)

An Achilles enthesopathy is more frequently described as an insertional Achilles tendinopathy and often shares many of the pathological characteristics of mid-substance pathology. The enthesis organ includes: the Achilles tendon; fibrocartilage; the periosteum of the posterior calcaneus; the retrocalcaneal bursa; and Kager's fat pad. Any of these structures can cause pain and may masquerade as a tendinopathy. Calcaneal apophysitis, also known as Sever's disease, in active children is one such condition. Posterior impingement of the talocrural joint from excessive plantar flexion is another condition with a similar presentation to insertional Achilles tendinopathy and is common during plantarflexion-based activities like dancing and swimming.

As previously described, the Achilles tendon is predominantly a tensile structure, but a compressive force can occur from the posterior calcaneus compressing the tendon via a cam-like mechanism when the ankle is dorsiflexed (**Figure 4.15**) (Cook and Purdam, 2011).

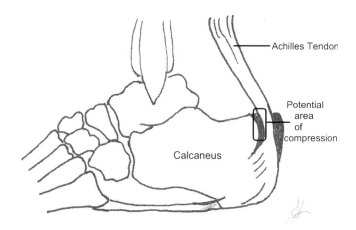

Achilles Tendon

Potential area of compression

Calcaneus

FIGURE 4.15   Image showing the potential location of tendon compression over the posterior superficial calcaneal tuberosity during dorsiflexion.

RUPTURES

Research indicates that all ruptures could potentially be the result of a pre-existing, and likely asymptomatic, tendinosis that is stressed by a sudden acute overload (Kujala, Sarna and Kaprio, 2005). A partial rupture is indicated by a sudden sensation of tearing or pulling that causes sudden pain. A partial rupture is difficult to detect on imaging and often has a tendinopathic presentation. A partial rupture should be managed like a tendinopathy. As previously discussed, a tear of the fascia cruris may also cause a similar presentation to a partial tendon tear.

PARATENDINOPATHY (OR PERITENDINITIS)

Paratendinopathy is characterised by an inflammatory response and can frequently be linked to friction from footwear or a direct impact from a hockey stick or shopping trolley, for example. Pathology of the paratenon often precludes intratendinous changes and involves the buildup of fibrotic adhesions in the underlying tendon (Józsa and Kannus, 1997). These adhesions increase with immobility and may explain the characteristic stiffness experienced during the first few steps in the morning and the creaking crepitus feeling at the back of the heel often felt and reported by patients. In addition, the underlying tendon often swells during tendinopathy, thereby further reducing the available space between tendon and paratenon.

The following assessment section is supported by the clinical guidance sheet in Appendix 1, which can be used as a quick reference guide when assessing patients in the clinic.

SUBJECTIVE ASSESSMENT

The aims of subjective assessment are: (1) identify intrinsic and extrinsic risk factors from the client's occupation, hobbies, or training programme that may predispose them to Achilles tendon pathology; (2) clarify pain behaviour, history, and severity; (3) make a detailed account of the client's loading history, potentially identifying the cause of the problem; and (4) begin to reason the nature of the condition, including the possibility of a rupture.

During the assessment, consider how many of these risk factors are present:

- previous injury;
- age >30 years;
- post-menopause;
- poor flexibility;
- reduced strength;
- increased weight;
- general weight-bearing;
- obesity;
- rheumatoid arthritis;
- diabetes mellitus (type 2);
- fluoroquinolones (antibiotic);
- increased loading;
- change in activity.

In addition to these evidence-based risk factors, an increased incidence of tendinopathy is seen in patients who have started a New Year's resolution to get fit by taking up running. Fit cyclists who decide to start running are another high-risk group. The demands of rapid loading placed on the lower limbs are considerably higher with running compared to cycling and the volume of running is often high because of cyclists' pre-existing fitness levels.

WHAT ABOUT THE PAIN?

If there is no morning stiffness and pain in the Achilles tendon, then it is highly unlikely to be a tendinopathy and further assessment is indicated.

The absence of this key symptom should cause the therapist to question the pathology and further investigate any masquerading pathologies, such as irritation of the plantaris muscle. Achilles tendinopathy pain should also be of a more focal nature; diffuse pain is again indicative of other structures. Any referred pain should also lead to consideration of a rare irritation of the sural (lateral) or medial fascial accessory nerve. Again, both are rare. **Table 4.1** outlines some of the pathologies found within the Achilles tendon region. Note that multiple pathologies may coexist.

PATHOLOGY		DESCRIPTION
MID-PORTION TENDINOPATHY		Morning pain and stiffness that rapidly reduces or 'warms up' with activity. Pain reduces when stretched into dorsiflexion.
INSERTIONAL TENDINOPATHY		Similar to mid-portion tendinopathy but with more distal symptoms located at or very near the calcaneal insertion. End of range dorsiflexion may increase pain.
RETROCALCANEAL BURSITIS		Symptoms more diffuse than a standard insertional tendinopathy and exacerbated by low-load dorsiflexion.
FAT PAD IRRITATION		Similar presentation to retrocalcaneal bursitis; may be differentiated from tendon pathology using simple palpation for tenderness behind the tendon.
PARATENON INFLAMMATION		Causes by repetitive low-load activity. Highly irritable on palpation around the tendon. More diffuse than intratendinous pathology. Unaffected by passive dorsiflexion.

PLANTARIS TENDINOPATHY		Rare source of pain often over the medial tendon. Pain increases with dorsiflexion.
POSTERIOR IMPINGEMENT		Pain with passive end range plantar flexion. History of plantar-flexion based activity.
SURAL NERVE IRRITATION		Lateral Achilles pain; shooting pain that may refer to the toes or further up the lower leg.
FLEXOR HALLUCIS LONGUS PAIN		Medial Achilles pain often higher than mid-tendon that increases with hallux extension or resisted hallux flexion.
ACCESSORY SOLEUS		Rare pathology; pain deep to the Achilles tendon and often a palpable muscle bulk. Pain may increase with activity due to a compartment-type syndrome.
PARTIAL RUPTURE		Sudden onset of pain followed by significantly reduced function.
FASCIA CRURIS RUPTURE		Very similar to a partial rupture, likely pre-existing muscle tension.

TABLE 4.1

Sudden pain

Sudden pain can indicate a full or partial tear, which often occurs in the pathological zone. A full rupture is often reported as a loud "shot"-like noise and the feeling of being kicked in the back of the heel. Pain and significant dysfunction is usually felt immediately. A partial rupture is less severe and partial function is maintained, with the main limitation being from pain inhibition.

Other anatomical causes

A tear to the fascia cruris is another suggested cause of pain from the Achilles region. Pain is usually of a sudden onset; it is experienced medial, lateral, or both around the mid-substance of the tendon. Confirmation requires an ultrasound (US) to identify the tear to the tissue (Webborn et al., 2015).

Clinical examination

A clinical examination of the Achilles tendon consists of the following six elements:

1. observation;
2. direct muscle and tendon loading;
3. joint testing;
4. palpation;
5. special tests and differentiation;
6. gait and movement analysis.

Observation requires the clinician to note the patient's overall posture, with a final focus on the lower limbs. General muscle bulk and visual muscle mass asymmetries should be noted, as should any evident tendon thickening. A more objective approach is achieved by measuring the circumference around the gastrocnemius muscle bellies on both legs. Taking a photo of any tendon thickening may also be helpful as a positive reference point following successful rehabilitation guidance.

Loading of the Achilles tendon and gastrocnemius-soleus muscle complex is an important part of the assessment because it indicates the ability of the structures to tolerate and control load. If the gastrocnemius-soleus muscle complex demonstrates poor strength that is not caused by acute pain inhibition, then it is likely that the Achilles tendon may also be in poor structural condition.

Heel raises (**Figure 4.16**) allow a very simple but important assessment of the strength of the gastrocnemius-soleus muscle complex. Begin by asking your patient to perform one slow repetition on a flat surface, lifting the heel up and down with a controlled movement. This should be followed by attempting 10 repetitions per leg. It is advisable to alter the number of repetitions depending on the individual's baseline fitness levels, possibly using the other leg for comparison.

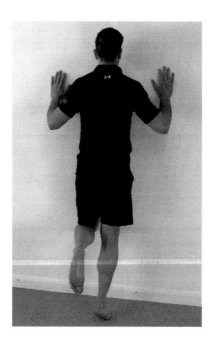

FIGURE 4.16   This simple heel raise action should be repeated in a slow controlled fashion approximately 10 times.

Following the heel raises, a continuous and functional loading should be performed if pain allows it. Functional assessment should allow an assessment of the integrated function the lower-limb kinetic chain. This can begin with a progression from the repeated heel raises to single-leg hopping.

Single-leg hopping
A strong Achilles tendon with suitably strong lower-limb musculature should produce a series of small hops (**Figure 4.17**) with little load absorption through range; there should also be evident force production through ankle joint plantarflexion and no heel contact with the ground during each landing phase. A weak or painful muscle or tendon will

result in a much slower hop with compensatory mechanisms, such as heel contact with the ground, increased knee flexion, and excessive lowering of the torso to absorb and then produce enough upward momentum of the body to leave the ground. Finally, "arm flapping" may be seen where patients use their arms to create extra upward lift.

You should expect to see a correlation between single-leg heel raise ability and the ability to produce single-leg hops.

FIGURE 4.17   A single-leg hop indicates higher-level function and ability

One important point should be considered. Do your patients need to single-leg hop? Do not ask them to hop if they cannot perform controlled single-leg heel raises or are morbidly obese.

To build a general picture of your patient's overall lower-limb function, a series of quick movement screening tests can be performed. These are: the squat; one-leg squat; and basic walking gait analysis.

For each of these basic movements you should be looking for three key things: an abnormality; the cause of that abnormality; and whether the abnormality is relevant.

Joint assessment need only be a brief assessment of the ankle joint range. The normal, full range from dorsiflexion to plantarflexion is approximately 55–60 degrees; however, this may be much higher in athletic individuals, such as dancers and swimmers. A limitation of dorsiflexion is not an identified cause of Achilles tendon pain; however, following the onset of pathology, dorsiflexion may be progressively reduced because of pain and muscle tension. This can be assessed and managed accordingly.

Palpation should cover the following structures, while noting any abnormalities and reports of pain:

- plantar fascia;
- posterior calcaneal region;
- tendon cord;

- retrocalcaneal region;
- upper tendon and MTJ;
- general muscle tone and focal painful areas.

SPECIAL TESTS

Test for posterior talocrural impingement with plantarflexion

Passive plantarflexion to the end of the available range will cause pain if posterior impingement is present. Further investigation is recommended. An X-ray can confirm the presence of an exostosis on the posterior talus, commonly referred to as os trigonum (**Figure 4.18**).

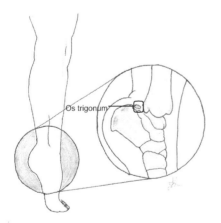 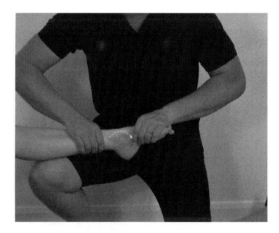

FIGURE 4.18   The posterior impingement test requires an assisted plantar flexion into the end of range. Impingement may be caused by several factors, including an os trigonum, or chronic bone

Dorsiflexion test for tendon and paratenon differentiation

A reduction in pain on palpation over the mid-tendon when the ankle is dorsiflexed helps to differentiate tendon from paratenon pathology. If the thickening or pain location is reduced by passive dorsiflexion, then it is indicative of an intratendinous problem (tendinopathy). If dorsiflexion does not influence the swelling or pain, then it is more likely to be a pathology affecting the paratenon. A mix of both pathologies may exist **(Figure 4.19a,b).**

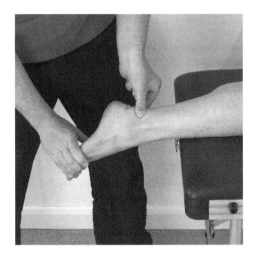 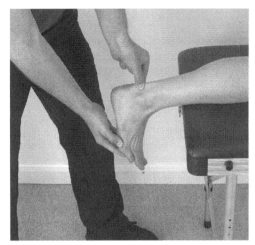

A   B

FIGURE 4.19 (a, b)   The Royal London Hospital test is performed to help differentiate between tendon and paratenon pathology.

Simmons test for Achilles tendon rupture

If pain in the Achilles region was of a sudden onset and caused by a rapid movement leading to an immediate loss of function, a full rupture should be suspected. The Simmons test (**Figure 4.20**) requires a simple squeeze of the gastrocnemius muscle bellies with the foot passively resting off the end of a treatment couch. A normal reaction would be a slight ankle plantarflexion movement when the muscle is squeezed. If this test does not produce ankle movement, an Achilles tendon rupture may be present. US scanning is often used as final confirmation and to assess the extent of the damage.

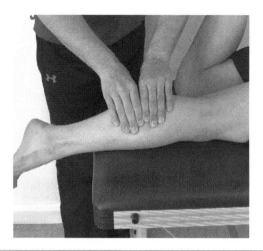

FIGURE 4.20   The Simmons squeeze test is used to test for a suspected Achilles tendon rupture. The results should be interpreted with the onset and history of injury details.

Foot posture

As mentioned previously, there is a tenuous link between overpronation and tendinopathy. Some clinicians have suggested that the opposite movement pattern of supination may cause the foot to become more rigid and less capable of absorbing force and thus place a greater and more sustained force on the tendon. A limited extension of the first metacarpophalangeal joint, known as hallux rigidus (stiff big toe), may also cause an increased force on the Achilles tendon through increased rigidity during propulsion. Despite the lack of research linking foot dysfunction with Achilles tendinopathy, many expert clinicians believe that foot and ankle pathology may contribute to Achilles tendon pain either through primary biomechanics or via a secondary pain inhibition and tissue offload mechanism leading to a reduced regional movement strategy and poor function.

Diagnostic imaging

Standard US scanners, Doppler scanners – which detect neovessels – and more recently US tissue characterisation devices, can be used to detect and monitor tendon pathology. (See Chapter 16 for more information.)

Gait analysis

The correlation between running form and injury has mainly focused on patellar tendinopathy, with some additional research on gluteal and hamstring tendon pain. Although there is no evidence directly linking gait style to Achilles tendinopathy risk, the theoretical underpinning for teaching good running form provides a clear rational for gait re-education. Chapter 10 provides detailed information on assessment and coaching points.

THE DIAGNOSIS

Following a full assessment, and the decision that an Achilles tendinopathy is the most likely cause of the pain, the tendinopathy stage should be determined using all the gathered subjective and objective information. This is not an easy task and may involve a few assumptions. The following patient presentations are typical examples of patients in each of the stages. Much crossover and variation may exist.

Patient A (reactive tendinopathy) has a history of a recent increase in loading or a period of lay-off followed by a rapid return to sport. A sudden switch to running from cycling or to a minimalist running style may also have caused Achilles pain. Muscle function appears to be good with no evident weakness. A history of repeated Achilles tendon pain is not likely.

Patient B (tendinopathy in a state of disrepair) has a history of recurrent tendinopathy. Heel raises are poor and general lower-limb function shows that a weakness is evident following a previous injury that was not properly rehabilitated. Previous treatment consisted of rest from all sporting activities but no rehabilitation.

Patient C (degenerative tendinopathy) has accepted their tendon pain and discomfort, which may have reduced while the tendon continues into a degenerative stage. This patient may not present for treatment because of the absence of pain. The onset of pain may indicate an overlapping reactive tendinopathy.

The clinical reasoning process involves an early attempt to categorise patients based on their overall presentation and their suspected tendinopathy stage; reactive, disrepair, or degenerative.

The reported severity and level of tendon irritation are also important and serve as a guide to inform the rehabilitation starting point. It also helps gain an empathetic understanding of what tendinopathy means to the patient and how it is affecting them.

Any identified biomechanical abnormalities, and the results of the loading and strength tests, should be considered in the context of the patient's sporting background and current participation levels.

Finally, individual training factors, medical condition, and any further personal factors should be considered when planning the patient's rehabilitation programme.

It is important to structure a programme that suits the patient's lifestyle and sporting endeavours because adherence to rehabilitation programmes is poor when the patient is not managed and monitored by a professional on a regular basis. For the patient to understand their tendinopathy and the rehabilitation required, the clinician must first get to know and understand the patient's needs and goals.

REHABILITATION CONSIDERATIONS FOR A REACTIVE, IN DISREPAIR, AND DEGENERATIVE TENDON

Specific loading principles are covered in Chapter 9 and rehabilitation guidelines are provided in Appendix 1. The following information outlines some of the key tendon rehabilitation principles.

Load management

The patient's current loading volume and type need to be identified and most likely reduced to allow a suitable environment for tendon recovery. However, this needs to be initiated in tandem with a suitable loading stimulus to either maintain tendon health or begin to improve it through load adaptation. The difference between aggravating and adaptive loading tasks is determined by the rate and volume of loading. For example, the rapid and repetitive loading that endurance running places on the tendon would aggravate the tendon, whereas a slow or sustained tendon load is thought to stimulate positive tendon adaptation. In summary, stop the rapid loading and begin the slow loading.

Continuum theory

Reactive

A tendon's status as reactive, in disrepair, or degenerative should also influence the treatment plan. A reactive tendon should return to normal if the initial stressor is removed and this is often achieved via a reduction in loading, training volume, training intensity, training frequency. Reducing the stress on the elastic properties of the tendon for a short period of time helps the recovery of the reactive tendon. High-volume eccentric training is not recommended for reactive tendinopathy because it simply repeatedly overloads an already overloaded tendon. Complete rest should also be avoided because a sudden return to the same activities following a period of relative immobilisation prevents the correct adaptation of the tendon.

Disrepair

Rehabilitation for a tendon in a state of disrepair requires a well-planned loading programme (isometric, concentric, eccentric). Resting the tendon ill-prepares it for future loading and may reduce tensile strength further.

A period, or multiple periods, of reactive tendinopathy are also likely to be identified in the patient's history; reducing any future exacerbations is paramount to a full and lasting rehabilitation programme. Strengthening the contractile gastrocnemius-soleus muscle complex and the non-contractile but elastic Achilles tendon, should be a primary goal. The gastrocnemius-soleus muscle complex should possess adequate endurance and maximal load capacity, which is often lacking in tendinopathic limbs.

Degenerative

Degenerative tendons have usually settled into a less symptomatic state or have become more "accepted" by the patient. For this reason, most degenerative tendons are not seen or managed clinically unless the tendon has succumbed to a more reactive tendinopathy in addition to the longer-standing underlying degenerative state. The reactive pathology should be reduced so that patients return to their baseline. From this point, a structured loading pattern can begin. The tendinopathic region may never return to normal structurally, but the surrounding tendon tissue and muscle units should still adapt positively to the correct loading stimulus.

The continuum stage also affects the suitability of additional tendon treatments, with more aggressive offerings considered less suitable, unnecessary, and even harmful for early reactive tendons.

EXERCISES FOR ACHILLES TENDON REHABILITATION

The following exercises are arranged in a progressive manner with the starting point and exercise suitability determined by individual patient presentation. Chapter 9 is a recommended read to understand the principles of exercise prescription and the underpinning theory.

Isometric heel raise

The isometric heel raise (**Figure 4.21**) is an excellent method of adding load with minimal symptom exacerbation. The benefits and theory of isometric loading are covered in more depth in Chapter 9.

FIGURE 4.21   Isometric heel raise.

Technique

Standing on one leg, raise the heel slightly off the ground to load the posterior muscle-tendon unit. A chair or wall can be used to aid balance.

Maintain the isometric hold for up to 60 seconds and repeat following a 2-minute rest interval up to 3 times. This exercise should be performed 3–4 times throughout the day.

Some pain and discomfort may be felt during the exercise. This should diminish and result in reduced pain from the Achilles region after each hold; if this does not occur after three attempts, the injury should be reassessed.

Seated calf press

The seated calf press (**Figure 4.22**) can be used for isometric and isokinetic loading. The stable seated position, safety features, and quick weight adjustments are favourable for specific isolation exercises.

FIGURE 4.22   Seated calf press.

Technique

Press the footplate forward using ankle plantarflexion followed by a controlled dorsiflexion movement.

Instruct your patient to keep their knees unlocked during the exercise and make sure the safety stops remain in place to stop the footplate travelling back too far. Be cautious of allowing too much dorsiflexion as the footplate retracts because this can irritate insertional pain.

Basic strength training guidelines

Use the following repetitions, sets, and frequencies as a guide only. Use the principles outlined in Chapter 9 to create personalised programmes:

REPETITIONS	SETS	FREQUENCY PER WEEK
6–10	2–4	× 2 for beginners and in-season; 3–4 for strength-trained individuals; 4+ for highly active individuals.

Standing heel raise

Perhaps the simplest and most effective way of loading the gastrocnemius-soleus muscle complex and Achilles tendon, this simple heel raise exercise (**Figure 4.23**) can be performed from a flat surface or a step to allow extra dorsiflexion.

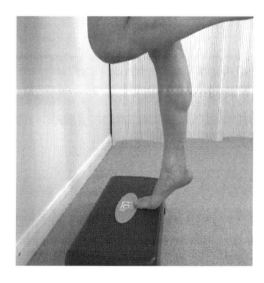

FIGURE 4.23   Standing heel raise.

Technique

Instruct your patient to perform slow repetitions to avoid using the tendon's energy-storing elasticity. Do not lower the heel off the back of a step if insertional Achilles pain is suspected.

Bent knee heel raise for a soleus bias

Bending the knee shortens the gastrocnemius muscle, placing it at a mechanical disadvantage. This allows increased force production from the soleus muscle fibres. The efficacy of the bent knee exercises (**Figure 4.24a,b**) is supported by the significant anatomical fibre contribution from the soleus to the Achilles tendon and the functional contribution of the soleus to walking and running.

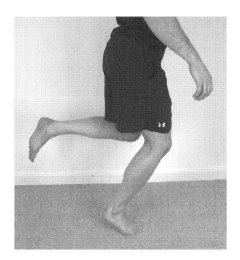

A   B

FIGURE 4.24   (a) Bent knee heel raise for a soleus bias (step). (b) Bent knee calf press for a soleus bias (seated).

Technique

Heel raise exercises with a bent knee can be performed from either a seated or standing position.

The seated version is much easier to perform if you have suitable equipment; simple heel raises can be performed with sufficient load. The standing bent knee exercise is easier to perform with the heel off the edge of a step, using a wall or rail for stability.

Weighted calf raise

Once the exercise techniques have been taught and practised, you need to add the correct load to stress the gastrocnemius-soleus muscle complex and promote contractile and connective tissue adaptation. Resistance can be added using machines, weights

(**Figure 4.25a**), or simply a rucksack (**Figure 4.25b**) with some weighted contents. Repetitions, sets, and frequency information is provided in the rehabilitation guidelines in Appendix 1 and are discussed in more detail in Chapter 9.

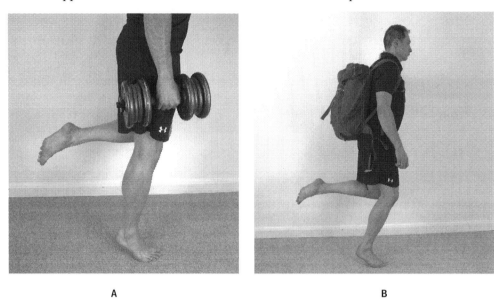

A   B

FIGURE 4.25   (a) Weighted heel raise using dumbbell. (b) Weighted heel raise using rucksack.

CROSS-TRAINING AND RUNNING

The addition of the loading exercises should be offset by a reduction of tendon rapid loading activities, mainly running and jumping. To maintain fitness and motivation, these activities can be replaced with non-impact activities, such as cycling, rowing, or swimming. I usually advise runners to reduce their running volume by 50% initially and then monitor the response to the rehabilitation programme after a few weeks.

ADJUNCT TREATMENTS

Further treatment and management options are described throughout this book in Chapters 10 (*Gait Manipulation*), 11 (*Massage for Tendon Pain*), 12 (*Taping Tendons*) 13 (*Extracorporeal Shockwave Therapy*), 14 (*An Introduction to Regenerative Biomedicine*), and 15 (*Miscellaneous Treatment Options for Tendinopathy*).

CONCLUSION

The unique elastic energy storage capacity of the Achilles tendon is its key function. However, it is also its highest level of function and one that makes the tendon susceptible to overload.

The assessment and treatment of Achilles tendinopathy has changed significantly, from an inflammatory model of injury to a less defined tendinopathy pathogenesis. While many passive treatments are proving useful, popular, and even fashionable, the core of a successful treatment programme unequivocally relies on the modification of loading. This approach is far from passive; for this reason, the willingness of the patient to adhere to a treatment plan is the final hurdle to clear for successful management. The evidence on isometric loading is still limited, but based on anecdotal reports, my own patient experiences, and the research supporting its use for patellar tendinopathy, I highly recommend teaching patients this technique for pain relief and rehabilitation.

REFERENCES

Albracht K, Arampatzis A, Baltzopoulos V (2008). Assessment of muscle volume and physiological cross-sectional area of the human triceps surae muscle in vivo. *J Biomech.* **41**:2211–2218.

Åström M and Westlin N (1994). Blood flow in chronic Achilles tendinopathy. *Clin Orthop Relat Res.* **308**:166–172.

Azevedo LB, Lambert MI, Vaughan CL, et al. (2009). Biomechanical variables associated with Achilles tendinopathy in runners. *Br J Sports Med.* **43**:288–292.

Brodie JT, Dormans JP, Gregg JR, et al. (1997). Accessory soleus muscle: a report of 4 cases and review of literature. *Clin Orthop Relat Res.* **337**:180–186.

Clement DB, Taunton JE, Smart GW (1984). Achilles tendonitis and peritendinitis: etiology and treatment. *Am J Sports Med.* **12**:179–184.

Cole BJ, Schumacher HR Jr (2005). Injectable corticosteroids in modern practice. *J Am Acad Orthop Surg.* **13**:37–46.

Cook JL, Purdam C (2011). Is compressive load a factor in the development of tendinopathy? *Br J Sports Med.* **46**:163–168.

Cronin NJ, Avela J, Finni T, et al. (2013). Differences in contractile behaviour between the soleus and medial gastrocnemius muscles during human walking. *J Exp Biol.* **216**:909–914.

Dorn TW, Schache AG, Pandy MG (2012). Muscular strategy shift in human running: dependence of running speed on hip and ankle muscle performance. *J Exp Biol.* **215**:1944–1956.

Duncan W, Dahm DL (2003). Clinical anatomy of the fabella. *Clin Anat.* **15**: 448–449.

Edama M, Kubo M, Onishi H, et al. (2015). The twisted structure of the human Achilles tendon. *Scand J Med Sci Sports.* **25**:e497–503.

Franettovich Smith MM, Honeywill C, Wyndow N, et al. (2014). Neuromotor control of gluteal muscles in runners with Achilles tendinopathy. *Med Sci Sports Exerc.* **46**:594–599.

Ishikawa M, Komi PV, Grey MJ, et al. (2005). Muscle-tendon interaction and elastic energy usage in human walking. *J Appl Physiol (1985).* **99**:603–608.

Józsa LG, Kannus P (1997). *Human Tendons: Anatomy, Physiology, and Pathology. Champaign, IL: Human Kinetics.*

Kouvalchouk JF, Lecocq J, Parier J, et al. (2005). [The accessory soleus muscle: a report of 21 cases and a review of the literature]. [Article in French]. *Rev Chir Orthop Reparatrice Appar Mot.* **91**:232–238.

Kujala UM, Sarna S, Kaprio J. (2005). Cumulative incidence of achilles tendon rupture and tendinopathy in male former elite athletes. *Clin J Sport Med.* **15**:133–135.

Lichtwark G, McGuigan R, Dorey N, et al. (2009). Achilles tendon compliance: implications for gait, injury and rehabilitation. *J Sci Med Sport.* **12**:S21.

Maganaris CN, Narici MV, Maffulli N (2008). Biomechanics of the Achilles tendon. *Disabil Rehabil.* **30**:1542–1547.

Moore KL, Agur AMR, Dailey AF (2008)**.** *Clinically Oriented Anatomy. 6th edn. Philadelphia, PA: Wolters Kluwer/*Lippincott Williams & Wilkins.

Myers TW (2001). *Anatomy Trains: Myofascial Meridians for Manual and Movement Therapists. Edinburgh: Churchill Livingstone.*

Sawicki GS, Lewis CL, Ferris DP (2009). It pays to have a spring in your step. Exerc Sport Sci Rev. **37**:130–138.

Simpson SL, Hertzog MS, Barja RH (1991). The plantaris tendon graft: an ultrasound study. *J Hand Surg.* **16**:708–711.

Stevenson N, Smeathers JE, Grigg NP, et al. (2009). Modelling activity dependent diametral strain in Achilles tendon. *J Sci Med Sport.* **12**:S18–19.

Theobald P, Bydder G, Dent C, et al. (2006). The functional anatomy of Kager's fat pad in relation to retrocalcaneal problems and other hindfoot disorders. *J Anat.* **208**:91–97.

Verheyen P (2011). *Corporis Humani Anatomia: In Qua Omnia Tam Veterum, Quam Recentiorum Anatomicorum Inventa Methodo Nova & Intellectu Facillima Describuntur, Ac Tabulis Aeneis Repraesentantur. [Latin]. Charleston, SC: Nabu Press.*

Vesalius A (1998). De Humani Corporis Fabrica. [Latin]. Palo Alto, CA: Octavo.

Webborn N, Morrissey D, Sarvananthan K, et al. (2015). Acute tear of the fascia cruris at the attachment to the Achilles tendon: a new diagnosis. Br J Sports Med. 49:1398–1403.

Wilson AM, Goodship AE (1994). Exercise-induced hyperthermia as a possible mechanism for tendon degeneration. *J Biomech.* **27**:899–905.

FURTHER READING

Alfredson H (2005). The chronic painful Achilles and patellar tendon: research on basic biology and treatment. *Scand J Med Sci Sports.* **15**:252–259.

Alfredson H, Bjur D, Thorsen K, et al. (2002). High intratendinous lactate levels in painful chronic Achilles tendinosis. An investigation using microdialysis technique. *J Orthop Res.* **20**:934–938.

Allison GT, Purdam C (2009). Eccentric loading for Achilles tendinopathy: strengthening or stretching? *Br J Sports Med.* **43**:276–279.

Antflick J, Myers C (2014). Management of tendinopathies with ultrasound tissue characterisation. *sportEX Med.* **6**:26–30.

Banes AJ, Tsuzaki M, Yamamoto J, et al. (1995). Mechanoreception at the cellular level: the detection, interpretation, and diversity of responses to mechanical signals. *Biochem Cell Biol.* **73**:349–365.

Bramble DM, Lieberman DE (2004). Endurance running and the evolution of *Homo. Nature.* **432**:345–352.

Cao H, Zhang YQ (2008). Spinal glial activation contributes to pathological pain states. *Neurosci Biobehav Rev.* **32**:972–983.

Cook JL, Purdam CR (2009). Is tendon pathology a continuum? A pathology model to explain the clinical presentation of load-induced tendinopathy. *Br J Sports Med.* **43**:409–416.

Coombes BK, Bisset L, Vicenzino B (2010). Efficacy and safety of corticosteroid injections and other injections for management of tendinopathy: a systematic review of randomised controlled trials. *Lancet.* **376**:1751–1767.

Danielson P, Alfredon H, Forsgren (2007). In situ hybridization studies confirming recent findings of the existence of a local nonneuronal catecholamine production in human patella tendon tendinosis. *Microsc Res Tech.* **70**:908–911.

Docking SI, Daffy J, vanSchie HT, et al. (2012). Tendon structure changes after maximal exercise in the Thoroughbred horse: use of ultrasound tissue characterisation to detect in vivo tendon response. *Vet J.* **194**:338–342.

Engebretsen L, Steffen K, Alsousou J, et al. (2010). IOC consensus paper on the use of platelet-rich plasma in sports medicine. *Br J Sports Med.* **44**:1072–1081.

Fallon K, Purdam C, Cook J, et al. (2008). A "polypill" for acute tendon pain in athletes with tendinopathy? *J Sci Med Sport.* **11**:235–238.

Firth BL, Dingley P, Davies ER, et al. (2010). The effect of kinesiotape on function, pain, and motoneuron excitability in healthy people and people with Achilles tendinopathy. *Clin J Sport Med.* **20**:416–421.

Furia JP, Rompe JD (2007). Extracorporeal shock wave therapy in the treatment of chronic plantar fasciitis and Achilles tendinopathy. *Curr Opin Orthop.* **18**:102–111.

Henriksen M, Aaboe J, Bliddal H, et al. (2009). Biomechanical characteristics of the eccentric Achilles tendon exercise. *J Biomech.* **42**:2702–2707.

Hoeger Bement MK, Rasiarmos RL, DiCapo JM, et al. (2009). The role of the menstrual cycle phase in pain perception before and after isometric fatiguing contraction. *Eur J Appl Physiol.* **106**:105–112.

Joseph MF, Taft K, Moskwa M, et al. (2012). Deep friction massage to treat tendinopathy: a systematic review of a classic treatment in the face of a new paradigm of understanding. *J Sport Rehabil.* **21**:343–353.

Kellenberger S, Schild L (2002). Epithelial sodium channel/degenerin family of ion channels: a variety of functions for a shared structure. *Physiol Rev.* **82**:735–767.

Kettunen JA, Kvist M, Alanen E, et al. (2002). Long-term prognosis for jumper's knee in male athletes. A prospective follow-up study. *Am J Sports Med.* **30**:689–692.

Khan KM, Cook JL, Bonar F, et al. (1999). Histopathology of common tendinopathies. Update and implications for clinical management. *Sports Med.* **27**:393–408.

Kosek E, Lundberg L (2003). Segmental and plurisegmental modulation of pressure pain thresholds during static muscle contractions in healthy individuals. *Eur J Pain.* **7**:251–258.

Kosek E, Ekholm J, Hansson P (1996). Modulation of pressure pain thresholds during and following isometric contraction in patients with fibromyalgia and in healthy controls. *Pain.* **64**:415–423.

McNeilly CM, Banes AJ, Benjamin M, et al. (1996). Tendon cells in vivo form a three dimensional network of cell processes linked by gap junctions. *J Anat.* **189**:593–600.

Maeda E, Yes S, Wang W, et al. (2012). Gap junction permeability between tenocytes within tendon fascicles is suppressed by tensile loading. *Biomech Model Mechanobiol.* **11**:439–447.

Maffulli N, Longo UG (2008). How do eccentric exercises work in tendinopathy? *Rheumatology (Oxford).* **47**:1444–1445.

Malliaras P, Barton CJ, Reeves ND, et al. (2013). Achilles and patellar tendinopathy loading programmes: a systematic review comparing clinical outcomes and identifying potential mechanisms for effectiveness. *Sports Med.* **43**:267–286.

Murrell GA (2007). Using nitric oxide to treat tendinopathy. *Br J Sports Med.* **41**:227–231.

Rio E (2014). Clinical perspective on isometric exercise for tendon pain. *sportEX Med.* **60**:21–26.

Rio E, Moseley L, Purdam C, et al. (2014). The pain of tendinopathy: physiological or pathophysiological? *Sports Med.* **44**:9–23.

Rosengarten SD, Cook JL, Bryant AL, et al. (2015). Australian football players' Achilles tendons respond to game loads within 2 days: an ultrasound tissue characterisation (UTC) study. *Br J Sports Med.* **49**:183–187.

Rowe V, Hemmings S, Barton C, et al. (2012). Conservative management of midportion Achilles tendinopathy: a mixed methods study, integrating systematic review and clinical reasoning. *Sports Med.* **24**:941–967.

Sayana MK, Maffulli N (2007). Eccentric calf muscle training in non-athletic patients with Achilles tendinopathy. *J Sci Med Sport.* **10**:52–58.

Smith RK (2008). Mesenchymal stem cell therapy for equine tendinopathy. *Disabil Rehabil.* **30**:1752–1758.

Tsai WC, Tang FT, Hsu CC, et al. (2004). Ibuprofen inhibition of tendon cell proliferation and upregulation of cyclin kinase inhibitor p21CIP1. *J Orthop Res.* **22**:586–591.

CHAPTER 5

PATELLAR TENDINOPATHY

INTRODUCTION

Patellar tendinopathy is defined as a clinical diagnosis of pain and dysfunction arising from the patellar tendon. The condition is often referred to as "jumper's knee" because it reflects the high prevalence in sports involving jumping, including volleyball and basketball. Like all tendinopathies, the treatment and management of patellar tendinopathy remains a challenge for coaches, therapists, and surgeons alike. This chapter provides evidence-based pathology, assessment, and treatment advice for clinical practice.

The knee joint consists of three bony articulations: the medial tibiofemoral compartment, lateral tibiofemoral compartment, and the patellofemoral joint (PFJ) (**Figure 5.1**). In-between the two tibiofemoral articulations, the cruciate ligaments provide stability in the sagittal plane while the collateral ligaments provide stability in the frontal plane. The surface of the joints is covered with hyaline cartilage and further supported by two fibrocartilage menisci, which improve the contact between the tibiofemoral joint.

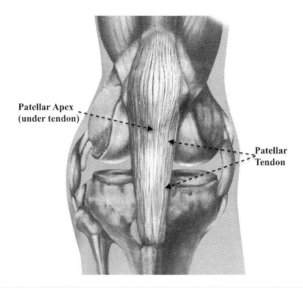

Patellar Apex
(under tendon)

Patellar
Tendon

FIGURE 5.1   The basic anatomy of the knee joint

The PFJ articulates with the anterior femoral condyles during knee flexion. Stability is provided laterally by medial and lateral retinacula and vertically by the quadriceps and patellar tendon.

A highly innervated infrapatellar fat pad sits between the patellar tendon and the PFJ. Multiple bursae are also found around the various knee joint structures. The three main anterior bursae are the prepatellar, infrapatellar, and suprapatellar.

MYOFASCIAL ANATOMY

The patellar tendon is one of the key structures in the lower half of the superficial front line (**Figure 5.2**) as described by Myers (2001). The rectus femoris muscle is anchored superficially from the anterior inferior iliac spine before combining with the three vasti muscles to form the quadriceps group. The muscles then converge into the centralised quadriceps tendon, which continues onto the patella and patellar tendon before inserting into the tibial tuberosity. Despite a definitive anchor onto the tibial tuberosity, there is also fascial continuity into the tibialis anterior compartment.

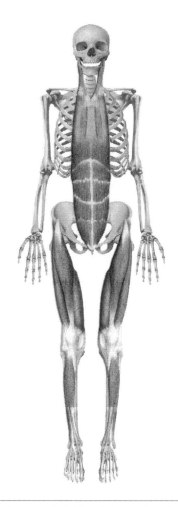

FIGURE 5.2   Representation of the superficial front line as described by Myers (2009).

PATELLAR TENDON ANATOMY

Most patellar tendon fascicles attach to the distal two-thirds of the anterior surface of the patella. The anterior fibres are longer than the posterior fibres because of the proximity of their tibial and patellar attachments (Basso, Johnson and Amis, 2001). The posterior fibres also take an increased share of tensile force and are therefore stronger (Basso, Amis and Race, 2002).

The medial and lateral fibres have a more proximal attachment than the central fibres; this creates a crescent-shaped attachment that reduces towards a more linear attachment posteriorly (Basso, Johnson and Amis, 2001). The attachment of the patellar tendon usually stops at the distal margin of the apex of the patella, with an occasional origin from the non-articular posterior aspect of the patella. The patellar tendon is thin and broad proximally, and thick and narrow distally. Basso and colleagues (2001) also reported a slightly asymmetrical tibial attachment with the apex of the patella slightly medial to the tendon midline.

The length of the patellar tendon is equal to the length of the patella with an approximate ratio of 1:1. Women may have a slightly longer tendon, but a ratio ≥1.3:1 is considered abnormal and termed patella alta (or a high-riding patella). This ratio is referred to as the Insall–Salvati index (Insall and Salvati, 1971). Patella alta is a very rare, visually identifiable condition that can be confirmed with an X-ray.

BIOMECHANICS OF THE KNEE

Knee joint structure must balance the required demand for stability with the necessity for mobility. With patellofemoral compressive forces of up to four times our body weight generated just from walking, and up to nine times our body weight while walking down stairs (Cox, 1990), it is easy to appreciate that the patella can dissipate the force transferred from the quadriceps tendon to the patellar tendon with a ratio of 8:5 (Evans, Benjamin and Pemberton, 1990). For example, a tensile force of 80 kg through the quadriceps tendon is reduced to 50 kg through the patellar tendon because the tensile force is partially transferred to patellar compressive force.

The patella works like a camshaft by successfully lengthening the moment arm that moves the line of pull generated from the quadriceps away from the joint and increases the ability of the muscles to generate a flexion torque (Levangie and Norkin, 2001), while reducing the compressive load.

The quadriceps are often required to work eccentrically when the leg is weight bearing. For example, the landing phase of running requires a powerful eccentric contraction to control and sustain knee joint position.

PATHOLOGY

Patellar tendinopathy is very similar to Achilles tendinopathy, but with a few key differences. Patellar tendinopathy usually occurs around the teno-osseus junction of the patellar apex. While tendinopathy has been reported in the mid-substance of the patellar tendon, it has mostly been in addition to tendinopathy at the teno-osseus junction.

General tendinopathy pathology has been described in Chapter 3. An outline of the continuum model is shown in **Figure 5.3.**

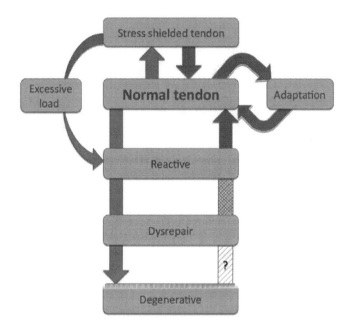

FIGURE 5.3   An algorithm of the tendinopathy continuum as proposed by Cook and Purdam (2009).

RISK FACTORS

A systematic review by van der Worp and colleagues (2011) reported the results of many studies investigating several potential patellar tendinopathy risk factors. Out of 368 studies, 9 risk factors were identified as showing "some" evidence of being associated with patellar tendinopathy. These were:

- weight;
- body mass index;
- waist-to-hip ratio;
- difference in leg length;
- foot arch height;

- quadriceps flexibility;
- quadriceps strength;
- hamstring flexibility;
- vertical jump performance.

Only some of the evidence supported these risk factors. Although the research reported in the systematic review was statistically significant, this may not denote clinical significance. Clearly, there are many other factors experts would add to this list. These include:

- general lower-limb strength (not just quadriceps);
- running form (e.g. overstriding; see Chapter 10);
- footwear (heeled shoes);
- running volume;
- jumping-based training and sports.

SUBJECTIVE ASSESSMENT

This assessment section is supported by the assessment guidance sheet that can be found in Appendix 1.

Any risk factors should be identified and documented, and a detailed history of pain behaviour and dysfunction should be taken. It is also vital to take extra care to fully question the patient about any recent changes in training and tendon loading. A detailed history should help to differentiate between suspected patellar tendinopathy and patellofemoral pain, fat pad irritation, or similar conditions.

Unlike Achilles tendinopathy, morning pain and stiffness are not defining symptoms of patellar tendinopathy, and may not be present.

PHYSICAL EXAMINATION

An objective physical examination is typically based on the suspected risk factors.

A brief observation of the patient's lower limbs and muscle bulk should be followed by tendon loading tests consisting of single- and double-leg squats (if appropriate), step downs, single-leg hopping (if appropriate), and squats on a decline board. While it is important to note pain during these tests, quality of movement and pain-free range are also significant factors and can serve as outcome measures for future treatment success.

Ankle dorsiflexion should be checked because plantar-to-dorsiflexion range below 45 degrees has been shown to increase patellar loading during jumping activities, due to the reduced dissipation of the ground reaction force (Malliaras, Cook and Kent, 2006).

Palpation should begin at the base of the patellar tendon from the insertion onto the tibia, then run up over the tendon, feeling for any thickening and noting any reported pain. This is most likely to occur over the superior tendon where it attaches to the patellar apex. Patellar mobility can be checked, particularly for the lateral tension commonly found with patellofemoral pain. The quadriceps may also show some focal areas of muscle sensitivity, also known as trigger points, which commonly influence patellar tendon pain.

Hamstring and quadriceps flexibility and strength should also be assessed to give a complete picture of lower-limb function.

GAIT ANALYSIS

Overstriding, heel striking, and excessive vertical displacement of the whole body are factors that individually or collectively cause an increase in force absorption through the knee. Because of this, a shorter stride and mid-foot loading are proven strategies to reduce knee stress when running. See Chapter 10 for further details and treatment approaches.

IMAGING

Doppler ultrasound can be useful to monitor the presence of neovessels that can help determine the tendinopathic stage, and the potential resolution or worsening of the structural changes. See Chapter 16 for more information on this and other imaging techniques.

DIFFERENTIAL DIAGNOSIS

Patellar tendinopathy has a similar presentation to other common knee pathologies, including: PFJ pain; fat pad irritation; and the less common Sinding-Larsen–Johansson (SLJ) syndrome. The key differentials between these are shown in **Table 5.1**. The presentation of patellar tendinopathy and SLJ syndrome are very similar; the key differential should be the patient's age. Many of the passive management strategies would be the same.

Signs & Symptoms	Patellofemoral Joint Pain	Patellar Tendinopathy	Fat Pad Irritation	Sinding Larsen Johansson Syndrome
ONSET	Any repetitive weight bearing activity that requires knee flexion. Most commonly running.	More common with jumping activities that produce a more rapid tendon loading of a repetitive nature.	Rapid onset following a single or repetitive knee hyperextension.	Children only, not adults, onset most common between ages 10 – 14 typically from excessive sport volume.
PAIN REPORTING	Diffuse pain that can be immediately aggravated by patella-femoral joint loading.	Pain localised to the inferior pole of the patella. Can be aggravated by a decline squat movement.	Sharp pain of a diffuse nature around and possibly behind the patellar tendon	Pain and swelling around the apex of the patella
OBSERVATIONS	Normal in the early stages with possible VMO wasting or inhibition.	Normal in the early (reactive) stages with possible quadriceps wasting with progression.	Likely swelling around the sides of the patellar tendon.	Muscle tension within the quadriceps. A limp may be present after exercise.
SWELLING	Small amount below the patella is common.	Unlikely	Likely swelling around the sides of the patellar tendon.	Low grade swelling around the patella.
CLICKING/CREPITUS	Occasional	No	No	No
GIVING WAY	Subluxation is rare but instability can occur from quadriceps inhibition	Quadriceps inhibition can also occur with tendinopathy.	Only as a result of pain.	Only if very painful.
KNEE ROM	Often normal in all but severe cases.	Normal	Pain into end of range extension and deep squatting.	Pain into end range flexion.
QUADRICEPS CONTRACTION IN FULL KNEE EXTENSION	Contraction in full extension does not load the PF joint so should not be painful.	Contraction in full extension would still load the patellar tendon but the load will be low and pain is uncommon.	Pain into end of range extension.	Pain with loading.
ACCESSORY PATELLO-FEMORAL JOINT MOVEMENT	Commonly tight lateral structures usually limited medial glide.	Usually normal. Patellofemoral pain could coexist with patellar tendinopathy.	May irritate the fat pad in the acute stages via a compressive mechanism.	Possibly tender on palpation of patella apex.
FUNCTIONAL TESTING	Decline squats and descending steps may aggravate both conditions.	Decline squats and descending steps may aggravate both conditions.	End of range knee extension or flexion movements will probably be symptomatic.	Decline squats and descending steps may aggravate both conditions.
TAPING	PFJ taping should reduce pain with functional testing.	PFJ taping will have little effect on Patellar tendinopathy related pain.	Fat Pad offload taping should reduce pain into end of range extension.	PFJ taping will have little effect on Patellar tendinopathy related pain.

TABLE 5.1

The success or failure of specific treatments can further inform or exclude a diagnosis. Two such treatment approaches are explained in the following sections.

Manual glide or taping to reduce PFJ pain

Technique

A sustained manual glide to the patella (**Figure 5.4a**) or using tape (**Figure 5.4b**) directed medially during a known pain-provoking movement, such as a squat or leg extension, often causes a reduction in symptoms, especially if patellar maltracking is present. If there is no change in symptoms, then PFJ pathology is considered less likely, but not excluded, and further assessment is required.

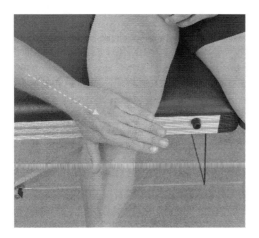
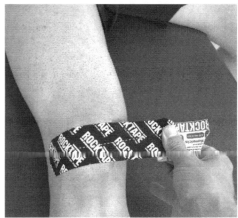

A   B

FIGURE 5.4   The patellar glide test can be used to test the influence of patellar gliding on knee pain during a typically pain-provoking test. (a) Manual glide. (b) Taping can be used.

Infrapatellar fat pad offload manoeuvre

Technique

If infrapatellar pain is felt when the knee is extended, a manual upward glide of the infrapatellar skin may impart a lifting effect on the fat pad. This can be achieved with hands (**Figure 5.5a**) or tape (**Figure 5.5b**). If the pain reduces, then the fat pad may be involved.

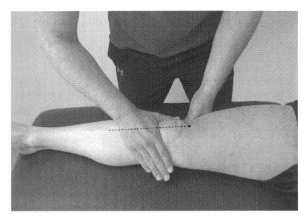
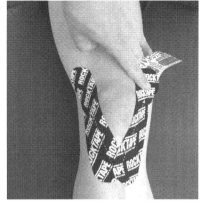

A   B

FIGURE 5.5   Performing a manual fat pad offload technique in combination with a typically painful knee extension can help to clarify pathology and aid diagnosis (manual glide (a) or taping (b) can be used).

Fat pad irritation most commonly occurs because of repeated full-knee extension and is aggravated by replicating these movements. Pain is often felt deep to the inferior pole of the patella and increases with quadriceps contraction when the knee is fully extended. Patients frequently have marked hyperextension of the knee. A swelling of the fat pad may also be visible. In the acute stages, fat pad irritation can be treated with activity modification and taping to offload the fat pad.

Although pathologies may coexist, placing one's hands on the knee may reduce pain from any knee pathology via a simple pain-modulating mechanism (gate control theory of pain). The results of the tests mentioned here should be considered along with full assessment and not in isolation.

THE DECLINE BOARD

I use a decline board less frequently in clinic these days to speed up the assessment process. However, the decline board offers the biomechanical benefit of increasing the load through the patellar tendon.

A decline board can be used for both assessment and treatment purposes (**Figure 5.6**). With a set and documented decline of between 15 and 30 degrees, the pain-free knee joint range can be measured with a goniometer. A pain scale at a set knee flexion angle can also be recorded.

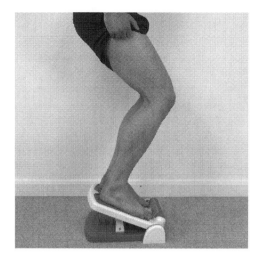

FIGURE 5.6   The decline board is a non-essential piece of equipment for anterior knee loading. It can be used for assessment and treatment purposes.

Decline board assessment instructions

(This test can be performed without a decline board.)

Equipment

A decline board set between 15 and 30 degrees is recommended. Make a note of the level of decline for future reference.

Test

Explain and demonstrate the test to your patient. Ask them to squat down slowly and stop as soon as they feel pain. Measure the range of movement with a goniometer. Repeat the test three times to get an average reading.

This test can be performed on both legs initially; optionally, each leg can be loaded individually – a wall or stick can be used for stability. If the movement appears too challenging, then stop immediately. This indicates some potential strength and balance issues that the rehabilitation programme needs to address.

Results

Pain is usually reported in early flexion. The result of this test often improves following many of the simple modalities described within this chapter; therefore, it is a good outcome measure for testing individual treatment outcomes and as a simple monitoring test to use during a rehabilitation programme.

ANALYSIS

Following the assessment process, it should be possible to form a diagnosis that considers the following factors:

1. Is the tendinopathy likely to be reactive, in a state of disrepair, or degenerative?
2. Has the patient had any notable changes in training and subsequent tendon loading?
3. Which risk factors are present? Are they contributory?

TREATMENT

Reducing loading

Reduction of tendon loading is an important part of an often-multifaceted treatment approach. Reduced loading does not constitute or include complete rest because this can often lead to deconditioning of the muscle and tendon, with an increased likelihood of future relapses. The patient should be advised to reduce jumping and running activities by 50% initially, and follow this with further reductions if required.

Strengthening

There are many strengthening exercises for patellar tendinopathy. Using the decline board to reduce ankle dorsiflexion and increase the force transmitted through the PFJ and patellar tendon is common in clinical practice. As previously mentioned, a decline board set to between 15 and 30 degrees optimally increases knee moment and reduces ankle and hip joint moment. Knee flexion range should be limited to 60 degrees because knee flexion <60 degrees increases the compressive force on the PFJ above that of the tensile forces transmitted through the patellar tendon (Zwerver, Bredeweg and Hof, 2007) and is therefore less helpful for tendon rehabilitation.

Tendon loading programmes for patellar tendinopathy have been well supported by the results of comparative studies over the last 10 years. The early work of Bahr and colleagues (2006) reported similar outcomes at 12 months between a surgical intervention group and an eccentric exercise group. More recent evidence demonstrated that both isometric and isotonic heavy slow leg extensions significantly reduced patellar tendon-related pain during the competitive season for a group of athletes participating in volleyball and basketball (van Ark et al., 2014). In another study, sustained isometric contractions of the quadriceps reduced patellar tendon pain and muscle inhibition in six volleyball players (Rio et al., 2015), further strengthening the case for using tendon loading, specifically isometric tendon loading, as a pain management tool. Isometric loading theory is discussed further in Chapter 9.

Making a start

Choosing when and how to begin a strengthening programme for patellar tendinopathy can be difficult. This short section alleviates some of these difficulties by providing some guidance. While a protocol may be easy to use and roll out, it neglects the use of proper clinical reasoning and may lead to poor or highly variable treatment outcomes.

Patients experiencing high levels of tendon pain can still benefit from some weight-based tendon loading. Isometric tendon loading may help to reduce tendon pain in the short term while maintaining or improving structural integrity.

Speed of progression should be governed by the reported symptoms. Pain should not be documented too frequently or only recorded approximately 24 hours after a loading session or participation in an aggravating activity. Immediate symptomatic differences are less valuable for what is often a lengthy rehabilitation process. Monthly use of the Victorian Institute of Sport Assessment-Patella (VISA-P) scale is also recommended to help the clinician and patient measure progress.

The experience of pain from patellar tendinopathy often leads to functional offloading of the limb, which results in alterations of motor patterns. In addition to potentially transferring loading onto the non-painful leg, compensation may also increase ankle or hip loading during jumping activities; it is important to remain aware of these potential adaptations during assessment and rehabilitation planning.

Early in the programme, single-leg exercises should take precedence over double-leg exercises because these ensure a specific unilateral loading without any habitual offloading onto the stronger limb.

An end goal should be set to determine the functional level acceptable to the patient. A triple jumper needs to regain a high level of ability that includes advanced strength training and plyometrics, while a "non-sporting" individual who wishes to participate in physical activity may only need to follow a basic strengthening programme for a few months followed by a recommended maintenance level of activity.

LOADING EXERCISES FOR PATELLAR TENDON REHABILITATION

The isometric decline squat

Technique

A decline angle of 15–30 degrees is recommended to focus the load on the anterior knee and patellar tendon. An isometric quadriceps contraction should be held by maintaining a knee flexion angle of <60 degrees for approximately 60 seconds, repeated 2 or 3 times with a 2-minute rest interval between contractions. The amount of knee flexion is often governed by initial pain levels, which can reach a level of 5/10 in severity before becoming unacceptable. The pain should then reduce on completion of the exercise. The exercise can be repeated several times during the day as a transient pain-reducing tool.

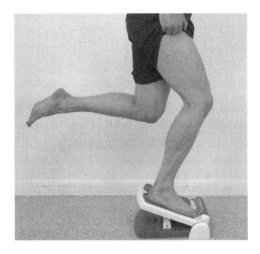

FIGURE 5.7   The isometric decline squat can be used to reduce pain and begin a strengthening programme with minimal tendon irritation.

The isometric decline squat (**Figure 5.7**) is an excellent method of adding load with minimal symptom exacerbation; it can also be performed without a decline board as a home exercise (**Figure 5.8**).

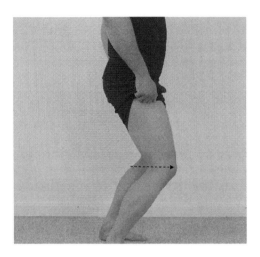

FIGURE 5.8   A knee bias squat movement is a suitable alternative technique for loading the anterior knee without a decline board.

Most patients do not have a decline board. To reduce any delay in beginning a loading programme, the isometric exercise can simply be performed with a knee-biased squat movement.

Some pain and discomfort in either the tendon or the quadriceps may be felt during the exercise. This should diminish and result in reduced pain from the patellar tendon region after each hold. If this does not occur after three attempts, it is advisable to reassess the injury and consider further assessment of alternative or additional pathologies.

Back squat

Simple squat exercises are often the best way to get started with lower-limb resistance training, especially for those unaccustomed to resistance training. The squat (**Figure 5.9**) is a fundamental movement pattern we master as infants, but unfortunately often unlearn as adults. Any squat technique performed correctly and under control that fatigues the quadriceps muscle group is sufficient to promote positive adaptive changes in both contractile and connective tissue. The finer details of strength and conditioning methods are covered in Chapter 9.

FIGURE 5.9   The basic back squat is a safe, functional, and easy exercise to perform.

Technique

The feet should be placed shoulder width apart, with the hips in slight external rotation. The head and chest should be kept up, looking forward. The ankles, knees, and hips should flex simultaneously, while the spine remains neutral with flexion occurring from the hips and not the lumbar spine. Half squats down to 60 degrees of knee flexion may be used initially before considering the rationale for full squats. Common errors include flexing the hips too much so that the bum sticks out and the torso leans forward or bending the knees excessively so that the heels lift off the floor.

Leg press

A leg press machine allows safe and stable loading and is an option for loading the quadriceps and patellar tendon (**Figure 5.10**).

FIGURE 5.10   A leg press machine offers more stability and safety features compared to free weight exercises.

Technique

Get your patient to sit in the machine with their feet on the footplate. Make sure your patient is familiar with the machine's safety features and perform a few test presses before adding the correct amount of weight. Discourage knee hyperextension when pushing the footplate away and make sure your patient carefully controls the weight when lowering it.

One-leg squat

The one-leg squat can be a very challenging exercise, but if you begin with a balance support, as shown in **Figure 5.11,** you can progress gradually. People with advanced strength and mobility should be able to deep squat on one leg, known as a pistol squat. For rehabilitation purposes, it may be more beneficial to perform slow half squats down to 60 degrees of knee flexion to focus the tension through the quadriceps and patellar tendon and lessen the balance and motor control requirements.

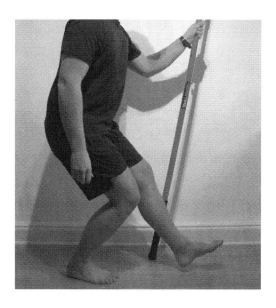

FIGURE 5.11   The one leg squat exercise is a challenging option to significantly load the patellar tendon.

Technique

Have your patient stand on one leg with the knee slightly bent. Allow a controlled ankle, knee, and hip flexion down to approximately 60 degrees of knee flexion before returning to the start position. The unweighted leg can be placed either in front or behind the body. Performing the exercise off a step or box makes positioning the unweighted leg easier. The exercise is also made easier with a heel lift or decline board. When you are trying to achieve focused tendon loading, this exercise can sometimes be too challenging for your patient; if this is the case, bilateral or machine-based exercises may be preferred.

MASSAGE

Any form of soft tissue treatment can be used to help reduce hypertonus in the lower limbs, promote an increase in muscle extensibility, and increase joint range of movement. Soft tissue techniques are described in Chapter 11; a specific fascial manipulation study and technique are described in the following section.

FASCIAL MANIPULATION

According to a fascia-based theory, patellar tendon pain is often due to uncoordinated quadriceps muscle contraction. Based on this theory, the therapist who chooses to focus on the fascia would examine and aim to treat the myofascial region of the thigh as the cause of the pathology and pain experienced in the patellar tendon (Pedrelli, Stecco and Day, 2009).

According to a pilot study by Pedrelli, Stecco and Day (2009), who reported the pain outcomes of 18 patients following fascial manipulation of the thigh, the following treatment approach proved to be successful at reducing patellar tendon pain immediately and in the short term for most of the group.

The key area to treat was referred to as the centre of coordination (CC), while the patellar tendon was referred to as the centre of perception. The CC is located on the mid-thigh over the vastus intermedius muscle, which interestingly overlaps with acupuncture point ST22 and with one of the known trigger points of the quadriceps group (Travell, Simons and Simons, 1999). The treatment consisted of a sustained deep manual pressure between the rectus femoris and vastus lateralis muscles on the mediolateral thigh, followed by an intermittent friction massage for a total of approximately 5 minutes.

Pedrelli, Stecco and Day (2009) suggested that the positive outcomes may be due to improved fascial mobility reducing the stimulation of the free nerve endings. Corrected quadriceps coordination may allow the correct deposition of new collagen fibres according to the forces placed on them.

In conclusion, fascial manipulation theory differs considerably from the cellular changes and loading model proposed by Cook and Purdam (2009). While the management of tendinopathy using current evidence in sports medicine may be largely based on patient education, there is great scope for manual therapy intervention as part of a comprehensive treatment plan.

EXTRACORPOREAL SHOCKWAVE THERAPY FOR PATELLAR TENDINOPATHY

A literature review published in the *British Journal of Sports Medicine* in 2008 reviewed the effectiveness of extracorporeal shockwave therapy (ESWT) for patellar tendinopathy using seven articles published after 2000 involving a combined total of 203 pa tients. While the studies varied in the quality of their methodology, overall ESWT appeared to be an effective treatment for patellar tendinopathy with no serious side effects being reported (van Leeuwen, Zwerver and van den Akker-Scheek, 2009). (See Chapter 13 for more information on ESWT.)

SURGICAL OPTIONS

Surgery should not be considered as a quick fix for tendinopathy and may not provide better outcomes than conservative management strategies (Bahr et al., 2006). If surgery is planned, there is no consensus regarding the optimal surgical technique to use. Most techniques aim to disrupt neovessels, stimulate a healing response, or remove abnormal tissue. Patients are often naively optimistic when electing surgery because they feel the objectivity and complexity of the procedure coupled with the attention from highly qualified and respected professionals is their best option to cure their symptoms. Convincing a patient that they should cancel a planned surgical procedure in favour of uncomfortable squatting exercises is quite a challenge. Patients should be aware that while symptomatic benefit is likely – depending on the tendinopathic stage – full return to previous function varies from 60 to 80% and rehabilitation to a previous level of function may take between 6 and 12 months (Coleman et al., 2000a,b).

STRETCHING AND MUSCLE ENERGY TECHNIQUES

Of the many forms of stretching, muscle energy techniques are fast and effective methods of improving flexibility. As mentioned previously, reduced flexibility in the hamstrings and quadriceps, and reduced ankle dorsiflexion, are easily identifiable risk factors for patellar tendinopathy and thus they are areas that may benefit from stretching methods. I find the following simple technique (**Figure 5.12**) highly effective at reducing pain. Interestingly, it also involves isometric contractions.

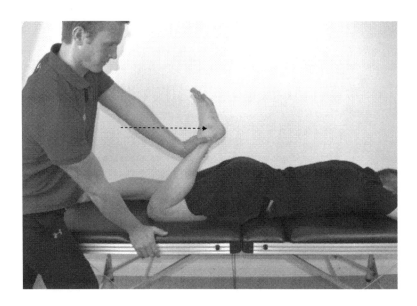

FIGURE 5.12   The simple knee flexion muscle energy technique can be highly effective for pain relief.

Technique

Begin with your patient lying in a prone position. Passively bend their knee by moving their foot towards their buttock. When muscle tension is felt in the quadriceps, begin an isometric contraction by resisting your patient's attempted knee extension for 10 seconds. After 10 seconds, instruct your patient to stop contracting against your resistance. After a couple of seconds, slowly move the foot further towards the buttocks until muscle tension is reported again. Repeat the process between 2 and 5 times. Correct therapist positioning is important to control knee extension.

Your patient is not required to produce a maximal contraction and should be guided to increase the contraction gradually rather than "fight" against the therapist's resistance.

TAPING

In addition to the traditional rigid taping methods used in the treatment of fat pad irritation and PFJ joint pain, kinesiology tape can also be used to reduce pain and improve knee function (**Figure 5.13**) (Chen et al., 2008; Vithoulk, Beneka and Malliou, 2010). (See Chapter 12 for more information and knee taping instructions.)

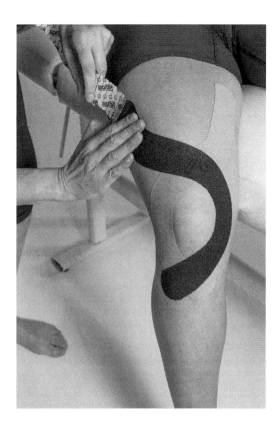

FIGURE 5.13   Knee taping using RockTape kinesiology tape. One of many options for taping the knee.

INFRAPATELLAR STRAPS

Infrapatellar straps (**Figure 5.14**) have been widely used by patients to reduce the pain and discomfort caused by patellar tendinopathy. The suggested mechanism of action is the reduced patellar tendon strain on the superior tendon near the patellar pole (Lavagnino et al., 2011). An alternative theory is that increased sensory input from compression may modulate the pain response. The straps are cheap to purchase and simple to apply. A quick "pain-free" range of movement squat test before the onset of pain can be used to test if the strap is effective.

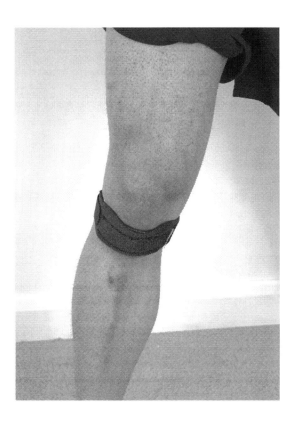

FIGURE 5.14 Infrapatellar straps can help reduce patellar-related pain.

CONCLUSION

As with any tendon, the patellar tendon should be viewed as part of a musculotendinous unit, which forms a key component of the lower limbs. All forces placed on the lower limbs should be considered in unity during assessment and treatment planning.

Patellar tendinopathy shares many similarities with Achilles tendinopathy and current research is supportive of similar treatments. More soft tissue massage, and supportive strapping and taping options, seem to exist for patellar tendinopathy. However, the mainstay of successful management is activity modification and load management.

REFERENCES

Bahr R, Fossan B, Løken S, et al. (2006). Surgical treatment compared with eccentric training for patellar tendinopathy (Jumper's Knee). A randomized controlled trial. *J Bone Joint Surg.* **88**:1689–1698.

Basso O, Johnson DP, Amis AA (2001). The anatomy of the patellar tendon. *Knee Surg, Sports Traumatol Arthrosc.* **9**:2–5.

Basso O, Amis AA, Race A, et al. (2002). Patellar tendon fiber strains: their differential responses to quadriceps tension. *Clin Orthop Relat Res. 246–253.*

Chen PL, Hong WH, Lin CH, et al. (2008). *Biomechanics effects of kinesio taping for persons with patellofemoral pain syndrome during stair climbing.* In: Abu Osman NA, Ibrahim F, Wan Abas WAB, et al. eds. *Fourth Kuala Lumpur International Conference on Biomedical Engineering. IFMBE Proceedings.* Vol 21. Berlin, Heidelberg: Springer. pp. 18–21.

Coleman BD, Khan KM, Kiss ZS, et al. (2000a). Open and arthroscopic patellar tenotomy for chronic patellar tendinopathy. A retrospective outcome study. Victorian Institute of Sport Tendon Study Group. *Am J Sports Med.* **28**:190–190.

Coleman BD, Khan KM, Maffulli N, et al. (2000b). Studies of surgical outcome after patellar tendinopathy: clinical significance of methodological deficiencies and guidelines for future studies. Victorian Institute of Sport Tendon Study Group. *Scand J Med Sci Sports.* **10**:2–11.

Cook JL, Purdam CR (2009). Is tendon pathology a continuum? A pathology model to explain the clinical presentation of load-induced tendinopathy. *Br J Sports Med.* **43**:409–416.

Cox AJ (1990). Biomechanics of the patello-femoral joint. *Clin Biomech (Bristol, Avon).* **5**:123–130.

Evans EJ, Benjamin M, Pemberton DJ. (1990). Fibrocartilage in the attachment zones of the quadriceps tendon and patellar ligament of man. *J Anat.* **171**:155–162.

Insall J, Salvati E (1971). Patella position in the normal knee joint. *Radiology.* **101**:101–104.

Lavagnino M, Arnoczky SP, Dodds J, et al. (2011). Infrapatellar straps decrease patellar tendon strain at the site of the jumper's knee lesion: a computational analysis based on radiographic measurements. *Sports Health.* **3**:296–302.

Levangie PK, Norkin CC (2001). *Joint Structure and Function: A Comprehensive Analysis. 3rd edn. Philadelphia, PA: FA Davis Company.*

Malliaras P, Cook JL, Kent P (2006). Reduced ankle dorsiflexion range may increase the risk of patellar tendon injury among volleyball players. J Sci Med Sport. **9**:304–309.

Myers T (2001). *Anatomy Trains: Myofascial Meridians for Manual and Movement Therapists.* *Edinburgh: Churchill Livingstone.*

Pedrelli A, Stecco C, Day JA (2009). Treating patellar tendinopathy with fascial manipulation. J Bodyw Mov Ther. **13**:73–80.

Rio E, Kidgell D, Purdam C, et al. (2015). Isometric exercise induces analgesia and reduces inhibition in patellar tendinopathy. *Br J Sports Med.* **49**:1277–1283.

Travell JG, Simons DG, Simons LS (1999). *Myofascial Pain and Dysfunction: The Trigger Point Manual. Vol. 1. 2nd edn. Baltimore, MD: Williams & Wilkins.*

van Ark M, Cook J, Docking S, et al. (2014). 14 exercise programs to decrease pain in athletes with patellar tendinopathy in-season: a randomised controlled trial. Br J Sports Med. **48**:A9–10.

van der Worp H, van Ark M, Roerink S, et al. (2011). Risk factors for patellar tendinopathy: a systematic review of the literature. *Br J Sports Med.* **45**:446–452.

van Leeuwen MT, Zwerver J, van den Akker-Scheek I (2009). Extracorporeal shockwave therapy for patellar tendinopathy: a review of the literature. *Br J Sports Med.* **43**:163–168.

Vithoulk I, Beneka A, Malliou N (2010). The effects of Kinesio-Taping® on quadriceps strength during isokinetic exercises in healthy non athlete women. *Isokinet Exerc Sci.* **18**:1–6.

Zwerver J, Bredeweg SW, Hof AL (2007). Biomechanical analysis of the single-leg decline squat. *Br J Sports Med.* **41**:264–268.

FURTHER READING

Laforgia R, Capocasale N, Saracino N, et al. (1992). A clinical and ultrasonoraphic study of jumper's knee and the Achilles tendon in volleyball players. *J Sports Traumatol Relat Res.* **14**:127–138.

Lian O, Holan KJ, Engebretsen L, et al. (1996). Relationship between symptoms of jumper's knee and the ultrasound characteristics of the patellar tendon among high level male volleyball players. *Scand J Med Sci Sports.* **6**:291–296.

Purdam CR, Cook JL, Hopper DM, et al. (2003). Discriminative ability of functional loading tests for adolescent jumper's knee. *Phys Ther Sport.* **4**:3–9.

Young MA, Cook JL, Purdam CR, et al. (2005). Eccentric decline squat protocol offers superior results at 12 months compared with traditional eccentric protocol for patellar tendinopathy in volleyball players. *Br J Sports Med.* **39**:102–105.

CHAPTER 6

PROXIMAL HAMSTRING TENDINOPATHY

INTRODUCTION

Proximal hamstring tendinopathy is not as common as the other tendinopathies reviewed in this book and less information is available in textbooks and research literature. The condition typically causes the gradual onset of deep buttock pain; it is prevalent in both athletic and sedentary individuals as is typical of most tendinopathies.

This chapter begins with a general review of hamstring anatomy and function before focusing on identifying proximal hamstring tendinopathy, how it can be treated, and the kind of therapeutic exercises available.

ANATOMY

The hamstring muscle group is a component of a long strip of myofascial tissue that runs up and down the back of the body. This continuity of tissue is often referred to as the posterior chain or superficial back line (Myers, 2001) (**Figure 6.1**).

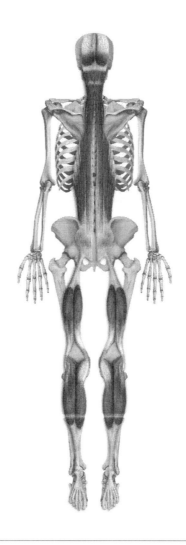

FIGURE 6.1   Representation of the continuity of posterior myofascial tissue, which includes the hamstring muscle group and is referred to as the superficial back line by Myers (2001).

According to myofascial anatomy, the proximal hamstring tendons attach to the ischial tuberosity and show a fibrous continuity with the superficial fibres of the sacrotuberous ligament, which in turn continues to blend with the erector spinae muscles. Inferiorly, the hamstrings have some continuity with the gastrocnemius muscle when the knee is extended; a flexed knee unlocks the transmission of tension between the two muscle groups.

The three muscles of the hamstring group are: the biceps femoris muscle; the semimembranosus muscle; and the semitendinosus muscle (**Figure 6.2**).

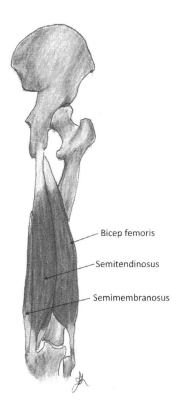

Bicep femoris

Semitendinosus

Semimembranosus

FIGURE 6.2   The three hamstring muscles: biceps femoris, semimembranosus and semitendinosus.

The innervation of these three muscles comes from the common tibial portion of the sciatic nerve. The biceps femoris muscle has two heads, a long and a short head. The short head of the biceps femoris has a different origin at the femoral linea aspera and a different innervation from the common peroneal portion of the sciatic nerve. Both the long and short head of the biceps femoris muscle share a common tendon at their distal attachment. The adductor magnus muscle shares the same innervation and similar functional alignment as the hamstring group, which makes it a "functional hamstring" muscle, even if not officially a member of the hamstring group.

The proximal origin of the hamstring tendons is more complex than most textbooks describe. An understanding of the soft tissue organisation within this region further aids our understanding of hamstring injuries (**Figure 6.3**). The long heads of the biceps femoris and semitendinosus muscles share a common proximal tendon that arises from the medial facet of the ischial tuberosity. The semitendinosus muscle fibres originate from the ischial tuberosity and the medial proximal tendon they share, while the biceps femoris muscle fibres originate from the lateral aspect of the common tendon approximately 6 cm below the ischial tuberosity. The proximal semimembranosus tendon is not part of the common tendon and arises from the lateral facet of the ischial tuberosity; it then runs deep and medial to the semitendinosus and biceps femoris muscles.

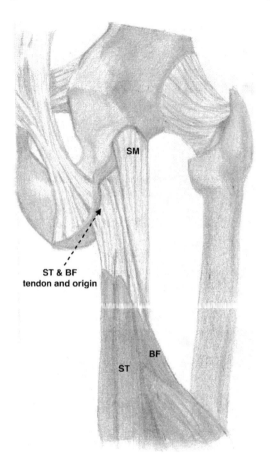

FIGURE 6.3   Representation of the specific tendon arrangement at the ischial tuberosity. SM = semimembranosus; ST = semitendinosus; BF = bicep femoris.

Distally, the semitendinosus muscle inserts onto the anteromedial surface of the proximal tibia; along with the gracilis and sartorius muscles, it makes up the three structures labelled the pes anserinus ("goose foot"). The semimembranosus muscle inserts onto the medial epicondyle of the tibia. The short and long head of the biceps femoris muscle form a common tendon that has multiple insertions, including the lateral epicondyle of the tibia, styloid process of the fibular head, popliteus tendon, and arcuate popliteal ligament (Tubbs et al., 2006).

The adductor magnus muscle has two distinct proximal attachments that give rise to the functionally separate adductor and hamstring portions of the muscle. The adductor portion attaches to the pubic ramus and the hamstring portion attaches to the ischial tuberosity inferior and anterior to the proximal hamstring tendons. The adductor magnus muscle inserts distally onto the adductor tubercle on the medial condyle of the femur, and is connected by a fibrous expansion to the line leading upwards from the tubercle to the linea aspera.

The sciatic nerve exits the sciatic notch in the pelvis. It then tracks deep to the piriformis muscle, but superficial to the short external rotators, the superior gemellus, inferior gemellus, and obturator internus muscles. It then runs down the posterior leg in-between and deep to the biceps femoris and semitendinosus muscles. The nerve splits into its main divisions at the level of the mid-thigh. The terminal branches are the common peroneal and tibial portion, which innervate the hamstring and the adductor magnus muscles.

The hamstring muscle fibres have a pennate (feather-like) structure, consisting of predominantly type II (fast-twitch) muscle fibres. This structure allows a more powerful, but shorter contraction distance in comparison to a more linear fibre arrangement (Lieber, 2010). This anatomical set-up supports the required muscle action of rapid deceleration and isometric power transfer from the hip to the knee during the stance phase of the gait cycle or during stair climbing, for example.

Hamstring strains most frequently occur in the lateral muscle belly of the biceps femoris muscle adjacent to the proximal musculotendinous junction (MTJ).

The MTJ, and the adjacent muscle tissue, is the most common site of excessive mechanical loading. The MTJ features a folding membrane that increases the surface area and dissipates the transmitted forces. This configuration allows the membrane to experience more shear and less tensile force as shown in **Figure 6.4.** Finally, the sarcomeres near the MTJ are stiffer than more distal ones (Noonan and Garrett 1992; Whiting and Zernicke, 2008), which may contribute to an increased risk of injury within the MTJ region.

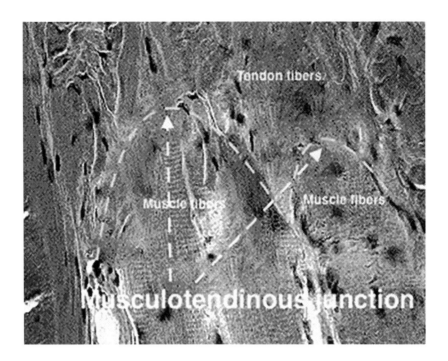

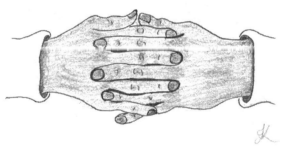

FIGURE 6.4   (a) Microscopic view of a musculotendinous junction. (b) The blending of the muscle with the tendon can be demonstrated with the interlocking of fingers, which represent the overlapping membranes.

To summarise, the hamstring muscle group consists of a complex anatomy specific to its function, but with some key areas of weakness. The hamstring muscle group is also an important and integral part of the myofascial system.

BIOMECHANICS

As a group, the hamstring muscles span both the hip and knee joints. In isolation, the hamstring muscle group can flex the knee and extend the hip. The most important and highest level of function of the hamstring group is to decelerate the leg during the late swing phase (deceleration) when running, sprinting, or kicking. At this point, the muscle group reaches its maximum strain and produces its peak force after a period of considerable eccentric contraction (Schache et al., 2012). Depending on body position, the hamstring muscle group also works concentrically to help pull the torso over the pelvis from heel strike to terminal stance; this is particularly apparent when striding uphill with a heel strike gait pattern. Some sporting movements may also load the hamstrings differently or more aggressively. For example, cycling requires the hamstrings to repeatedly flex the knee, leading to a typical functional shortening of the hamstring muscle group.

Electromyography studies using inverse dynamics have indicated that the hamstrings are most active from mid-swing until terminal stance (Yu et al., 2008; Higashihara et al., 2010; Chumanov, Heiderscheit and Thelen, 2011). This transition requires a rapid change in muscle activity from eccentric deceleration (power absorption) to terminal swing, and then to concentric contraction (power generation) just before and during the stance phase.

When comparing the work done by each specific muscle in the hamstring group, Schache and colleagues (2012) reported that the biceps femoris muscle had the largest peak strain, the semitendinosus muscle displayed the greatest lengthening velocity, and the semimembranosus muscle produced the highest force and did more work than the other two hamstring muscles.

PROXIMAL HAMSTRING TENDINOPATHY

Proximal hamstring tendinopathy is much less common than Achilles, patellar, or gluteal tendinopathy. Hamstring tendinopathy usually occurs at the ischial tuberosity origin of the tendon, thereby making diagnosis difficult among the many other pain-generating structures within or related to this area. Symptoms usually include a localised deep ischial tuberosity or posterior thigh pain that is exacerbated by running, squatting, and lunging, and is made more noticeable by sitting because this can place pressure directly onto the pathological region of the proximal hamstring tendons, at the ischial tuberosity origin.

Tendinopathy of the proximal hamstring tendon is increasingly being acknowledged by sports people. It was originally identified by Puranen and Orava (1988), who referred to it as the "the hamstring syndrome". The condition is more prevalent in middle-to-long-distance runners and in sports that involve running (e.g. hockey, football) (Fredericson et al., 2005).

The condition may involve irritation of the sciatic nerve as it passes the ischial tuberosity. Histological evaluations have shown a chronic tendinopathy with dense fibrosis around the ischial tuberosity, which can entrap or adhere to the sciatic nerve (Lempainen et al., 2009). This supports using the slump test during the assessment process.

While onset is generally insidious, there might be a link between gradual onset and a history of hamstring strain. Changes to the musculotendinous unit post-strain might unload the tendon and lead to degenerative changes.

RISK FACTORS

Hamstring tendinopathy is a lesser-researched condition; therefore, fewer risk factors have been reported. The following factors include those identified in both practice and extrapolated from other tendon-related research.

Intrinsic factors

Age, a high body mass index, type 2 diabetes, the menopause, and fluoroquinolone antibiotics have been identified as risk factors for negative tendon changes.

Compression

Tendon compression can occur at the ischial tuberosity from dynamic hip flexion activities that are either sustained (yoga positions) or repetitive (high repetitions of deep squats).

Running

When running, the force on the proximal hamstring tendon may be increased by biomechanical factors including: increased anterior pelvic tilt; poor lumbopelvic control; increased stride length; and reduced muscle-tendon extensibility.

GAIT ANALYSIS

Patients may display an overstriding gait pattern when running. This places an increased demand on the hamstrings to contract concentrically to bring the body for ward following a heel strike. This demand is increased by striding uphill, and is also a typical movement pattern used by race walkers.

Inhibition of the gluteus maximus muscle can lead to a compensatory hamstring action that leads to fatigue due to poor movement patterns. This is often found in combination with a loss of full hip extension, which is due to hip flexor tension at the end range. I often see this imbalance in hip flexor–extensor moments when treating novice runners. Some runners demonstrate a heel/foot contact considerably anterior to the body's centre of mass, which is followed by a limited extension during the stance phase. This presents as a hip flexion-dominant running style, where the patient seems to be pulling themselves forward rather than extending the hips and pushing their bodies forward. This type of gait pattern places more load on the hamstrings, especially when running uphill. This pattern is also inefficient; some running coaches state that it is not running but shuffling! Gait and running is discussed further in Chapter 10.

ASSESSMENT

As mentioned in the introduction, localised deep buttock and posterior thigh pain is often reported as the main symptom of proximal hamstring tendinopathy. The reporting of symptoms shares a pattern like that seen in other tendinopathies. Pain and stiffness is felt after inactivity and during activity onset; pain and stiffness then subsides with prolonged activity but may return during prolonged endurance running or, more specifically, when fatigue sets in. Morning pain and stiffness may be reported, but it is not such a key symptom as it is with Achilles tendinopathy. Pain when sitting for prolonged periods on a firm surface is a key symptom.

Following widespread use of the Victorian Institute of Sport Assessment-Achilles (VISA-A) and Patellar (VISA-P) assessments, the Victorian Institute of Sport developed an adapted version for hamstring tendinopathy. In line with the VISA-A and VISA-P, the Victorian Institute of Sport Assessment-Hamstring questionnaire is a valid and reliable patient-reported outcome measure (Cacchio, De Paulis and Maffulli, 2014). As with the other VISA assessments, the questionnaire is best used for medium-to-long-term reporting and should not be over-assessed. Daily or sessional pain diaries that document the initial pain, time to pain-free, or pain behaviours should be used in the short term.

Tenderness is usually felt with palpation directly over the ischial tuberosity, at the proximal hamstring attachment. As with other tendinopathies, palpation is a poor prognostic indicator of severity and should not be used as a definitive diagnostic sign (Malliaras and Purdam, 2014). Normal or near-normal hamstring strength is usually found with specific muscle testing. Localised discomfort may be felt with passive stretching and functional movements (squatting, lunging), which should form part of the assessment.

Because of the potential sciatic nerve adhesion, the slump test is recommended. However, this test lacks specificity and can often lead to false positive readings and differing results with retesting. The standard slump test should be modified by maintaining an anterior pelvic tilt, with the hip in adduction and internal rotation to sensitise the sciatic nerve around the hip and provoke any neural symptoms. This test can often provoke pain from the hamstring origins; however, sciatic nerve entrapment is more likely to produce the diffuse pain and paraesthesia commonly seen with standard neural tension testing (**Figure 6.5**).

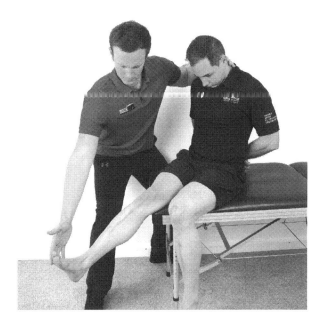

FIGURE 6.5   The standard slump test can be modified by maintaining an anterior pelvic tilt and keeping the hip in adduction and internal rotation, to sensitise any sciatic nerve involvement.

Multiple pathologies can give rise to buttock pain; a differential diagnosis is key to beginning the correct treatment programme. Malliaras and Purdam (2014) proposed a differential diagnosis in their report on proximal hamstring tendinopathy (see **Table 6.1**)

DIAGNOSIS	FEATURES
SCIATIC NERVE ENTRAPMENT AT THE ISCHIAL TUBEROSITY.	Sciatic tenderness. May be provoked by hamstring slump with diffuse symptoms and paraesthesia.
PIRIFORMIS SYNDROME	May be provoked with piriformis stretch, contraction, or slump testing. Diffuse thigh symptoms. Pain on palpation.
ISCHIOGLUTEAL BURSITIS	Irritable symptoms with sitting. MRI or ultrasound imaging for confirmation.
LUMBAR FACET ARTHROPATHY (DISC DEGENERATION)	Diffuse leg referral. Inconclusive hamstring loading tests.
ISCHIOFEMORAL IMPINGEMENT	Possible reproduction with femoral external rotation in hip neutral. MRI may be required.
UNFUSED ISCHIAL GROWTH PLATE (RARE OCCURRENCE)	Avulsion history in teenage years. MRI diagnosis required.
APOPHYSITIS OR AVULSION	Sudden onset following rapid hip flexion (kicking, splits).
CHRONIC COMPARTMENT SYNDROME OF THE POSTERIOR THIGH (RARE)	Diffuse whole hamstring discomfort. Pain does not reduce with activity. Pain may increase with activity.
POSTERIOR PUBIC OR ISCHIAL RAMUS STRESS FRACTURE	Tenderness over the posterior pubic or ischial ramus. Night pain.

TABLE 6.1   Differential diagnosis of proximal hamstring tendinopathy (adapted from Malliaras and Purdam, 2014).

Physical examination of the lumbar spine, sacroiliac joint, and hip joints should be performed to aid a correct diagnosis. The lumbar spine can simply be assessed with palpation of the musculature and passive mobilisation of intervertebral movement.

The following set of sacroiliac joint (SIJ) tests, commonly referred to as Laslett's provocation tests, are recommended to rule out any SIJ involvement (**Table 6.2**).

TEST	DESCRIPTION

DISTRACTION

Patient supine. The therapist then applies posterolateral-directed pressure to bilateral pelvis at the level of the anterior superior iliac spine. A positive finding would be a reproduction of pain.

COMPRESSION

Patient side-lying with hips and knees flexed to 90°. The therapist needs to get their upper body over the pelvis to allow the application of enough pressure over the iliac crest, with the force directed down to the opposite iliac crest. A positive finding would be a reproduction of symptoms.

THIGH THRUST

Patient supine. The therapist places the patient's hip into 90° of flexion and into adduction. The therapist should then apply a compressive force down through the femur at varying angles of adduction and flexion. The therapist can place one hand under the sacrum to stabilise the pelvis on a soft couch. The reproduction of posterior pain would be a positive finding.

SACRAL THRUST

Patient prone. The therapist applies a central and anteriorly directed thrust over the sacrum. A positive finding would be a reproduction of symptoms.

GAENSLEN'S

Patient supine with both legs extended. The test leg is passively brought into full hip flexion, while the opposite hip is in extension off the side of the couch. Overpressure is then applied to the flexed extremity. A positive finding would be the reproduction of pain.

TABLE 6.2   Provocation tests

The hamstring stretch test

The hamstring stretch test can be used to stress the proximal attachment for pain provocation under load (**Figure 6.6**). To perform the test, with the patient supine, the therapist rapidly flexes the hip and extends the knee. This is like Askling's H-test, but it is achieved passively and without a knee brace to lock the knee into extension.

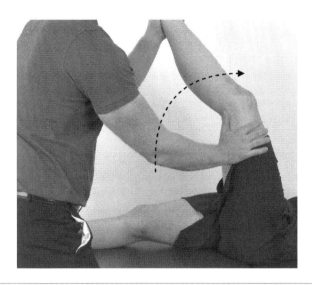

FIGURE 6.6   The simple hamstring stretch test may provoke pain from the hamstring origin and could be used to determine pain sensitivity.

The H-test

Askling's H-test (Askling, Nilsson and Thorstensson, 2010) can be used when standard strength and flexibility tests are asymptomatic and before returning to sport (**Figure 6.7**). This active test seems sensitive enough to detect small deficits in hamstring flexibility, recruitment, and apprehension during the important deceleration of the leg. The leg needs to be locked at the knee using a brace. The patient is then asked to flex their hip from a supine position to produce a kicking action at full speed and full range. Pain or a functional deficit are evidenced by lack of range, power, and apprehension.

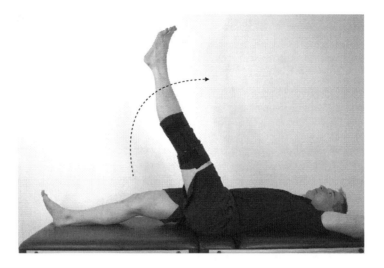

FIGURE 6.7 The H test can be used to determine the ability of the hamstrings to control deceleration of the limb before returning to sprint-based activities. It also gives an indication of patient apprehension for muscle and tendon loading.

Hip extension testing

A limitation of hip extension resulting from hip flexor tension and poor gluteus maximus activation should be identified and treated. The modified Thomas test and the standing hip extension test can be used to identify hip flexor tension (**Figure 6.8**).

Modified Thomas test

Instruct your patient to lie on the couch with their buttocks at the end of the couch, so that hip extension is not blocked by the couch under their thighs when they lie back. Instruct them to pull one leg into their chest with the knee bent; this tilts the pelvis posteriorly and increases the contralateral hip flexor stretch. A limited contralateral hip extension with reported anterior hip tension is a sign of limited hip extension. If the extended leg is abducted, this indicates lateral tension from the hip abductors.

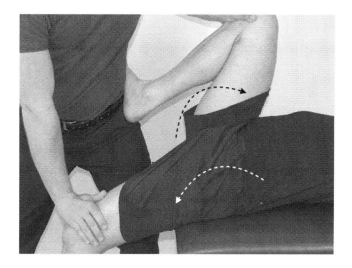

FIGURE 6.8   The modified Thomas test provides an indication of passive hip extensibility.

Standing hip extension test

This test demonstrates the range and control of standing, unweighted hip extension. Instruct your patient to extend one leg from the hip (**Figure 6.9**). Their habitual method of achieving this movement should be noted; lumbar spine extension is a common compensation for poor hip extension. Then, instruct them to stabilise the torso and repeat the hip extension movement. This test is useful for detecting restrictions and movement dysfunction and to reassess them after exercise intervention strategies.

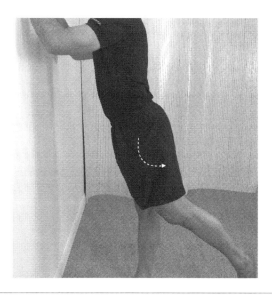

FIGURE 6.9   Standing hip extension test.

Prone hip extension test

Poor gluteal function is a common problem. This may be due to sitting too much, or because of flexion-based activities and poor training methods. If the gluteus maximus muscle is inhibited or hindered by tight hip flexors, then hamstring compensation and hip flexor dominance typically become evident. This is often assessed with a prone hip extension test to evaluate a delayed gluteal response to hip extension, and noticeable hamstring or erector spinae muscle dominance.

With your patient lying prone on the treatment table, put one hand on the upper gluteal region and one on the belly of the hamstring muscle. The erector spinae muscle should also be visible up to the lower thoracic region to observe muscle activation. Ask your patient to extend the leg from the hip (**Figure 6.10**). Note the pattern of recruitment of the hamstring, gluteal, and erector spinae muscles. Typical patterns are suggested in the literature, but the key thing to observe is whether the gluteus maximus muscle activates early to initiate and maintain hip extension. Poor gluteal activation is usually compensated by increased erector spinae and hamstring muscle contraction.

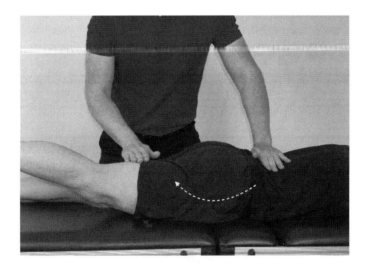

FIGURE 6.10   The prone hip extension test is an active test that allows the assessment of hip extension, range, and power.

Other factors to consider

Hip extension may also be limited by weakness in the knee extensors and plantar flex-ors, as well as by limitations in ankle dorsiflexion and hallux limitus. All these would reduce the ability of the lower limb to extend behind the torso during the stance and push-off phases of the gait cycle.

MAGNETIC RESONANCE IMAGING

Magnetic resonance imaging (MRI) findings typically include tendon thickening, intrasubstance signal heterogeneity, and oedema around the ischial tuberosity. The use of ultrasound imaging is also becoming increasingly popular. While a significant amount of research continues to be done on Achilles and patellar tendinopathy, the research that focuses on hamstring tendinopathy remains sparse, although MRI and histological findings appear to demonstrate the same abnormalities, including rounding of tenocyte nuclei and increased tendinous proliferation, as discussed in Chapter 3.

TREATING PROXIMAL HAMSTRING TENDINOPATHY

The treatment of high hamstring tendinopathy may involve a range of typical tendinopathy interventions including analgesic treatments, gait re-education, and strengthening exercises. As with other tendinopathies, the simple option of rest and inactivity does not provide a long-term solution.

Extracorporeal shockwave therapy

There is a very low volume of research on the use of extracorporeal shockwave therapy (ESWT) for hamstring tendinopathy. Despite this, ESWT has been shown as a safe and effective treatment for chronic hamstring tendinopathy (Cacchio et al., 2011). However, if ESWT is used, it should be administered alongside a managed loading programme.

Surgery for hamstring tendinopathy

Hamstring tendinopathy can be more problematic to resolve conservatively, and surgery may be indicated more readily than would be expected for Achilles or patellar tendinopathy. The outcome from surgery is poorly documented, but research suggests a reasonable success rate (Lempainen et al., 2009). Surgery usually involves a transverse tenotomy of the semimembranosus tendon 3–4 cm distal to the origin followed by a suture to the biceps femoris tendon to prevent retraction. The release of any thickened tissue around the sciatic nerve is also a surgical option. Both may be done if required.

Potential adherence of the sciatic nerve is likely responsible for the poor response to conservative treatment.

PREVENTION AND REHABILITATION

A large amount of recent research into the prevention of all types of hamstring injuries remains largely inconclusive (Goldman and Jones, 2010). The current trends include: Nordic hamstring curls (Petersen et al., 2010); a balance programme (Kraemer and Knobloch, 2009); and soft tissue therapy (Hoskins and Pollard, 2010). The specific treatment and management of proximal hamstring tendinopathy has not been well documented. Malliaras and Purdam (2014) recently provided some management guidelines which have helped to inform the following sections in this chapter.

Currently, the most effective management of proximal hamstring tendinopathy has been extrapolated from Achilles and patellar tendon management programmes and involves two main objectives: reduction of pain; and improvement in function. Usually, the patient's main concern is to reduce the pain and discomfort rather than making structural changes through loading and mechanotransduction. A loading programme will be less successful, if adhered to at all, if pain is not controlled. The prospect of initiating a loading management programme while the patient is still experiencing pain is very challenging and often negatively influences the outcome. Exercise adherence is discussed in Chapter 9.

MONITORING

Before beginning a management programme, choose a few key outcome measures that can be measured on a weekly basis to gauge progress. A few have been included in the following sections.

Morning pain diary

Pain commonly increases at the beginning of a loading programme and should be expected and tolerated to a small degree. By explaining this to a patient and using a pain diary, you can monitor and chart the delayed (12–24 hours) pain response rather than any immediate correlations to activity. Your patient may need to choose a key function that usually causes discomfort during their morning routine, such as bending forward or squatting.

The maximum voluntary contraction test

The maximum voluntary contraction (MVC) test is a useful method of detecting a developing weakness within a unilateral hamstring muscle group, potentially providing advanced warning of an increased injury risk for an athlete (**Figure 6.11**). The test may also be used as a simple strength outcome measure to monitor rehabilitation progress. It is simple to perform and only requires a set of scales or similar measuring equipment. To perform the test, position your patient supine with their feet up on a chair or stool. This position should be standardised for test/retest reliability. Place the scales under one heel and instruct your patient to push their heel down as hard as possible without letting their hips lift off the ground; the contraction should be held for 3 seconds and the maximum pressure recorded. A reading should be taken for each leg. The test's creators, Schache and colleagues (2011), recommend that it should be performed weekly 1 or 2 days after a competition or intensive training event. Any reduction in MVC is taken as a warning sign of injury risk. I have changed the test to use a set of standard bathroom scales rather than the original pressure cuff. It is much simpler to set up and the patient can easily perform the test at home.

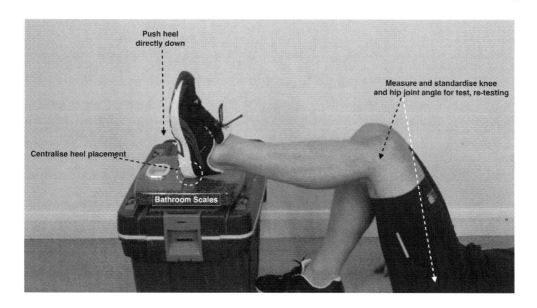

FIGURE 6.11   The maximum voluntary contraction test is an active test that allows the assessment of hamstring strength using simple equipment.

REDUCING PAIN AND CONTROLLING SYMPTOMS

Soft tissue therapy

For symptomatic relief, many patients report a reduction in symptoms following massage of the hamstring region. Many different massage styles exist, and no evidence is available to suggest any specific type. (See Chapter 11 for further discussion and description of massage techniques.)

Improving hip extension

A comprehensive plan should be used to improve hip extension. Attention should be given to the following factors: (1) hip extension is commonly limited by hip flexor tension (techniques to reduce this are shown in **Figures 6.12–6.14**); (2) hip extensors should be strengthened into the end range with isolation and compound exercises, such as supine hip extension, double leg, single leg, weighted (see **Figures 6.15–6.17**).

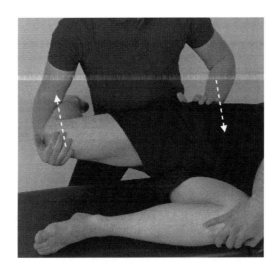

FIGURE 6.12   The side-lying-assisted hip extension allows the correct positioning of the lumbar spine, to avoid hyperextension. Muscle energy techniques can also be added when stretching from this position.

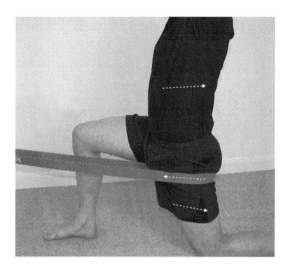

FIGURE 6.13 Banded hip stretch. This active stretch includes a soft tissue stretch and an element of joint mobilisation. The stretch can be taught and used in clinic before being prescribed as a routine home exercise.

FIGURE 6.14 Hip flexor stretch (kneeling). If the patient has a reasonable level of hip and knee flexibility, they may find this hip flexor and knee extensor stretch effective. Contraction of the glutes on the stretched leg will also help to push the hip further into extension.

A

B

C

FIGURE 6.15   The supine hip extension exercise can be performed with (a) both feet on the ground, (b) just one or, for a more advanced exercise, (c) as a resistance exercise.

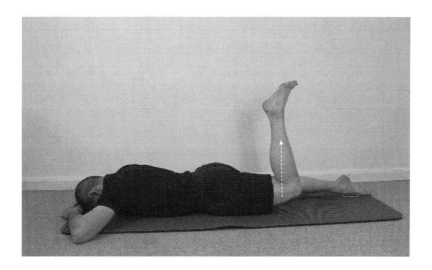

FIGURE 6.16   The prone bent knee hip extension activates the gluteal musculature with a reduced hamstring contribution because of the flexed knees shortening the hamstrings towards the end of the contractile range.

FIGURE 6.17   Prone straight leg hip and arm extension. The hip is extended while simultaneously extending the opposite arm. This exercise activates much of the posterior extensor musculature and encourages hip extension and inner range gluteal activation.

Squats and deadlifts

These compound exercises are excellent for strengthening the lower limbs and trunk, but be cautious when prescribing them for some individuals because both exercises can place a significant strain on the hamstrings in a lengthened position, potentially irritating symptoms. Without proper guidance, the exercises may be repeated incorrectly, thereby insufficiently loading the gluteal muscles.

Hip extension drills should be integrated into training to alter movement patterns and make full use of the hip extension range (see **Figures 6.18–6.20**).

FIGURE 6.18   Standing hip extension aims to mimic hip extension during running gait to assist in retraining movement patterns.

FIGURE 6.19   Hip thrusts can be helpful for understanding the required pattern of end of range hip extension.

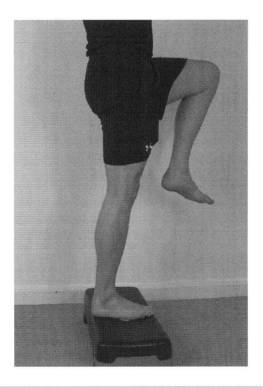

FIGURE 6.20   The step-up exercise brings the hip from a flexed position to one of full extension under load.

Hip extension running drills

Running technique and drills are covered in Chapter 10. Please be cautious when recommending running drills and gait changes; without proper guidance and management, novice runners are likely to increase their risk of injury. I have included some simple advice for patients in Chapter 10.

REDUCING LOADING

Research supports the notion that simply resting is insufficient to rehabilitate tendons because it further reduces the loading capacity of the muscle-tendon unit; this provides poor preparation for a return to training. However, the identification and reduction of specific aggravating loading patterns should be one of the first priorities. Identification, reduction, or removal of the risk factors identified earlier in this chapter should lead to a rapid reduction in symptoms, especially in early-stage reactive tendinopathy.

TENDON LOADING PROGRAMME

Phase 1: isometric loading

The aim is to reduce pain and introduce a loading stimulus. It is sensible to consider the analgesic benefits of isometric loading for the treatment of hamstring tendinopathy, bearing in mind the treatment success to date with its use in the management of Achilles and patellar tendinopathy. Isometric exercises are often performed alongside some of the other previously mentioned treatments. Patient education and compliance are key drivers for a successful start to a loading programme.

Hamstring isometric contractions should be performed with the hips in or near to neutral; significant hip flexion should be avoided to reduce the chances of tendon compression over the ischial tuberosity. For general tendinopathy-related pain, 30–60-second holds should be repeated up to 3 or 4 times within 1-minute intervals and performed around 4 times each day (Rio, 2014; patellar tendinopathy research). Following completion of the isometric holds, the patient should experience a period of reduced pain from the hamstring origin. The loading should also stimulate positive structural changes through cellular adaptation within the tendon.

Exercise positions include: prone leg curl hold (**Figure 6.21**); long lever bridge holds (**Figure 6.22**); and straight leg pull downs (**Figure 6.23**).

FIGURE 6.21   Prone leg curl hold. The leg curl machine can be used for isometric hamstring loading, maintaining a contraction with the muscle in a mid-range position.

FIGURE 6.22   The long lever bridge position allows hamstring loading in a neutral hip position. It is also simple to complete and requires no exercise equipment.

FIGURE 6.23   The leg is pulled down against resistance from an elastic exercise band. This is very similar to the long lever bridge exercise and essentially achieves the same loading affect.

To progress the rehabilitation plan, isometric exercises can be continued alongside phase 2 exercises and can be reduced in volume accordingly. My patients have reported that both phase 1 and 2 exercises are helpful for pain relief.

Phase 2: developing strength

The aim is to stimulate musculotendinous adaptation and strength gains. Much of the hamstring rehabilitation research supports the use of eccentric exercises, but tendinopathy loading research is steering us towards heavy slow resistance training with less concern for an eccentric or concentric bias. One rationale for biasing the eccentric component during a hamstring programme, is the potential to influence the length-tension relationship of a muscle group that is often lacking in flexibility and strength. This "lengthening through strengthening" approach is an effective strength and conditioning technique.

Eccentric hamstring muscle training has been shown to increase the maximal strength of the hamstring muscle group and has the additional advantage of partially mimicking one of the muscle group's main functional actions. It is also the muscle action that causes most hamstring injuries (Askling, Karlsson and Thorstensson, 2003). Theoretically, the stronger the muscle the more energy it can absorb before failing (Garrett, 1996).

Before starting an eccentric hamstring training programme, there are some important points to consider. Focused eccentric overload can often be more physically taxing than the usual concentric training and can, particularly in the early stages, lead to detrimental changes in the form of stiffness and increased muscle tone as components of delayed onset of muscle soreness. In the short term, this type of training could increase the risk of hamstring injury in the post-adaptive period (Clark et al., 2005). To minimise any short-term problems, the initial exercise programme should use low repetition and low resistance, beginning with an initial twice-weekly session. An intensity approximately 50% below maximum ability should be used before gradually progressing towards a more maximal performance over several weeks (Clark et al., 2005).

Nordic hamstring exercises

One of the most recommended hamstring exercises is the eccentric Nordic exercise (**Figure 6.24**), which is associated with increased performance and protective benefits (Clark et al., 2005). Despite its successful use in preventive programmes, the Nordic exercise has been challenged for its lack of functional relevance to usual hamstring function. Another popular exercise with poor rationale is the prone leg curl exercise. This simple exercise is useful for low-load training but has a poor correlation with typical hamstring function.

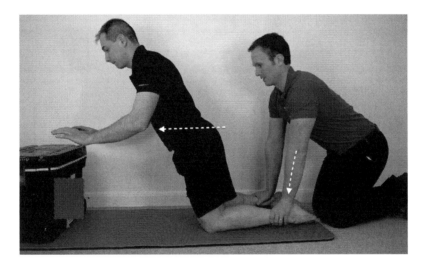

FIGURE 6.24   The Nordic hamstring exercise. (a) An eccentric load is placed through the hamstring muscles as the patient controls a forward fall into a press-up position. (b) Modified version. This is an advanced exercise and not suitable for sedentary, non-athletic patients.

Long lever bridge exercise

This simple exercise does not require any equipment and has many variations.

Technique

Begin with your patient lying supine with legs straight and feet up on a raised surface. Instruct your patient to keep their knees slightly bent, then ask them to push the heels down so that their hips lift off the floor (**Figure 6.25**). The exercise should be performed slowly and under control. A more advanced version of the exercise can be performed using only one leg.

FIGURE 6.25   The long lever bridge exercise (one leg version). This exercise is simply a progression of the isometric version in phase 1.

Modified trunk extensions

This exercise can be performed using a back extension machine and provides an excellent hamstring stimulus (**Figure 6.26**).

Technique

The upper pad should sit below the pelvis so that hip flexion can be achieved while maintaining neutral spinal posture. The exercise should be performed with a fast, controlled, concentric contraction followed by a slow, controlled, eccentric lowering of the upper torso. No weight should be added until the patient can perform 15 or more repetitions while maintaining the correct position.

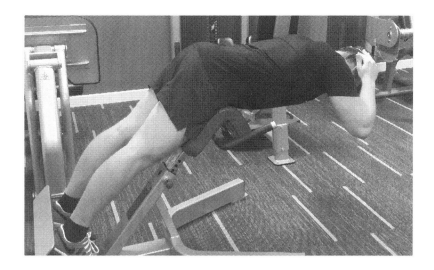

FIGURE 6.26   Modified trunk extensions. A standard adjustable trunk extension bench can be used for this exercise.

Half-range straight leg deadlift

The standard straight leg deadlift (**Figure 6.27**) can be modified and performed with the knees bent approximately 20 degrees to mimic the position during the support phase of sprinting (Panariello, 1999). This exercise is designed to recruit the posterior musculature and focuses on the hamstring involvement over the hip joint. The exercise begins with a half-range deadlift to avoid too much hip flexion that may exacerbate a compressive mechanism of hamstring tendinopathy. Although this exercise is demanding on the spinal musculature, it is very functional because of the natural movement pattern. Attention should be paid to the technique before adding resistance is considered. Further modifications of this exercise include end-of-range contractions to actively increase the available range and the isometric holds.

Technique

Begin by asking your patient to stand up straight with the feet shoulder width apart and the knees slightly bent. Ensure your patient maintains a neutral spine while flexing forward from the hips. It is an option to only perform half-range exercises for the reasons stated previously. Get your patient to perform the exercise slowly and under control, focusing on hamstring lengthening and contraction.

FIGURE 6.27   Half-range straight leg deadlift. With this exercise, it is important to maintain the correct form with a neutral spine and a slight knee bend.

Phase 3: functional strength

The focus of this phase is strength adaptation of the muscle-tendon unit during integrative functional movement patterns.

This phase can begin after symptoms have been reduced and there is evident adaptation from phase 1 to 2. Begin by replacing one exercise set from phase 2 with a phase 3 exercise and progress to a 50/50 split between phase 2 and the new phase 3 exercises.

To allow more functional movement exercises, hip flexion needs to be increased; the patient's response to this should be carefully monitored.

Functional exercises

Many functional exercises have been unearthed from an extensive range of books, research, and literature. Several techniques claim to simulate the performance requirements of the athlete; some involve difficult body positioning in the process, thus reducing the likelihood of patients showing exercise adherence.

The challenge of focusing on the hamstring muscle group without disrupting the efficiency of functional biomechanics should form the basis of training programme design. The following exercises have been included for this reason. They also require minimal equipment.

Full-range straight leg deadlift

This is simply the progression from the half-range deadlift exercise in phase 2, with an increased range of movement (**Figure 6.28**).

Technique

Begin by having your patient stand up straight with the feet shoulder width apart and the knees slightly bent. Ensure your patient maintains a neutral spine while flexing forward from the hips. Get your patient to perform the exercise slowly and under control, focusing on hamstring lengthening and contraction.

FIGURE 6.28   Full-range straight leg deadlift. Performing this exercise under load provides a stimulus to the hamstring muscle group into a lengthened position.

Arabesque

The arabesque (**Figure 6.29**) requires advanced balance and coordination, placing an increased demand on the lateral hip stabilisers when compared with the double-leg stance deadlift. If the posterior unweighted leg can extend backwards, then this provides an advantageous counterbalance when performing the movement.

Technique

This exercise should be performed on one leg. The supporting knee should be slightly flexed. From an upright position, ask your patient to flex forward from the hips while maintaining a neutral spinal posture. Begin without additional weight and a small amount of forward flexion. Increase the range of flexion and additional weight to progress.

FIGURE 6.29   The arabesque movement is essentially a single-leg, straight leg deadlift. The stability demands on the loaded hip are increased, but the posterior leg provides some assistance to the movement in the form of a counterbalance.

Kettlebell swings

The kettlebell swing (**Figure 6.30**) is an excellent hip extension exercise. Start with your patient adopting a wide stance and a slight bend in the knees, which should be maintained during the swing. Ensure your patient maintains a neutral spine throughout the movement by flexing and extending from the hips, commonly described as "hip hinging", because the back and knees should remain in the same position while the hips provide the movement. The kettlebell should be swung upwards from beneath the thighs and up in front of the body. The power for the upswing should be generated from a hip thrust into extension; the control during the descent phase should also come from the hips and the kettlebell should swing back down beneath the legs. Knee flexion and trunk flexion are common technique faults, especially when fatigued.

FIGURE 6.30   The kettle bell swing is an excellent conditioning exercise. It loads the hip extensors and promotes the development of lumbopelvic control and coordination.

Standing leg curl

This is an excellent exercise for runners. It is easily set up as a home exercise with a resistance band, or can be carried out with a cable machine in the gym (**Figure 6.31**).

Ask your patient to stand on one leg with or without a balance aid depending on ability. Use a resistance band secured at floor height and around the ankle to provide a resistance to hip extension and knee flexion. Ask your patient to extend the hip and flex the knee to bring the foot posteriorly before allowing a controlled return to hip flexion and knee extension.

FIGURE 6.31   The standing leg curl loads the hamstring muscle group through a range of movement like that seen with running and sprinting.

Phase 4: developing speed

The aim of this phase is neuromuscular stimulation and energy storage loading to stress the elastic properties of the tendon.

Rapid loading can commence when pain has been reduced with phases 2 and 3 exercises and strength adaptation is evident. To reduce the risk of exacerbation, speed exercises should initially be performed without resistance and with assistance, if required. Repetitive loaded deep hip flexion should be reduced initially to limit tendon compression.

Exercises to develop speed should be performed every 4 days. A typical training cycle would be:

- day 1: speed training (high load);
- day 2: isometrics and symptom reduction treatment (low load);
- day 3: strength training including functional exercises (medium load);
- day 4: rest day.

Getting started with speed training

Begin by reducing weight and adding speed, but without leaving the ground. The exercises can be faster versions of the functional exercises because these movement patterns have already been practised and progression can be achieved at a faster rate.

Advanced exercises

Advanced exercises use plyometric movements and usually involve jumping and landing to achieve a rapid contraction and subsequent force absorption. Plyometric exercises carry a higher risk of injury and should not be performed under muscular fatigue, instead stopping the exercise when technique starts to falter.

Advanced athletic training

The hamstring muscle group is maximally recruited at two specific points in the gait cycle: at the end of the swing phase to decelerate the leg; and following heel or foot strike to bring the body forward over the centre of gravity. Based on this knowledge, these two specific actions can form the focus of specific athletic drills.

Squats and deadlifts are commonly used off-season to improve strength and thus performance on the field or track during sprinting. Problems arise when transferring the strength gains from squatting exercises to sprinting because of the different movement patterns, and due to imbalance in the quadricep/hamstring strength ratio; this may produce a more powerful hip flexion and knee extension and one that is mismatched with the deceleration ability of a lesser-conditioned hamstring group. For this reason, resistance training should include exercises for the posterior chain (deadlifts, kettlebell swings) and sprint drills should continue to be used off-season to support the coordination of the movement pattern and identify any early limitations to range of movement from other training methods. For example, hip flexor tension limiting hip extension at the end of the stance phase, as discussed earlier in this chapter.

Acceleration/deceleration drills

Easy

Walk > jog > run drill: from a brisk walk, begin to jog and then continue to increase your pace towards approximately 75% of your maximum speed, then reduce your pace gradually. Begin with a gradual acceleration and progress towards a more rapid increase and decrease in speed.

Medium

Walk > sprint > walk drill: accelerate from a walking pace to a full sprint, once you feel you have achieved your maximal or near maximal speed, reduce your pace back to a brisk walk before preparing to repeat the drill. Progression can be made by shortening the rest time between sprints and aiming to increase sprint repetitions.

Hard

From a standing or crouched start accelerate to full speed as quickly as possible; on reaching a maximal pace, immediately begin to decelerate before repeating the drill and progressing the repetitions.

Incline drills

Hill running should be introduced cautiously because of the sustained hamstring contraction from a flexed hip and associated tendon compression at the ischial tuberosity. A shortened stride length and increased cadence may be a useful technique to reduce hamstring loading. See Chapter 10 for more information on gait re-education.

CONCLUSION

Hamstring injuries continue to plague both professional and amateur athletes, with hamstring tendinopathy making up a small portion of the more chronic cases. Previous injury is a major risk factor for re-injury. This justifies focusing on full rehabilitation and prevention during off-season and preseason training.

As with other lower-limb tendinopathies, isometric testing and loading of the whole musculotendinous unit can be successfully used within the management approach. Because both active and inactive patients can suffer from tendinopathy, it is important to select the most suitable exercises for each individual patient, to avoid any aggravating positions, monitor progress, and adapt the programme in response to mutually agreed outcome measures. Gait analysis is also recommended for runners of all abilities. Conscious changes to gait will likely allow an earlier return to running and possibly serve as a viable preventive method.

Despite the large amount of data relating to loading and movement patterns, it is the pain and discomfort that has led patients to seek help and advice. Simple analgesic methods should be administered before other management strategies to promote adherence to a more comprehensive programme.

REFERENCES

Askling C, Karlsson J, Thorstensson A (2003). Hamstring injury occurrence in elite soccer players after preseason strength training with eccentric overload. *Scand J Med Sci Sports*. **13**:244–250.

Askling CM, Nilsson J, Thorstensson A (2010). A new hamstring test to complement the common clinical examination before return to sport after injury. *Knee Surg Sports Traumatol Arthrosc*. **18**:1798–1803.

Cacchio A, De Paulis F, Maffuli N (2014). Development and validation of a new visa questionnaire (VISA-H) for patients with proximal hamstring tendinopathy. *Br J Sports Med*. **48**:448–452.

Cacchio A, Rompe JD, Furia JP, et al. (2011). Shockwave therapy for the treatment of chronic proximal hamstring tendinopathy in professional athletes. *Am J Sports Med*. **39**:146–153.

Chumanov ES, Heiderscheit BC, Thelen DG (2011). The effect of speed and influence of individual muscles on hamstring mechanics during the swing phase of sprinting. *J Biomech*. **40**:3555–3562.

Clark R, Bryant A, Culgan J-P, et al. (2005). The effects of hamstring strength training on dynamic jumping performance and isokinetic strength parameters: a pilot study on the implications for the prevention of hamstring injuries. *Phys Ther Sport*. **6**:67–73.

Fredericson M, Moore W, Guillet M, et al. (2005). High hamstring tendinopathy in runners: meeting the challenges of diagnosis, treatment, and rehabilitation. *Phys Sportsmed*. **33**:32–43.

Garrett WE Jr (1996). Muscle strain injuries. *Am J Sports Med*. **24(6 Suppl)**:S2–8.

Goldman EF, Jones DE (2010). Interventions for preventing hamstring injuries. *Cochrane Database Syst Rev. CD006782*.

Higashihara A, Ono T, Kubota J, et al. (2010). Functional differences in the activity of the hamstring muscles with increasing running speed. J Sports Sci. **28**:1085–1092.

Hoskins W, Pollard H (2010). The effect of a sports chiropractic manual therapy intervention on the prevention of back pain, hamstring and lower-limb injuries in semi-elite Australian Rules footballers: a randomized controlled trial. *BMC Musculoskelet Disord*. **11**:64.

Kraemer R, Knobloch K (2009). A soccer-specific balance training program for hamstring muscle and patellar and Achilles tendon injuries: an intervention study in premier league female soccer. *Am J Sports Med*. **37**:1384–1393.

Lempainen L, Sarimo J, Mattila K, et al. (2009). Proximal hamstring tendinopathy: results of surgical management and histopathologic findings. *Am J Sports Med.* **37**:727–734.

Lieber RL (2010). *Skeletal Muscle Structure, Function, and Plasticity. 3rd edn. Baltimore, MD: Lippincott Williams & Wilkins.*

Malliaras P, Purdam G (2014). Proximal hamstring tendinopathy assessment and management. Sports Health. **32**:21–30.

Myers T (2001). *Anatomy Trains: Myofascial Meridians for Manual and Movement Therapists. Edinburgh: Churchill Livingstone.*

Noonan TJ, Garrett WE Jr. (1992). Injuries at the myotendinous junction. Clin Sports Med. **11**:783–806.

Panariello RA (1999). CKC Exercises for Rehabilitating Hamstring Injuries. *Athl Ther Today.* **4:11–12.**

Petersen J, Thorborg K, Nielsen MB, et al. (2010). Acute hamstring injuries in Danish elite football: a 12-month prospective registration study among 374 players. *Scand J Med Sci Sports.* **20**:588–592.

Puranen J, Orava S (1988). The hamstring syndrome. A new diagnosis of gluteal sciatic pain. *Am J Sports Med.* **16**:517–521.

Rio E (2014) Clinical perspective on isometric exercise for tendon pain. *SportEX Med.* **60**:21–26.

Schache AG, Crossley KM, Macindoe IG, et al. (2011). Can a clinical test of hamstring strength identify football players at risk of hamstring strain? *Knee Surg Sports Traumatol Arthrosc.* **19**:38–41.

Schache AG, Dorn TW, Blanch PD, et al. (2012). Mechanics of the human hamstring muscles during sprinting. *Med Sci Sports Exerc.* **44**:647–658.

Tubbs RS, Caycedo FJ, Oakes WJ, et al. (2006). Descriptive anatomy of the insertion of the bicep femoris muscle. *Clin Anat.* **19**:517–521.

Whiting WC, Zernicke RF (2008). *Biomechanics of Musculoskeletal Injury. 2nd edn. Champaign, IL: Human Kinetics.*

Yu B, Queen RM, Abbey AN, et al. (2008). Hamstring muscle kinematics and activation during overground sprinting. J Biomech. **41**:3121–3126.

FURTHER READING

Askling C, Saartok T, Thorstensson A (2006). Type of acute hamstring strain affects flexibility, strength, and time to return to pre-injury level. *Br J Sports Med.* **40**:40–44.

Askling CM, Tengvar M, Saartok T, et al. (2007a). Acute first-time hamstring strains during slow-speed stretching: clinical, magnetic resonance imaging, and recovery characteristics. *Am J Sports Med.* **35**:1716–1724.

Askling CM, Tengvar M, Saartok T, et al. (2007b). Acute first-time hamstring strains during high-speed running: a longitudinal study including clinical and magnetic resonance imaging findings. *Am J Sports Med.* **35**:197–206.

Connell DA, Schneider-Kolsky ME, Hoving JL, et al (2004). Longitudinal study comparing sonographic and MRI assessments of acute and healing hamstring injuries. *AJR Am J Roentgenol.* **183**:975–984.

Croisier J, Ganteaume S, Binet J, et al. (2008). Strength imbalances and prevention of hamstring injury in professional soccer players: a prospective study. *Am J Sports Med.* **36**:1469–1475.

Devlin L (2000). Recurrent posterior thigh symptoms detrimental to performance in rugby union: predisposing factors. *Sports Med.* **29**:273–287.

Engebretsen AH, Myklebust G, Holme I, et al. (2010). Intrinsic risk factors for hamstring injuries among male soccer players: a prospective cohort study. *Am J Sports Med.* **38**:1147–1153.

French D (2008). Conditioning the hamstrings: Training considerations for performance and injury prevention. *SportEx.* **15**:18–22.

Gabbe BJ, Bennell KL, Finch CF, et al. (2006). Predictors of hamstring injury at the elite level of Australian football. *Scand J Med Sci Sport.* **16**:7–13.

Goom T, Malliaras P, Reiman MP, et al. (2016). Proximal hamstring tendinopathy: clinical aspects of assessment and management. *J Orthop Sports Phys Ther.* **46**:483–493.

Heiderscheit BC, Sherry MA, Slider A, et al. (2010). Hamstring strain injuries: recommendations for diagnosis, rehabilitation, and injury prevention. *J Orthop Sports Phys Ther.* **40**:67–81.

Herrington L (2009). Hamstring muscle injuries. *SportEX.* **20**:20–22.

Kubo K, Kanehisa H, Fukunaga T (2002). Effects of resistance and stretching training programmes on the viscoelastic properties of human tendon structures in vivo. *J Physiol.* **538**:219–226.

Kubo K, Komuro N, Ishiguro N, et al. (2006). Effects of low-load resistance training with vascular occlusion on the mechanical properties of muscle and tendon. *J Appl Biomech.* **22**:112–119.

Kubo K, Yata H, Kanehisa H, et al. (2006). Effects of isometric squat training on the tendon stiffness and jump performance. *Eur J Appl Physiol.* **96**:305–314.

Massoud Arab A, Reza Nourbakhsh M, Mohammadifar A (2011). The relationship between hamstring length and gluteal muscle strength in individuals with sacroiliac joint dysfunction. *J Man Manip Ther.* **19**:5–10.

Orchard JW, Farhart P, Leopold C (2004). Lumbar spine region pathology and hamstring and calf injuries in athletes: is there a connection? *Br J Sports Med.* **38**: 502–504.

Petersen J, Thorborg K, Nielsen MB, et al. (2011). Preventative effect of eccentric training on acute hamstring injuries in men's soccer: a cluster-randomized controlled trial. *Am J Sports Med.* **39**:2296–2303.

Proske U, Morgan DL, Brockett CL, et al. (2004). Identifying athletes at risk of hamstring strains and how to protect them. *Clin Exp Pharmacol Physiol.* **31**:546–550.

Rio E, Moseley L, Purdam C, et al. (2014). The pain of tendinopathy: physiological or pathophysiological? *Sports Med.* **44**:9–23.

Seward H, Orchard J, Hazard H, et al. (1993). Football injuries in Australia at the élite level. *Med J Aust.* **159**:298–301.

Tooley A (2009). The role of exercise in the prevention of hamstring injury. *SportEX Med.* **39**:12–16.

Verrall GM, Slavotinek JP, Barnes PG, et al (2003). Diagnostic and prognostic value of clinical findings in 83 athletes with posterior thigh injury: comparison of clinical findings with magnetic resonance imaging documentation of hamstring strain. *Am J Sports Med.* **31**:969–973.

Warren P, Gabbe BJ, Schneider-Kolsky M, et al (2010). Clinical predictors of time to return to competition and of recurrence following hamstring strain in elite Australian footballers. *Br J Sports Med.* **44**:415–419.

Whatman C, Knappstein A, Hume P (2006). Acute changes in passive stiffness and range of motion post-stretching. *Phys Ther Sport.* **7**:195–200.

Witvrouw E, Mahieu N, Danneels L, et al. (2004). Stretching and injury prevention: an obscure relationship. *Sports Med.* **34**:443–449.

CHAPTER 7

GLUTEAL TENDINOPATHY

INTRODUCTION

Lateral hip pain is often diagnosed as trochanteric bursitis, but research over the last 15 years has increasingly challenged the notion of bursal inflammation. Instead, imaging, histological, and surgical investigations have identified a non-inflammatory insertional tendinopathy (Kingzett-Taylor et al., 1999; Bird et al., 2001; Fearon et al., 2010). The pain and dysfunction from this condition reported by patients are said to be like advanced hip osteoarthritis in severity (Fearon et al., 2014); other studies have reported more moderate symptoms. In practice, you are likely to see a range of reported symptom severities. Gluteal tendinopathy most commonly affects women >40 years of age (Segal et al., 2007) and is the most common lower-limb tendinopathy (Albers, Zwerver and van den Akker-Scheek, 2014). This high prevalence may be partially due to the increased participation in running events by older age groups or because of a generally increasing size of this demographic.

This chapter provides evidence-informed and clinically useful guidance for the treatment of gluteal tendinopathy, also termed trochanteric pain syndrome or, simply, lateral hip pain.

ANATOMY

Gluteal tendinopathy has been identified in both the gluteus medius and minimus. The anatomy of the iliotibial band (ITB), including its superior attachments to the gluteus maximus and tensor fasciae latae (TFL), are also important structures to assess and are covered in this anatomical section.

Pelvis and hip joint

The basic muscular anatomy of the pelvis and hip joint is shown in **Figure 7.1**. There are notable differences between the adult male and female pelvis, which are relevant to the increased incidence of gluteal tendinopathy among women. In comparison to the male pelvis, the female pelvis is wider, has a smaller, more anterior acetabulum, and a less vertical ilium (**Figure 7.2**).

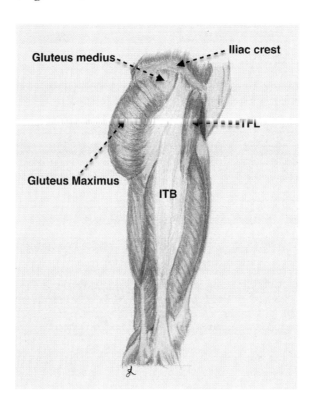

FIGURE 7.1   Musculature of the lateral hip.

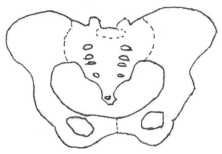

Adult human female (above)

Adult human male (below)

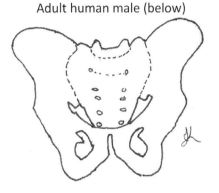

FIGURE 7.2   Comparisons between the adult human male and female pelvis.

Evolution

The increased lateral orientation of the ilia during evolution was likely necessary to allow us to stabilise the pelvis during single-leg stance as required during the normal bipedal gait cycle. In primates, the ilia have less lateral orientation and their equivalent gluteal muscles function predominantly as extensors during quadrupedalism (Earls, 2014). In theory, this means that primates and other quadrupeds should be unable to walk on two legs like humans. There are many reports of quadrupeds (from monkeys to dogs) performing bipedalism, but even when they do, a lack of trunk stability and hip extension and the inefficiency of the movement is evident.

The role of the gluteal muscles during the gait cycle

Walking and running are full body movements that involve a complex interplay of controlled joint movements. Poor function of the hip and pelvis during gait has been identified as a key area to assess because of its potential links to the onset of gluteal tendinopathy. The bony arrangement and joint mechanics of the pelvis, femur, and hip joint fulfil multiple functions during the gait cycle, while preserving the ability to allow less common movements more akin to our arboreal (tree-dwelling) ancestors. Hip joint function is reviewed in Chapter 10 and it is also discussed in Chapter 2.

Located under the gluteal tendons are three key lateral hip bursae: the subgluteus maximus (trochanteric) bursa; the subgluteus medius bursa; and the subgluteus minimus bursa (**Figure 7.3**). The large trochanteric bursa is the most superficial bursa located beneath the gluteus maximus and iliotibial tract, covering the posterior and lateral facets of the greater trochanter and gluteus medius tendon (Pfirrmann et al., 2001). Historically, this was implicated as the main pathological structure causing lateral hip pain. Gluteal tendinopathy is now considered the most likely pathology, although the two may coexist. A recent retrospective review of the sonography results of 877 individual patients for lateral hip pain reported that 80% did not demonstrate a bursitis on ultrasound (Long, Surrey and Nazarian, 2013).

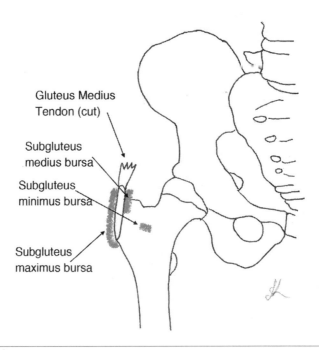

FIGURE 7.3   The three subgluteal bursae.

The gluteal muscles

Gluteus minimus

The gluteus minimus is shown in **Figure 7.4.**

A

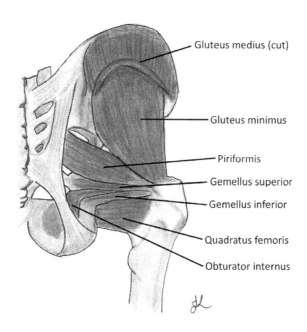

Gluteus medius (cut)

Gluteus minimus

Piriformis

Gemellus superior

Gemellus inferior

Quadratus femoris

Obturator internus

B

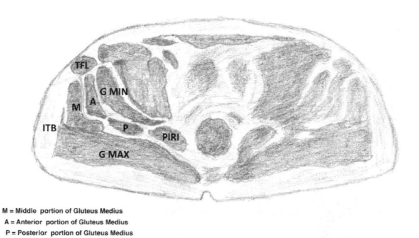

M = Middle portion of Gluteus Medius
A = Anterior portion of Gluteus Medius
P = Posterior portion of Gluteus Medius

FIGURE 7.4   (a) The anatomy of the gluteus minimus and medius. (b) Cross-section of the hip musculature showing the separations within the contractile tissue. Recreated line drawing, adapted from (Grimaldi, 2011).

The proximal attachment is at the lateral ilium, between the anterior and inferior gluteal lines. The muscle is also directly attached to the superior hip joint capsule. The distal attachment is at the anterior facet of the greater trochanter.

The gluteus minimus is the deepest muscle of the hip abductor muscle group and the smallest gluteal muscle. The attachment to the hip joint capsule may offer dynamic stabilisation to the otherwise passive capsular and ligamentous tissue.

The gluteus minimus is innervated by the superior gluteal nerve associated with the L4-S2 spinal and sacral vertebrae. This nerve separates into two branches: cranial (L4-S1); and caudal (S1-S2). The gluteus minimus may receive innervation from both branches (Duparc et al., 1997) or solely from the cranial branch (Flack, Nicholson and Woodley, 2012).

Gluteus medius

The gluteus medius is attached to the lateral ilium, between the anterior and posterior gluteal lines. Some texts also note attachments to the iliac crest and gluteal aponeurosis (Flack, Nicholson and Woodley, 2012). The gluteus medius tendon is composed of two parts: a strong, round tendon that attaches to the superoposterior facet of the greater trochanter; and a thin, lateral part that attaches to the lateral facet of the greater trochanter (Pfirrmann et al., 2001).

Grimaldi (2011) reported that the gluteus medius has three fascially distinct portions (**Figure 7.4b**): anterior, middle and posterior.

Therapeutically, it is more helpful to be aware of the separate functions of the anterior and posterior portions of the muscle, with the middle (superficial) portion receiving little attention in the literature and not reported in some anatomical texts. The posterior and anterior portions appear to be the most important functionally.

The gluteus medius is innervated by the superior gluteal nerve associated with the L4-S2 spinal and sacral levels. The superior gluteal nerve separates into two branches, one of which innervates the posterior gluteus medius (cranial branch L4-S1) and the other innervates the anterior gluteus medius (caudal branch S1-S2).

Tensor fasciae latae

The proximal attachment of the TFL is the anterior lateral portion of the ilium, often extending laterally to the anterior superior iliac crest and often attaching on the ilium below the iliac crest.

The distal attachment of the TFL involves the contractile fibres of the TFL inserting into the fascia latae and ITB. The fascia latae and ITB then blend with the patellar retinaculum and insert onto the tubercle of the tibia distally. There is anatomical variation in this arrangement (Standring et al., 2008), but the TFL along with the ITB span both lateral hip and knee joints.

Less information exists on the anatomy of the TFL muscle. The long, slender muscle is about 15 cm long (Moore and Dalley, 1999), but this varies with height. The muscle is very superficial and easy to palpate; it is often tender to the touch in runners and those with lateral hip pain.

The TFL is innervated by the superior gluteal nerve associated with the L4-S2 spinal and sacral levels. (Flack, Nicholson and Woodley, 2012).

The fasciae latae and iliotibial band

The fasciae latae is the deepest of the three divisions of fascia over the lateral thigh; it resides under the lateral intermuscular septa of the thigh, which thickens superficially into the ITB.

The proximal origin of the ITB is a bony attachment from the middle to the anterior iliac crest. The ITB also has muscular attachments to the superficial fibres of the gluteus maximus and the TFL.

The vastus lateralis muscle increases ITB tension by pushing the band out laterally, providing a mechanical advantage for the TFL and superior gluteal fibres.

PATHOLOGY

The biological contents of a tendon are primarily structured to tolerate tensile forces while allowing the necessary pliability needed to bend and become compressed during joint movements. A tendinopathic response begins at the lateral hip following unaccustomed tensile force, a compression mechanism, or a combination of both. The gluteus medius or minimus tendons at their attachment to the greater trochanter are most at risk and potentially affected by additional compressive force from the overlying ITB. A tendinopathy continuum is likely to occur; the continuum theory is covered in Chapter 3.

BIOMECHANICS

To prevent the "hip drop" that is typical of the Trendelenburg gait pattern and excessive leg adduction during the single-leg stance phase of the gait cycle, two key lateral hip stabiliser mechanisms work in synergy (**Figure 7.5**).

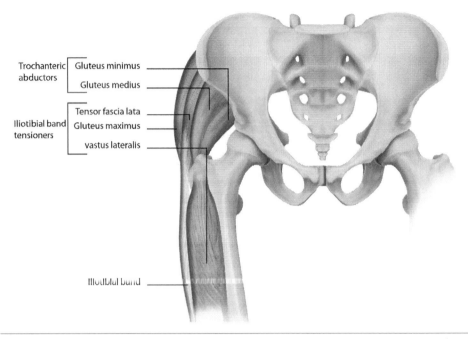

FIGURE 7.5   The trochanteric and iliotibial band stabilisers as described by Grimaldi et al. (2015).

The abductor mechanisms

The gluteus medius and minimus provide 70% of the abductor force required for pelvic stability during single-leg stance (Kummer, 1993). The ITB stabilisation mechanism provides the remaining 30% of abductor force during single-leg stance (Kummer, 1993). ITB tension is increased by the contraction of the fibres of the upper gluteus maximus, the TFL and the lateral expansion of the vastus lateralis muscle during its concentric contraction.

A likely mechanism for gluteal tendinopathy is an imbalance between the two abductor mechanisms, with atrophy of the gluteus medius and minimus causing an increased load on the ITB stabilisers, resulting in potential compensatory hypertrophy of the TFL (Sutter et al., 2013) and the associated gluteus maximus fibres. Increased tension through the ITB coupled with a likely increase in hip adduction during stance leads to an increased compressive force over the greater trochanter and gluteal tendons. This may also present as "snapping hip syndrome" as the ITB is plucked over the greater trochanter during loaded hip extension from a position of flexion.

These changes indicate the need for specific testing procedures and provide guidance for therapeutic intervention. Potential options are discussed later in this chapter.

BONY ANATOMY

Specific anatomical measurements or "anthropometrics" have been correlated with an increased incidence of lateral hip pain due to the increased stress on the supporting soft tissues during the single-leg stance phase of gait.

The first of these is a lower femoral neck-to-femoral shaft angle, commonly termed coxa vara. This reduced angle places the greater trochanter in a more lateral position, effectively widening the hips but not the pelvis; thus, the ITB must bow out around the greater trochanter. This leads to an increased compressive force on the greater trochanter from the overlying ITB. Birnbaum and collaborators (2004), supported by Fearon, Stephens and Cook (2012), identified that patients with more severe gluteal tendon pathology have lower femoral neck shaft angles than pain-free individuals or those with hip osteoarthritis.

Assessing for coxa vara

The measurement of the femoral neck-to-shaft angle should be assessed with radiography, but some clinical signs of bilateral coxa vara may be evident. These include: increased prominence of the greater trochanters relative to the iliac crests (Viradia, Berger and Dahners, 2011); a waddling gait pattern; and limited abduction and internal rotation.

Coxa vara is uncommon and these are simple tests that lack specificity. Be cautious not to diagnose all wide-hipped patients with coxa vara.

ASSESSMENT

The Victorian Institute of Sports Assessment-Gluteal Tendon (VISA-G) questionnaire is an excellent clinical tool for measuring the severity of gluteal tendinopathy during the initial assessment and for monitoring purposes. The gluteal version of the well-known VISA-A questionnaire, is reliable and valid (Fearon et al., 2015). As recommended for the other VISA questionnaires, it is best used at monthly intervals and should not be used too often to avoid over-assessment.

There is no single test with high sensitivity and specificity for diagnosing gluteal tendinopathy; instead, a battery of tests is suggested to aid a correct differential diagnosis. Symptoms and the associated tests are described here.

Lateral hip pain

Pain and tenderness is often reported on or around the greater trochanter, possibly radiating down the lateral thigh. Pain onset is often insidious and tends to progressively worsen or be exacerbated by certain activities such as running and walking, or postures such as deep-seated positions, sitting cross-legged or prolonged standing while leaning on one leg (**Figure 7.6**).

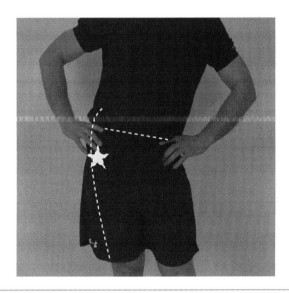

FIGURE 7.6   Standing in hip adduction places direct pressure on the lateral hip structures of the loaded leg and is an aggravating or causative factor for gluteal tendinopathy.

SLEEP DISTURBANCE

Gluteal tendinopathy typically disturbs sleep and can be especially uncomfortable for the patient when side-lying. With the painful side down, an external compressive mechanism is applied over the lateral hip by the bed; having the painful side on top places the hip in an adducted position that increases internal soft tissue compression over the greater trochanter.

Functional tasks

Moving from hip flexion to hip extension often causes pain, so simple activities such as standing up from a chair or walking up steps often cause pain over the lateral hip. Single-leg stance during the gait cycle can provoke pain in patients with significant hip instability.

Provocation tests

Testing that initiates both an active contraction of the hip abductors and provides a compressive mechanism over the greater trochanter is most likely to reproduce symptoms. The following tests can be used for assessment.

The 30-second single-leg stance test

Instruct your patient to transfer their weight onto the affected leg and allow some hip adduction to occur (**Figure 7.7**). Have them remain standing on the affected leg for up to 30 seconds or until lateral hip pain is reproduced.

FIGURE 7.7   The single-leg stance test can be used for assessment and monitoring purposes; its primary function is to provoke pain, with a secondary function of detecting hip stability.

The timing of the onset of pain can be documented and used for monitoring purposes. This test differs from the Trendelenburg test, which assesses the maintenance of pelvic stability rather than pain and is of shorter duration; however, an inability to maintain stability of the pelvis should also be noted as an associated outcome measure.

The single-leg stance test has not been extensively researched, but a study by Lequesne and collaborators (2008) reported a test sensitivity of 100% and specificity of 97.3% in a small (17 people), predominantly female cohort with long-standing greater trochanteric pain syndrome with magnetic resonance imaging serving as the gold standard. Despite the paucity of research, the biomechanical basis of pain provocation logically fits with changes in normal biomechanical function (pathomechanics).

The resisted external de-rotation test

The resisted external de-rotation test (**Figure 7.8**) is used to provoke pain over the lateral hip and indicates the presence of gluteal tendinopathy. Lequesne and collaborators (2008) reported a sensitivity of 88% and a specificity of 97.3% for this test when they tested it alongside the 30-second single-leg stance test mentioned earlier.

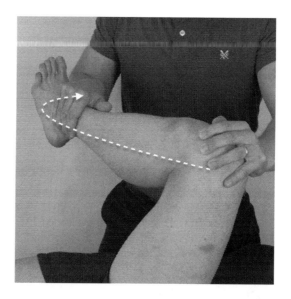

FIGURE 7.8   The resisted external de-rotation test can also be described as outer range-resisted internal rotation.

Passively flex the hip to 90 degrees and then externally rotate the hip to the end of available external rotation range. Full external rotation is often painful for patients with lateral hip pain; if this is the case, external rotation should be gradually reduced to a pain-free position. From here, you should instruct your patient to resist further external rotation, effectively attempting to internally rotate their leg in response. A positive outcome is determined by the immediate onset of pain over the lateral hip.

DIFFERENTIAL DIAGNOSIS

Patients with hip osteoarthritis commonly share a similar clinical presentation to gluteal tendinopathy; however, those with hip osteoarthritis will have difficulty putting on socks and shoes when dressing because of hip joint limitation when flexing, whereas gluteal tendinopathy does not limit flexion (Fearon et al., 2013). This can be tested clinically with a simple passive hip flexion test or a FABER (Patrick's) test (**Figure 7.9**).

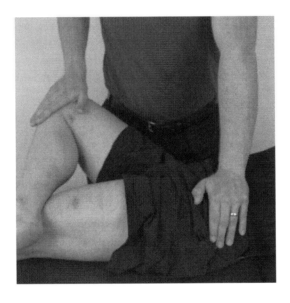

FIGURE 7.9   The FABER test is widely used for a variety of suspected hip and pelvic pathologies. FABER = Flexion, ABduction, and External Rotation.

The FABER (Patrick's) test begins with the patient supine; this is followed by the passive positioning into hip **F**lexion, **AB**duction and **E**xternal **R**otation (FABER). The test is widely used for a variety of suspected hip and pelvic pathologies. The test can be used to help differentiate between an arthritic hip and gluteal tendinopathy. If these pathologies coexist, which is not uncommon, the FABER test is not as effective.

Patients with gluteal tendinopathy, but without osteoarthritis, do not have a limited range during the FABER test, although they may experience pain at the end of the range. Patients with osteoarthritis present with a reduced range during the FABER test, again making it difficult to put on shoes and socks.

Assessing lateral hip stability

The modified Trendelenburg test is recommended over the standard Trendelenburg test, which insufficiently tests lateral hip stability and may lead to false results because other body segments, such as trunk alignment, are not routinely screened.

Modified Trendelenburg test

This test is adapted from the work of Grimaldi (2011). The test consists of two parts: self-select; and prompted correction.

Single-leg stance: self-select

Instruct your patient to stand on one leg with the non-weight-bearing hip in neutral. The presence or absence of a few key compensations should be noted. The ideal position is for the weight-bearing hip to stabilise with minimal adduction (5 degrees) while the trunk is kept upright over the pelvis with the arms relaxed (**Figure 7.10a**). The following compensations may occur: (1) lateral pelvic tilt and hip drop on the non-weight-bearing side (**Figure 7.10b**), which indicates instability and represents a positive test result; and (2) lateral trunk flexion towards the weight-bearing side (**Figure 7.10c**), which represents a positive result due to the trunk compensation for the lateral pelvic drop.

A   B   C

FIGURE 7.10 (a) Correct and stable one-leg stance. (b) Hip adduction showing contralateral pelvic drop. (c) Compensatory trunk flexion.

Single-leg stance: prompted correction

After assessing your patient's self-selected single-leg stance, you can glean further useful information by prompting specific movements to assess the availability and control of movement and correct any compensations. The following actions should be prompted:

1. Lateral hip lift: whether the lateral hip has dropped or not, the ability to lift the non-weight-bearing side of the pelvis with the loaded abductors indicates the strength, control, range, and willingness of the loaded abductors. The onset of pain should also be noted. Watch out for compensatory trunk side flexion with this test.

2. If the trunk has flexed during the initial self-select test, then the patient should be encouraged to correct this. It is common for the pelvis to drop again when the trunk returns to an upright position; the onset of any lateral hip pain should be noted.

3. If compensation can be corrected without pain, this indicates a more modifiable movement pattern. If pain occurs with the reduction of the compensatory pattern, then this offloading mechanism remains until the associated pain can be reduced. Although movement patterns and corrective exercises can be performed in the presence of pain, patient compliance and exercise adherence are greatly reduced by poor pain management.

RISK FACTORS

Identifying potential risk factors for tendinopathy can help inform the diagnosis and treatment plan. Risk factors and their mechanisms include:

*   Female gender: anatomical differences in pelvic anatomy may account for the gluteal tendinopathy gender bias towards women at a suggested ratio of 4:1 (Segal et al., 2007).

*   Age: gluteal tendinopathy is commonly reported in people over 40 years of age.

*   Poor lateral hip stability: the intrinsic and extrinsic reasons for this are explained within this chapter.

*   Gluteal weakness: there may be poor gluteal function overall from a lack of conditioning, a sedentary occupation or lifestyle, and non-bipedal exercise habits. The synergistic function of the muscles is also a factor, as discussed in this chapter.

*   Overstriding during running (and walking): an excessive stride length leads to an increased vertical ground reaction force and braking force per foot contact,

plus increased adduction from the end of the swing phase and during stance, all of which can be contributing factors.

- Hip to pelvic girth: this may be gender-related and may be classed as coxa vara if the femoral shaft-to-neck angle is below the normal range.

- High body mass index (BMI): excessive weight increases the stability demands on the lateral hip stabilisers and a high BMI is indicative of inactivity. In addition, blood lipids may increase the risk of tendon pathology at a cellular level.

- Hip osteoarthritis: osteoarthritis and pain lead to gluteal muscle inhibition followed by atrophy, which reduces hip stability and increases the risk of tendinopathy within this region.

- Leg length discrepancy: in clinical practice, this seems to have become an all-too-popular diagnosis. A significant leg length discrepancy would logically be a risk factor for many biomechanically driven issues, but this may not be the cause of the pain.

- Poor lower-limb muscle strength: if a patient has generally poor lower-limb muscle strength this would likely include the lateral hip stabilisers.

- Posture: standing habitually on an adducted leg "hanging on the hip". This pain-provoking position may be a cause of gluteal tendinopathy by altering the length/tension relationship of the hip stabilisers and allowing a constant compression of the ITB over the gluteus medius and minimus tendons.

MANAGEMENT

Modifying the risk factors
The most useful risk factors are the ones easily identified and modified. A high BMI is easily identified but not so simple to modify. Advice regarding standing posture, not "hanging on the hip", and sleeping with a pillow between the knees may provide some quick relief. The mainstay of treatment is based on strengthening the lateral hip region and avoiding aggravating postures.

Strengthening programmes
A variety of gluteal exercises can improve hip stability and reduce pain, but the targeted activation of the trochanteric abductors is most likely to be beneficial if it can be achieved without further strengthening the ITB mechanism or habitually recruiting it. While the gluteus medius and minimus remain inhibited. The habitual motor

pattern will continue to activate the ITB mechanism if this has become dominant. Reversing these aberrant recruitment patterns is potentially achievable by using the correct exercise positions. In addition, reducing muscle tone in the ITB tensioners appears to support the same outcome.

Isometrics

These exercises are designed to bias the trochanteric abductor mechanism and avoid ITB compression over the greater trochanter. Isometric loading aims to provide an exercise-based analgesic option in addition to a mechanical loading stimulus, which forms the beginning of a more dynamic and specific loading programme.

The benefits of isometric exercises for analgesia have been reported for a variety of conditions including patellar tendinopathy (Rio, Kidgell and Moseley, 2013), fibromyalgia (Kosek, Ekholm and Hansson, 1996) and in healthy individuals (Kosek and Lundberg, 2003; Hoeger Bement et al., 2009), but not specifically for lateral hip pain. I have found them to work clinically in most cases. Isometrics are a popular pain management tool for lower-limb tendon pain.

Abductor wall push

The aim is to isometrically contract the gluteus medius and surrounding muscles in a stable position.

With your patient supine, the hips should be flexed, and the knees bent. The inner leg should abduct out towards the wall. Place a cushion between the knee and the wall to reduce the amount of necessary abduction. Instruct your patient to abduct the leg towards the wall for 45–60 seconds and repeat 3–4 times (**Figure 7.11**).

This exercise can be tested when lateral hip pain has been exacerbated to see if it provides an analgesic effect.

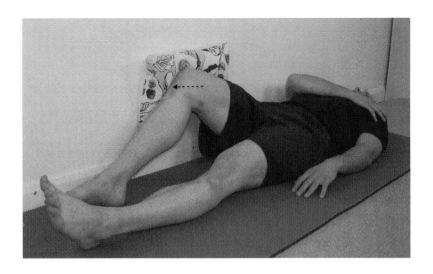

FIGURE 7.11   The abductor wall push is a simple isometric exercise to load the hip abductors from a stable and relaxed posture.

Double-abductor hold

This bilateral exercise can be performed sitting down or lying with a belt or band to provide resistance. It is an excellent option for people who sit for long periods during the day.

Your patient should be lying or sitting with their hips flexed and knees bent. Apply a band or belt around their knees to resist hip abduction. Get your patient to abduct their legs by parting their knees and maintaining an isometric resistance against the band for 45–60 seconds, repeating this 3– 4 times (**Figure 7.12**).

This is a great exercise to get less active people to perform isometric exercises in the hope that they will progress to more dynamic exercises if pain is reduced.

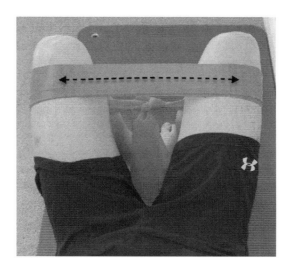

FIGURE 7.12   The double abductor hold is a simple exercise that can be performed in a variety of comfortable positions.

Gluteal activation research

Most of the gluteal muscle activation studies have used surface electromyography (EMG) measurements to determine the best exercises to activate the gluteus maximus and medius. Some of these studies used EMG to measure the TFL, based on the premise that the TFL can become overactive; therefore, exercises with a higher gluteal muscle/TFL ratio would be beneficial for correcting this imbalance. Based on EMG research, the consensus is that single-leg squats and deadlift exercises provide the highest activation of both gluteus maximus and medius (Distefano et al., 2009). To bias the gluteus medius, a hip abduction-based movement is required, potentially benefiting further from a small amount of internal rotation as the hip abducts (McBeth et al., 2012). For a more isolated gluteus maximus contraction, a hip extension exercise can be used.

Isolation exercises

The clam

In contrast to the research supporting the clam, McBeth and collaborators (2012) found that the clam exercise produced high EMG output for the TFL and low EMG output for the gluteus medius. They concluded that the exercise has poor efficacy for gluteal retraining. Their findings are supported by the literature describing the altered function of the gluteus medius after 40 degrees of hip flexion (DiStefano et al., 2009).

Despite this, Lee and collaborators (2014) found that the gluteus medius dominated over the TFL during the clam exercise, with the hip flexed at different ranges between 30 and 60 degrees. The research does not show a consensus; in practice, the clam remains one of the most commonly prescribed gluteus medius exercises. The aim of the clam exercise is to stimulate contraction of the gluteus medius and associated muscles.

Your patient should be side-lying with the hips flexed to 30 degrees and the knees bent to approximately 90 degrees (**Figure 7.13a**). From side-lying, they should tilt the pelvis forward so that their upper knee slightly overhangs their lower knee. Do not allow the pelvis to rock backwards during the exercise. Place a pillow between your patient's knees to reduce hip adduction.

Have your patient keep their pelvis stable and heels together while lifting their upper knee up until the pelvis begins to rock backwards, then lower their leg back to the starting position under control.

Get your patient to focus on controlling their movement and maintaining the correct form. Repetitions are not the focus of these exercises.

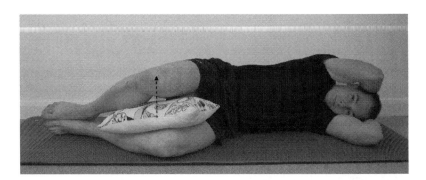

A

B

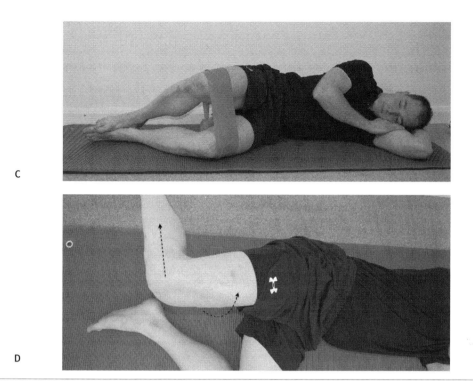

C

D

FIGURE 7.13   (a) The clam exercise is a common exercise for hip stability. Although simple to complete, attention should be given to the correct positioning so that the gluteus medius and minimus can be targeted effectively. (b) Abducted clam. (c) Banded clam. (d) Extension clam.

Clam progressions

Abducted clam

By getting your patient to slightly lift their upper foot and maintain this abducted position, gluteus medius activation is increased significantly (**Figure 7.13b**).

Banded clam

Using a resistance band around the knees increases muscle activation. It is important for the patient to maintain the correct technique (**Figure 7.13c**).

Extension clam

Starting from the abducted clam position, have your patient move their upper leg back into hip extension and then perform internal-to-external hip rotations from this extended hip position (**Figure 7.13d**).

Side-lying hip abduction

This is one of the most commonly used exercises, supported by EMG studies, to facilitate the gluteus medius. Performing it with internal hip rotation may allow a reduced contribution from the TFL (**Figure 7.14a**).

Your patient should be side-lying in a similar position to the clam but with their upper leg extended in line with their torso. Get them to abduct the upper leg to approximately 30 degrees of abduction.

The exercise is more challenging if the leg is not lowered fully. The length-tension relationship of the gluteus medius muscle may be positively influenced by repeating the movement within the muscle's inner range.

A

B

FIGURE 7.14   (a) The side-lying hip abduction exercise is a simple alternative to the clam exercise. The author prefers to focus on the clam exercise with most patients, but it is important to have different exercise options available. (b) The side plank hip abduction is not easy. Patient selection is important.

Hip abduction progressions

Side plank hip abduction

The side plank with hip abduction exercise provides a challenging progression (**Figure 7.14b**). The side plank can also be performed in isolation with or without bending the knee.

Kneeling hip stability

This is a challenging hip stability exercise for more physically able patients. Balancing on a bent knee reduces the contribution from the ITB tensioners (**Figure 7.15**).

Your patient should be kneeling on one knee on a raised surface with cushioning. The unweighted leg should not be weight-bearing during the exercise. Actively hitching the lateral pelvis with the loaded abductors should provide a challenging isometric hold for your patient, while further reducing the compressive mechanism associated with adduction. Hip flexion and extension can also be performed, as can further balance challenges.

It is important for your patient to maintain an upright trunk and avoid too much compensation from the trunk lateral flexors. A stick can be used for stabilisation and to help teach the correct positioning.

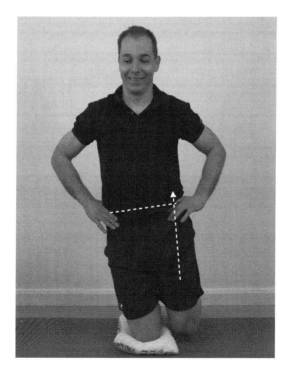

FIGURE 7.15   This exercise is an effective way to challenge hip stability. Make sure the set-up is safe and cushioning is provided under the knee for comfort.

Abduction steps

This is a dynamic exercise, which loads the lateral rotators (**Figure 7.16**). Your patient should be standing with a resistance band securely attached around the knee.

Ask your patient to walk sideways using a controlled abduction movement of the leading leg against the resistance of the band.

Make sure the band is secure and does not roll up the leg. Teach your patient how to achieve this before they do this as a home exercise.

FIGURE 7.16   A resistance band is used to provide resistance into abduction during this dynamic exercise.

Abduction resistance squat

Attaching a resistance band around your patient's knees during squat and deadlift activities stimulates an increased abductor moment to maintain the external rotation of the lower limbs (**Figure 7.17**).

FIGURE 7.17   Abduction resistance squat. Adding a resistance band to a simple squat motion to increase abduction resistance can increase the contribution of the gluteus medius.

Single-leg squat and single-leg straight leg deadlift

These two exercises require maximum hip stability. As discussed earlier, the EMG recordings for both gluteus maximus and medius are consistently reported to be high for these two exercises. These exercises should only be performed by patients assessed as suitably physically fit and capable of performing the activity. They are not the goal of all strength training programmes for gluteal tendinopathy. Essentially, they are presented as an advanced "option" (**Figure 7.18a,b**).

A   B

FIGURE 7.18   (a) Single-leg squat. (b) Single-leg straight leg deadlift.

Strengthening summary

I recommend reading Chapter 9 before prescribing a strengthening programme for the gluteal musculature. Reducing lateral hip pain can be achieved by placing the hip away from adduction during exercise and rest. A strengthening programme should begin with simple isometric exercises followed by progressive isolation exercises leading to compound exercises and then functional rehabilitation, including gait changes if required. This suggested order of progression is one used within many rehabilitation plans, but it is not a golden rule. Experimenting with a mixture of exercise types at the same point in a rehabilitation plan is also possible.

OTHER TREATMENTS

Massage options

The key areas to massage that often decrease lateral hip pain from tendinopathy are: (1) TFL; (2) posterior superior gluteal muscles; (3) vastus lateralis muscle; and (4) the quadratus lumborum muscle, which may also benefit from massage treatment if it has been compensating for hip instability (**Figure 7.19a-d**).

Massage theory and options are discussed further in Chapter 11.

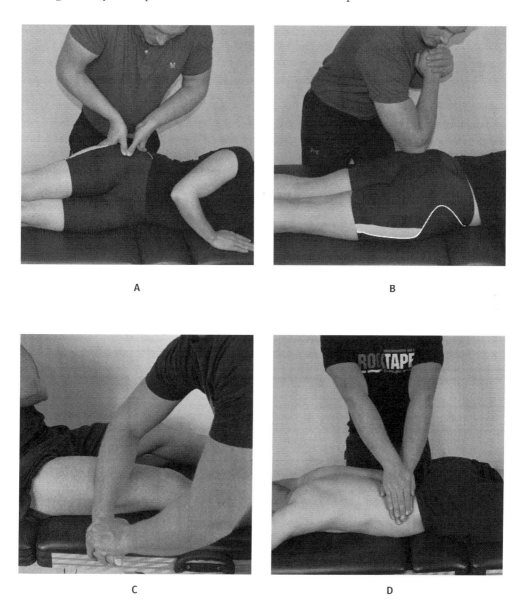

A

B

C

D

FIGURE 7.19   Massage options for (a) tensor fasciae latae, (b) gluteal muscles, (c) vastus lateralis, and (d) quadratus lumborum.

Extracorporeal shockwave therapy

Although two studies have reported positive outcomes for lateral hip pain using extracorporeal shockwave therapy (ESWT) (Furia et al., 2009; Rompe et al., 2009), further review of the methodology highlighted that it was radial wave and not shockwave. Chapter 13 on ESWT explains the important difference.

Corticosteroid injections

Corticosteroid injections are popular because they often reduce the pain from chronic musculoskeletal conditions quickly and their effect can be maintained for anywhere between a few weeks and a few months. They are also quick, cheap, and easy for doctors to administer. Unfortunately, corticosteroids provide poor long-term outcomes, mainly due to the failure to address the underlying cause of the problem. If the aggravating factor remains, the pain is likely to return when the effects of the corticosteroid have reduced. One option is to simply continue injecting the lateral hip. A systematic review of the efficacy of trochanteric bursitis treatments reported on one patient group that had received five lateral hip injections over a 4-year period (Lustenberger et al., 2011). The efficacy of corticosteroid injections for gluteal tendinopathy remains questionable and is not clear. They seem to provide medium-term pain relief (Labrosse et al., 2010), but they may also have a negative impact on the tissue response to load and loading (Coombes et al., 2013).

Surgery

Surgery should be considered after conservative physical therapy methods have failed.

Different surgical options exist for lateral hip pain and gluteal tears. Repairs can be performed endoscopically or as open procedures. Post-surgical follow-up reports after ≥1 year are very positive (Walsh, Walton and Walsh, 2011), even though control groups for comparison are not available. Common procedures for lateral hip pain focus on trochanteric bursectomy and ITB release techniques (e.g. Z-plasty). The longer-term follow-up from ITB release methods is poor and there is valid concern for the disruption of the ITB hip stabilisation mechanisms.

Taping

Kinesiology taping has become increasingly popular for the management of musculoskeletal conditions. Some research has documented the advantages of taping around the buttock region to improve local muscle activation (Dowarah, 2011; Mostert-Wentzel et al., 2012; Miller et al., 2013). From my experience, kinesiology taping for lateral hip pain can be used as a simple analgesic tool and to facilitate gluteal activation. This may be achieved with one application, different applications, or a combination of applications, such as a lateral hip decompression and a lateral line ITB taping. Gluteal taping options are described in Chapter 12.

Gait manipulation

Overstriding causes a more anterior and midline-oriented foot strike that increases ITB compression over the greater trochanter. Overstriding is often coupled with a low step rate that increases the ground reaction force per foot contact. The pelvis needs to control this loading and may allow an increased adduction to absorb the higher impact forces from increased vertical displacement. The initial strike pattern (heel or mid-foot) also influences force absorption further up the kinetic chain. Gait manipulation is a valuable tool for managing gluteal tendinopathy (**Figure 7.20**). Chapter 10 reviews the research and techniques.

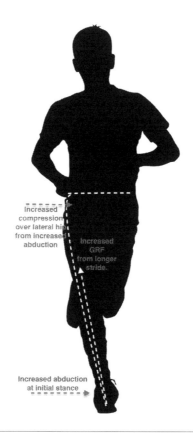

Increased compression over lateral hip from increased abduction

Increased GRF from longer stride.

Increased abduction at initial stance

FIGURE 7.20   An increased stride length leads to an increased hip adduction at the terminal swing, and initial stance along with an increased load through the lateral hip tissues.

CONCLUSION

Evolutionary biology informs us that our hips and pelvis have evolved to allow an upright stance as our default posture and position of ambulation, while preserving our ancestral mobility by allowing us to squat down or climb. Functional anatomy research allows us to identify the specific muscles likely to require intervention, for example, an overactive TFL or inhibition of the gluteus medius. The trochanteric and ITB stabiliser mechanism proposed by Kummer (1993) provides a practical rationale for assessment and treatment planning.

What potentially makes this condition distinct from the other common lower-limb tendinopathies is the compressive mechanism over the greater trochanter, which may be a larger contributory mechanism than it is for other tendinopathies. This highlights the importance of movement correction, from static posture to gait changes.

A selection of simple tests with good validity and sound biomechanical underpinning, plus the VISA-G questionnaire, increases the ability to assess and monitor this pathology.

REFERENCES

Albers IS, Zwerver J, van den Akker-Scheek I (2014). Incidence and prevalence of lower extremity tendinopathy in the general population. *Br J Sports Med.* **48**(Suppl 2). Available from http://bjsm.bmj.com/content/48/Suppl_2/A5.1 (accessed 29 June 2017).

Bird PA, Oakley SP, Shnier R, et al. (2001). Prospective evaluation of magnetic resonance imaging and physical examination findings in patients with greater trochanteric pain syndrome. *Arthritis Rheum.* **44**:2138–2145.

Birnbaum K, Siebert CH, Pandorf T, et al. (2004). Anatomical and biomechanical investigations of the iliotibial tract. *Surg Radiol Anat.* **26**:433–446.

Coombes BK, Bisset L, Brooks P, et al. (2013). Effect of corticosteroid injection, physiotherapy, or both on clinical outcomes in patients with unilateral lateral epicondylalgia: a randomized controlled trial. *JAMA.* **309**:461–469.

Distefano LJ, Blackburn JT, Marshall SW, et al. (2009). Gluteal muscle activation during common therapeutic exercises. *J Orthop Sports Phys Ther.* **39**:532–540.

Dowarah BP (2011). A study of effects of gluteal taping on TD-parameters following chronic stroke patients. *Indian J Physiother Occup Ther.* 5:36–39.

Duparc F, Thomine JM, Dujardin F, et al. (1997). Anatomic basis of the transgluteal approach to the hip-joint by anterior hemimyotomy of the gluteus medius. *Surg Radiol Anat.* **19**:61–67.

Earls J (2014). *Born to Walk: Myofascial Efficiency and the Body in Movement. Chichester: Lotus Publishing.*

Fearon A, Stephens S, Cook J, et al. (2012). The relationship of femoral neck shaft angle and adiposity to greater trochanteric pain syndrome in women. A case control morphology and anthropometric study. Br J Sports Med. **46**:888–892.

Fearon AM, Cook JL, Scarvell JM, et al. (2014). Greater trochanteric pain syndrome negatively affects work, physical activity and quality of life: a case control study. *J Arthroplasty.* **29:383–386.**

Fearon AM, Ganderton C, Scarvell JM, et al. (2015). Development and validation of a VISA tendinopathy questionnaire for greater trochanteric pain syndrome, the VISA-G. *Man Ther.* **20**:805–813.

Fearon AM, Scarvell JM, Cook JL, et al. (2010). Does ultrasound correlate with surgical or histologic findings in greater trochanteric pain syndrome? A pilot study. *Clin Orthop Relat Res.* **468**:1838–1844.

Fearon AM, Scarvell JM, Neeman T, et al. (2013). Greater trochanteric pain syndrome: defining the clinical syndrome. *Br J Sports Med.* **47**:649–653.

Flack NA, Nicholson HD, Woodley SJ (2012). A review of the anatomy of the hip abductor muscles, gluteus medius, gluteus minimus, and tensor fascia lata. *Clin Anat.* **25**:697–708.

Furia JP, Rompe JD, Maffulli N (2009). Low-energy extracorporeal shock wave therapy as a treatment for greater trochanteric pain syndrome. *Am J Sports Med.* **37**:1806–1813.

Grimaldi A (2011). Assessing lateral stability of the hip and pelvis. *Man Ther.* **16**:26–32.

Hoeger Bement M, Rasiarmos R, DiCapo JM, et al. (2009). The role of the menstrual cycle phase in pain perception before and after isometric fatiguing contraction. *Eur J Appl Physiol.* **106**:105–112.

Kingzett-Taylor A, Tirman PF, Feller J, et al. (1999). Tendinosis and tears of gluteus medius and minimus muscles as a cause of hip pain: MR imaging findings. AJR Am J Roentgenol. **173**:1123–1126.

Kosek E, Lundberg L (2003). Segmental and plurisegmental modulation of pressure pain thresholds during static muscle contractions in healthy individuals. *Eur J Pain.* **7**:251–258.

Kosek E, Ekholm J, Hansson P (1996). Modulation of pressure pain thresholds during and following isometric contraction in patients with fibromyalgia and in healthy controls. *Pain.* **64**:415–423.

Kummer B (1993). Is Pauwels' theory of hip biomechanics still valid? A critical analysis, based on modern methods. *Ann Anat.* **175**:203–210.

Labrosse JM, Cardinal E, Leduc BE, et al. (2010). Effectiveness of ultrasound-guided corticosteroid injection for the treatment of gluteus medius tendinopathy. *Am J Roentgenol.* **194**:202–206.

Lee JH, Cynn HS, Kwon OY, et al. (2014). Different hip rotations influence hip abductor muscle activity during isometric side-lying hip abduction in subjects with gluteus medius weakness. *J Electromyogr Kinesiol.* **24**:318–324.

Lequesne M, Mathieu P, Vuillemin-Bodaghi V, et al. (2008). Gluteal tendinopathy in refractory greater trochanter pain syndrome: diagnostic value of two clinical tests. *Arthritis Rheum.* **59**:241–246.

Long SS, Surrey DE, Nazarian LN (2013). Sonography of greater trochanteric pain syndrome and the rarity of primary bursitis. *Am J Roentgenol.* **201**:1083–1086.

Lustenberger DP, Ng VY, Best TM, et al. (2011). Efficacy of treatment of trochanteric bursitis: a systematic review. *Clin J Sport Med.* **21**:447–453.

McBeth JM, Earl-Boehm JE, Cobb SC, et al. (2012). Hip muscle activity during 3 side-lying hip-strengthening exercises in distance runners. *J Athl Train.* **47**:15–23.

Miller J, Westrick R, Diebal A, et al. (2013). Immediate effects of lumbopelvic manipulation and lateral gluteal kinesio taping on unilateral patellofemoral pain syndrome: a pilot study. *Sports Health.* **5**:214–219.

Moore KL (1999). *Clinically Oriented Anatomy.* 4th edn. Philadelphia, PA: Lippincott Williams & Wilkins.

Mostert-Wentzel K, Sihlali BH, Swart JJ, et al. (2012). Effect of kinesio taping on explosive muscle power of gluteus maximus of male athletes. *SAJSM.* **24**:75–80.

Pfirrmann CW, Chung CB, Theumann NH, et al. (2001). Greater trochanter of the hip: attachment of the abductor mechanism and a complex of three bursae–MR imaging and MR bursography in cadavers and MR imaging in asymptomatic volunteers. *Radiology.* **221**:469–477.

Rio E, Kidgell D, Moseley L, et al. (2013). Exercise to reduce tendon pain: a comparison of isometric and isotonic muscle contractions and effects on pain, cortical inhibition and muscle strength. *J Sci Med Sport.* **16**:e28.

Rompe JD, Segal NA, Cacchio A, et al. (2009). Home training, local corticosteroid injection, or radial shock wave therapy for greater trochanter pain syndrome. *Am J Sports Med.* **37**:1981–1990.

Segal NA, Felson DT, Torner JC, et al. (2007). Greater trochanteric pain syndrome: epidemiology and associated factors. *Arch Phys Med Rehabil.* **88**:988–992.

Standring S (ed.) (2008). *Gray's Anatomy: The anatomical Basis of Clinical Practice. 40th ed. Edinburgh: Elsevier Churchill Livingstone.*

Sutter R, Kalberer F, Binkert CA, et al. (2013). Abductor tendon tears are associated with hypertrophy of the tensor fasciae latae muscle. Skeletal Radiol. **42**:627–633.

Viradia NK, Berger AA, Dahners LE (2011). Relationship between width of greater trochanters and width of iliac wings in trochanteric bursitis. *Am J Orthop (Belle Mead NJ).* **40**:E159–162.

Walsh MJ, Walton JR, Walsh NA (2011). Surgical repair of the gluteal tendons: a report of 72 cases. *J Arthroplasty.* **26**:1514–1519.

FURTHER READING

Gibbons J (2014). *The Vital Glutes: Connecting the Gait Cycle to Pain and Dysfunction.* Chichester: Lotus Publishing.

Grimaldi A, Mellor R, Hodges P, et al. (2015). Gluteal tendinopathy: a review of mechanisms, assessment and management. *Sports Med.* **45**:1107–1119.

Selkowitz DM, Beneck GJ, Powers CM (2013). Which exercises target the gluteal muscles while minimising activation of the tensor fascia lata? Electromyography assessment using fine-wire electrodes. *J Orthop Sports Phys Ther.* **43**:54–64.

Sidorkewicz N, Cambridge ED, McGill SM (2014). Examining the effects of altering hip orientation on gluteus medius and tensor fasciae latae interplay during common non-weight-bearing hip rehabilitation exercises. *Clin Biomech (Bristol, Avon).* **29**:971–976.

CHAPTER 8

BIOMECHANICS

INTRODUCTION

The aims of this chapter are twofold. First, several simple biomechanical terms and principles that may be helpful for therapists are introduced. Then, their relevance to lower-limb tendinopathies is discussed.

Applying mechanical principles to the human body helps us to measure and quantify the forces (kinetics) and motion (kinematics) that produce human movement. This chapter presents some of the key biomechanical principles; both normal and abnormal presentations are examined and their possible influence on lower-limb forces is discussed.

A knowledge of biomechanics is essential for the prevention, treatment, and management of injuries. An appreciation of normal movement patterns and structural alignment helps the clinician to spot anomalies and potentially problematic functional movement patterns.

Each sport has its own biomechanical blueprint of successful movement patterns. As therapists, we are often familiar with the sports practised by our client base. This chapter focuses specifically on the biomechanics of walking and running.

BIOMECHANICS AND FASCIA

Recently, biomechanical research has received some criticism because it overlays rigid mechanical principles over the transient biological web[9] of human form. Biomechanists often consider the body as the sum of separate parts that move in uniform patterns according to the planes and laws of motion. This mathematical summation has been challenged by some anatomists who see the body as functioning as a single unit with forces being transferred and absorbed throughout the tissues in a way that cannot be measured with mathematical instruments.

The emergence of this challenge is the product of the increasing interest in the human fascial web and its inherent properties as described by many authors including Myers (2009), Schliep (2012), and Stecco (2014).

Despite this challenge, biomechanical principles offer a method to quantify movement and function in a way that benefits injury prevention, treatment, and management. For example, the amount of measurable ground reaction force (GRF) through the fifth metatarsal head is not that useful as a single measurement; however, when used as a baseline against future changes with the addition of an orthotic device or a barefoot exercise programme, it can provide tangible objective evidence of treatment success.

BIOMECHANICAL PRINCIPLES

Anatomical planes of the body

Movements of the body (kinematics) occur in planes of motion (**Figure 8.1**). To visualise these movement planes, assume the position of the body shown in the Figure 8.1, with feet together and palms of the hands facing forward. If you flex your head and trunk forward, this is a movement in the sagittal plane; similarly, extending the head and trunk in the opposite direction would also be a movement in the same sagittal plane. The coronal (frontal) plane goes through the body as if you were magically stepping through a pane of glass. Lateral movements, such as leg abduction or side flexion of the trunk produce movement in this plane. Finally, the transverse plane transects the body and is used to refer to rotation movements such as trunk, limb, or total body rotation. When we move

---

[9] Human beings are structured using a range of tissues arranged in a web-like way. Whether it is the fascia in the soft tissues or the trabeculae in the bones, human beings are not structured along straight lines like machines. Here, transient refers to the fact that human beings are always metabolising and replenishing, unlike machines.

about in daily life, we usually move in all planes of motion simultaneously, with a primary movement in one plane and a secondary movement in the other two.

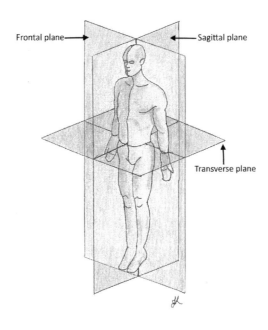

FIGURE 8.1   Planes of movement are often described using the three planes: frontal (coronal), sagittal, and transverse (axial). Movement can occur in one, two, or all three planes.

Which planes matter to tendons?

Tendons carry tensile forces from muscle to bone; thus, they are mainly influenced by alterations of movement in the sagittal plane, such as repetitive loading from running or jumping, or sagittal plane variants such as reduced dorsiflexion or overstriding. Alterations in the coronal (frontal) plane have been associated with instability of the loaded limb and may increase the risk of gluteal tendinopathy due to hip instability. The link between kinematics of the transverse plane and tendon strain is less clear, but excessive pronation may be linked to Achilles tendinopathy. Although this link has not been supported by current research, many clinicians believe that a prominently flattened arch must influence the stress on the Achilles tendon.

FORCES (KINETICS)

All human movement requires either an internal (muscle) or external (gravity) force to produce, sustain, and stop movement. A force can exert a push or pull action from one structure to another.

Gravity

From the moment we are born, our bodies respond to the force of gravity. Gravity is the most consistent force acting on the human body. One of the most common measurements for force analysis is the centre of gravity (COG). This is the theoretical point of concentrated force; it is sometimes referred to as the centre of mass (COM) or the balance point of an object. The COG can fall outside of the object mass, whereas the COM cannot. The final gravity vector to familiarise yourself with is the line of gravity (LOG) that runs vertically through the COG. As with the COG, the LOG regularly runs outside of the body (**Figure 8.2)**

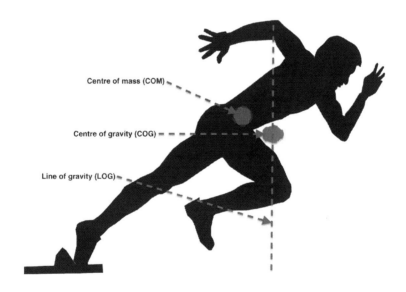

Centre of mass (COM)

Centre of gravity (COG)

Line of gravity (LOG)

FIGURE 8.2   Centre of mass, centre of gravity, and line of gravity.

On running blogs, the COG and COM are often referred to as reference points to improve running technique. Cueing a runner to make initial ground contact under their COG can help to reduce overstriding. However, video analysis shows that well-trained runners make contact in front of their COG. This allows time for the limb to become loaded and store energy before switching to propulsion and releasing energy from behind the COG. Another running form tip is to lean forward from the ankles to shift the COG forward and outside of the body and initiate what is often described as a controlled forward fall. Novice runners are often seen to bend forward from the waist, which would not shift the COG in the same way (see **Figure 8.3**).

Forward flexion from the ankles leading to a more erect posture and a foot placement below the body.

Flexion from the hips with anterior foot placement and heel strike pattern

FIGURE 8.3   (a) Forward lean from the ankles. (b) Forward lean from the hips.

The weight-bearing line (hip-to-ankle line)

The weight-bearing line (WBL) moves in the direction of the LOG while always remaining in the body as it passes through from the centre of the hip to the centre of the ankle joint and onto the ground. In a neutrally aligned lower limb, the WBL passes down each leg through the anterior superior iliac spine of the pelvis down through the patella and into the second metatarsal bone.

Gait cycle

The movement pattern of walking and running is referred to as the gait cycle and consists of a stance phase and a swing phase. These are divided into smaller sub-phases and are analysed when we review the gait cycles of walking and running individually later in the chapter.

Base of gait in walking and running

The base of gait determines the width of our support base when walking and running. It is the lateral distance between the midline of the footfall during normal gait, which is usually measured at the mid-point of the heel (**Figure 8.4**). A normal base of gait is usually around 3 cm when walking; it reduces to zero or close to it when running because the forward momentum increases stability and the reduced base width improves efficiency.

A reduced gait width requires increased limb and hip adduction, which is a key movement variant linked to gluteal tendinopathy and iliotibial band-related conditions such as "runner's knee".

Some running coaches find it helpful to instruct runners to either keep their knees apart or facing forward, which may consciously increase the gait width and may bring about changes that assist rehabilitation. Gait manipulation is discussed further in Chapter 10.

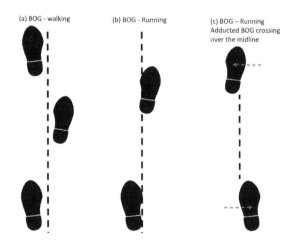

FIGURE 8.4   The base of gait for walking (a) is wider than the base of gait when running (b); this increases hip adduction, and if the base of support becomes too narrow it can lead to the legs crossing over the mid-line (c).

Ground reaction force and centre of pressure

The centre of pressure (COP) measurement is used in gait analysis to map the focal pressure point and pressure distribution in the foot during the stance phase. This can be represented in several forms (three-dimensional pressure mapping, colour-coded pressure mapping, simple line graphs) to help assess the area and timing of GRFs.

When running, during an average heel strike, the COP pattern is initially focused on the lateral heel before rapidly spreading an increasing load to the mid-heel and fore-foot. In the forefoot, the pressure peaks under the first and second metatarsals.

Key differences in COP measurements between barefoot and shod runners indicate that barefoot runners have an initial COP peak around the mid-foot, whereas shod runners have a COP peak around the rearfoot. COP is maintained more medially during the stance phase in the barefoot group (Becker et al., 2014). This alteration reflects the inability to heel strike without cushioned trainers and the increased use of ankle and foot dynamic stabilisers to absorb GRFs.

The loading pattern of the foot changes in the presence of lower-limb pathology. From foot-specific conditions, such as plantar fasciitis, to hip pathology, the COP changes as part of a protective and pain-avoiding gait strategy. As discussed in Chapter 10, any changes to a movement pattern in response to injury may be of short-term benefit but lead to longer-term implications for gait and joint loading.

The overall magnitude of the GRF for a typical rearfoot striker is shown in **Figure 8.5**. While most training shoe-related research focuses on the peak of the heel strike force (the first peak), the larger GRF occurs when the foot makes full contact with the ground. The GRF rapidly increases because the leg musculature controls the descending body and generates an opposing propulsive force.

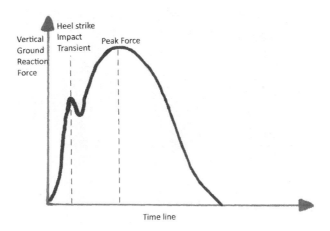

FIGURE 8.5   Vertical ground reaction force curve for a heel-toe runner.

THE LOAD–DEFORMATION RELATIONSHIP OR STRESS–STRAIN CURVE

The load–deformation behaviour of tissue is often represented as a curve plotted on a graph against the two measurements of stress (force) and strain (deformation). This curve is sometimes called the stress–strain curve (**Figure 8.6**).

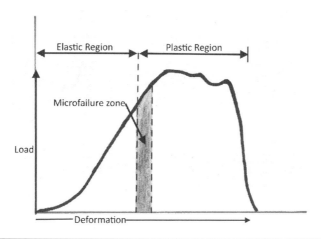

FIGURE 8.6   Soft tissue behaviour under load is demonstrated in this stress strain curve graph. The phases of deformation are influenced by many factors including age, injury, and fitness levels.

Tendons generally share the common features of soft tissue extensibility described here:

- Region 1: This is the toe region. It is associated with non-damaging forces that reduce the wavy "slack" (crimp) in the fibres.

- Region 2: This is the elastic or linear region that stretches the aligned fibres without causing damage. Towards the end of this region, some fibres may start to break.

- Region 3: Further stretching from region 2 enhances fibre damage and failure continues in an unpredictable manner. This would equate to a partial tear of a tendon.

- Region 4: This region is characterised by complete tendon failure, usually reported clinically as a full rupture or full thickness tear.

The shape of the graph would be different depending on the type of tissue, such as ligament, muscle, or tendon, and would also alter depending on a variety of factors, such as age, conditioning, or pathology. One of the most common variables is tendon stiffness measured with Young's modulus. This is measured in mega or giga pascals.

The original theory of tendinopathy involved an inflammatory microtrauma pathology. The more recent continuum model focuses on a cellular response rather than evident fibre damage. Some evidence still suggests that an inflammatory process is involved, despite wide acceptance of the continuum theory among professionals. (See Chapter 3 for more details.)

YOUNG'S MODULUS

Young's modulus or *modulus of elasticity* refers to the resistance offered by a material when subjected to tensile or compressive stress. For example, in the Achilles tendon, Young's modulus represents the resistance offered by the tendon when stretched. This is calculated by dividing the load by the deformation and is represented as an elastic curve on the graph. A steep rise represents a higher modulus and therefore higher stiffness, whereas a shallower rise indicates a lesser modulus and lower stiffness. Two contrasting examples would be a ligament having a high Young's modulus and body fat having a low Young's modulus.

Not surprisingly, tendon stiffness has been shown to reduce in the presence of tendinopathy and to improve with muscle strengthening. A stiffer musculotendinous unit with a higher Young's modulus of elasticity can store and release more energy and is ultimately more efficient.

THE BEHAVIOUR OF THE TENDON UNDER LOAD

Tendons have a unique property known as viscoelasticity. A viscoelastic substance or tissue alters its response to force depending on the speed with which the force is applied. For example, slow loading of a tendon leads to energy absorption and tendon deformation (a slow stretch), whereas rapid loading of a tendon increases its stiffness and the tendon returns most of the energy it absorbs. This energy-saving viscoelastic property reduces the required input from contractile tissue (Shin et al., 2008).

Each cycle of this energy-saving viscoelasticity loses approximately 10% of the stored energy (Maganaris, Narici and Maffulli, 2008). This energy loss is called hysteresis and a 10% loss per loading cycle is called the hysteresis loop. This energy is lost in the form of heat that can accumulate to a point which hinders tissue repair mechanisms. A temperature above 42.5° C is above the threshold for fibroblast viability (Wilson and Goodship, 1994), thus pointing to a possible mechanism for tendon degeneration.

THE WALKING GAIT CYCLE

The walking gait cycle consists of two phases called stance and swing. These phases are further divided into shorter sub-phases. The stance phase comprises: initial contact (heel strike); loading response (foot flat); midstance; terminal stance; and toe-off. The swing phase can be purely passive under the right initial conditions and comprises: follow through; forward swing; and descent (**Figure 8.7**). One of the key differences between walking and running is the switch from a double-stance phase, when both feet are in contact with the ground during walking, to a double-flight phase, when both feet are above the ground during running.

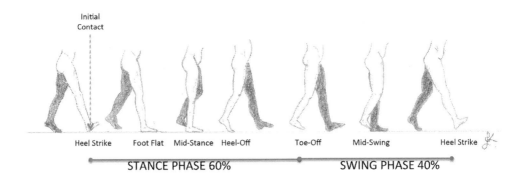

FIGURE 8.7   The complete gait cycle. Stance and swing phases are further divided into three shorter phases. The stance phase comprises the following phases: contact (heel strike); mid-stance (foot flat); and propulsive (toe-off). The swing phase is divided into the following phases: follow-through; forward swing; and descent.

An appreciation of normal joint motion during walking is an important point of reference for assessing lower-limb function. The motion of walking has been described as akin to an inverted pendulum swinging not from the hip joint, as you might initially assume, but from the 12th thoracic vertebra. From this point on, we can appreciate the subtle motion of the lumbar spine and the three-dimensional rhythm of the pelvic girdle. Our upright stance and bipedalism allows the upper body to be available for independent activities such as carrying, catching, or throwing when walking. However, the upper body may also be used to improve the efficiency of the gait pattern through counterrotation of the upper spine and arm swing.

Reduced movement in one of the lower-limb joints forces a compensation from local or more distal joints. For example, a weak knee joint may transfer load up to the hip and down to the ankle joint, increasing the repetitive loading of the supporting musculature and tendons.

The following descriptions of joint movement occur during a normal walking gait cycle.

Pelvis

When viewed from the side, during the single-leg stance phase of walking, the pelvis is seen to rock forward as the lumbar spine extends in unison.

Viewed from the front, during the single-leg stance phase, the pelvis dips down on the non weight bearing side.

Some rotatory movement can also be seen and should increase with walking speed.

Hip joint

The hip joint moves from a flexed position during the heel strike to an extended position during toe-off and slightly adducts in response to load.

Knee

At the beginning of the stance phase, the knee absorbs some of the GRF by allowing a controlled flexion of approximately 15 degrees.

Ankle

During walking, the ankle begins the contact phase in a dorsiflexed position to allow an initial heel strike to occur. (Some clinicians have argued that the ankle is in plantarflexion at heel strike when walking and that the heel strike occurs because of knee extension and tibial position.) Next, the ankle plantarflexes and then dorsiflexes again as the body passes over the base of support (the foot and ankle complex in this instance) before plantarflexing again to achieve toe-off propulsion.

Subtalar joint and foot

The subtalar joint places the foot in a slightly supinated position during heel strike, so that the foot appears to contact the ground on the lateral side of the heel. The subtalar joint then leads the foot into pronation to help absorb the GRFs and form a stable base of support. As the body passes over the foot and begins to move forward, the foot is then required to provide a propulsive force, achieved by supinating the foot through the subtalar joint into a more rigid position. The midtarsal joint is also locked by supination; this important mechanism adds considerable rigidity to the foot for propulsion.

The movement of the subtalar joint is shadowed by the rotation of the tibia, which rotates internally with pronation and externally with supination. Tibial rotation is much easier to observe and assess in situ than the smaller triplanar subtalar joint.

The walking system

Earls (2014) described the walking system in his book *Born to Walk: Myofascial Efficiency and the Body in Movement*. In the book, he links myofascial anatomy trains to human locomotion. He identified the use of the stretch-shortening cycle via pre-tensioning of the myofascial structures. It is a helpful way of understanding how the myofascial system contributes to walking and running; biomechanical textbooks tend to break down muscular function during gait into isolated movements.

THE RUNNING GAIT CYCLE

The increased momentum during running forces the double-stance phase to become a "flight" (or float) phase, where both lower limbs are momentarily suspended above the ground. This occurs twice per cycle; once at the beginning of the swing phase and once at the end. The timing ratio between stance and swing phases also changes from walking to running. With running, the stance phase becomes shorter and the float or flight phase increases with increased speed (**Figure 8.8**).

Heel-to-toe motion also changes with increased speed and the departure from running gait to sprinting gait is often marked by the switch from rear or mid-foot contact to forefoot contact throughout the initial contact, loading response, midstance, terminal stance, and toe-off phases.

FIGURE 8.8   The key phases of a running gait cycle are labelled in the diagram above.

Braking and bounding: absorption and generation

Alternate periods of acceleration and deceleration occur during running that lead to force generation during acceleration and force absorption during deceleration. The placement of the lead foot during the initial contact (weight acceptance) phase is often highlighted as a braking force and is considered detrimental to the goal of proceeding forward while running. An excessive braking force usually occurs when running downhill and when overstriding. This excessive braking force increases the forces absorbed by the lower limbs and appears to be highest at the knee joint. (This is discussed further in Chapter 10.)

The absorption and generation phases are also influenced by the vertical displacement of the body throughout the gait cycle. This vertical displacement occurs because of elastic energy stored and released as we maintain an upright posture. Vertical displacement is impossible to eliminate because we run on two legs and not four, and do not roll on wheels. (Running form coaches often teach runners to imagine their legs as wheels during the completion of specific running drills to reduce vertical displacement and focus on forward momentum.) Vertical displacement increases with some running styles, such as overstriding or bounding. An excessive vertical displacement has been associated with an increased incidence of lower-limb injury, specifically tibial stress fractures (Zadpoor and Nikooyan, 2011). Chapter 10 covers the techniques used to improve running form and reduce vertical displacement.

Muscle tension and tendon springs

When we run, muscles are most active in anticipation of and just after initial contact; their contraction following this period is of secondary importance (Novacheck, 1998). Far more injuries would occur if this situation was reversed and muscles generated larger forces than they could absorb. For example, it is far better to be poor at jumping and good at landing than good at jumping and poor at landing.

Runners expend a large proportion of their energy to stay upright against gravity. Unlike cyclists, who expend most of their energy fighting air resistance, for runners the major source of energy loss is the foot-to-ground collision. At this transition point, the COM must be redirected from moving down and forward to moving upwards and forward. A normal running gait pattern is reliant on push-off with ankle joint plantarflexion providing 35–45% of total hip, knee, and ankle work with each stride, and as much as 60% during the stance phase (DeVita, Helseth and Hortobagyi, 2007; Sawicki and Ferris, 2008). Most of this ankle force comes from stored "collisional" energy in the Achilles tendon (Sawicki, Lewis and Ferris, 2009), while the powerful hip and knee musculature relies on a fresher active power production with each cycle.

As speed increases, more power is generated proximally. This function is reflected in the anatomy of the lower limbs. The plantarflexors have relatively short muscle fibres with higher pennation angles and a long, compliant Achilles tendon. This contrasts with the muscular properties of the hip joint. In fact, one of the most notable differences between a sprinter and a distance runner is the size of their hip musculature (i.e. the gluteus maximus) as opposed to the size of their plantarflexor muscles (i.e. the gastrocnemius). Observe the musculotendinous arrangement of horses and other quadrupeds to appreciate this anatomical make-up.

The Achilles tendon as a spring

When running, the Achilles tendon acts like a spring while the muscles act as tensioners. Running has been compared to the springing of a pogo stick, except that the Achilles tendon is like an elastic cord and not a spring; it pulls but does not push. Another method of maintaining efficiency is the transfer of energy through isometrically contracted biarticular muscles that act like guy ropes between joints. For example, as the hip extends, the rectus femoris muscle is stretched passively. If it maintains its length through static contraction, then the force will cause the knee to extend thus lengthening the gastrocnemius muscle and increasing the force through the Achilles tendon to produce ankle plantarflexion for propulsion at toe-off.

Thus, full lower-limb function should be assessed and not just the immediate painful region of the tendon.

PRONATION

This section briefly outlines what pronation is. Pronation is mentioned again in Chapter 10.

Pronation is a triplanar motion that occurs predominantly through the subtalar joint of the ankle. It comprises the following three motions: dorsiflexion; eversion; and abduction (**Figure 8.9**).

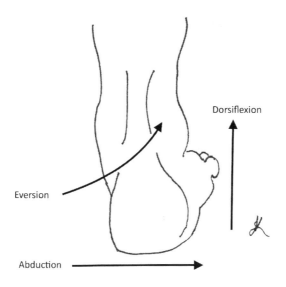

FIGURE 8.9   Pronation consists of eversion, dorsiflexion, and abduction occurring through the foot and ankle.

Pronation is a natural function of the foot-ankle joint complex that serves to alter the function of the foot during the stance phase of gait. From heel strike to midstance, the foot allows a controlled pronation that includes unlocking of the midtarsal joint; to help dissipate forces, a neutral position is achieved just after midstance (70% stance). From this point on, the midtarsal joint locks and moves into a supinated position to provide a rigid lever for successful propulsion (toe-off).

Achilles tendon and pronation

In theory, hyperpronation of the foot past its normal range and beyond its normal stance time would lead to an increased tendon loading period. The gastrocnemius and soleus muscles would have to contract eccentrically for longer to decelerate the leg and absorb the GRF.

Under normal conditions, peak pronation should occur just before midstance (40% of stance), then begin to supinate back into a supinated foot (McCrory et al., 1999). If the foot remains in a pronated position with the midtarsal joint unlocked past the point of midstance, then the plantarflexor muscles would begin to load the non-rigid foot through the Achilles tendon. The foot would be a less effective lever arm and the Achilles tendon would lose some of its recoil power via the dampening influence of pronation. This would require an increased amount and duration of force that could overload the Achilles tendon. To put it another way, if the Achilles tendon tension increases while the foot is unlocked, then the two structures are not supportive of each other and much energy is wasted.

Clement, Taunton and Smart (1984) suggested that excessive pronation could cause a twisting of the spiraled Achilles tendon fibres. This twisting may reduce the tendon's vascular supply through a wringing or blanching effect. So far, the mechanics of this theory have not been supported by any further evidence.

EXCESSIVE SUPINATION

Excessive supination or underpronation occurs when the foot strikes the ground in an excessively supinated, or normal, position but then fails to pronate enough to attenuate the GRFs appropriately. Lack of pronation often leads to an increased incidence of stress fractures of the lateral metatarsals, calcaneus, tibia, or fibula. Van Ginckel and collaborators (2009) identified that patients with Achilles tendinopathy demonstrated a more lateral foot loading pattern with a delayed, but sustained, pronation.

ABNORMAL PELVIC MECHANICS

Instability of the pelvis often occurs in more than one plane of motion. The two most common abnormalities are excessive anterior tilt and excessive lateral sway.

While a certain degree of bilaterally balanced movement should occur with normal running, any excessive movement, unilateral or bilateral, may be due to poor control of the stabilising muscles. This lack of control often attenuates the forces distally and to less suitable structures, thus causing a variety of overuse injuries. Reduced force absorption or movement around the hip and pelvis may place an increased demand on the musculature of the knee and ankle joint.

Excessive anterior pelvic tilt

A certain degree of anterior pelvic tilt is considered normal, but a combination of hip flexor tension and dysfunctional gluteal muscles, hamstrings, and abdominal muscles, can cause the pelvis to tilt forward excessively when running. It is tempting to assume that the lengthened muscles must also be weaker, but they are often forced to work harder, thus increasing their contractile tone in a resting position. For example, the hamstring muscles are stretched from their ischial tuberosity attachments while their continual tone is required to help stabilise the pelvis from further anterior pelvic tilt. An increased lumbar lordosis is also evident and may be the first thing that draws your attention to increased pelvic tilt. Depending on the athleticism of your patient, a more protruding or distended abdomen may also serve as a giveaway. The position places an increased strain on the lumbar spine as the lumbar erector spinae muscles provide some extensor compensation for the hip joints.

Excessive lateral pelvic tilt

Excessive lateral dipping of the pelvis is caused by the inability of the hip abductors to isometrically and eccentrically stabilise the pelvis. This places increased stress on the lateral hip structures and surrounding joints. Hip instability is covered in depth in Chapter 7.

MYOFASCIAL CONSIDERATIONS

When viewing the lines of tissue described by Myers (2009), you can appreciate the links and relationships between the muscle groups and the joints on which they act. The lines can be used to guide assessment, soft tissue work, and exercise interventions. A few examples of common patterns are described here:

- Anterior pelvic tilt: causes an increase in tension through the lower superficial backline, which includes the hamstrings and Achilles tendons.

- Tension in the lower half of the superficial frontline: reduces hip extension and favours flexion-based exercise habits. Running form would be affected, resulting in poor efficiency and force absorption.

- Lateral line dysfunction: the lateral line stabilises the body unilaterally. Dysfunction of the lateral hip stabilisers can often cause symptoms around or below the hip joint because other lateral line structures can become overloaded in a compensatory pattern.

- For treatment purposes, it is also helpful to review the spiral, front, and back functional lines. *Anatomy Trains: Myofascial Meridians for Manual and Movement Therapists* by Myers (2009) is a must-read for anyone interested in clinically relevant myofascial anatomy.

REFERENCES

Becker J, Pisciotta E, James S, et al (2014). Center of pressure trajectory differences between shod and barefoot running. *Gait Posture.* **40**:504–509.

Clement DB, Taunton JE, Smart GW (1984). Achilles tendinitis and peritendinitis etiology and treatment. *Am J Sports Med.* **12**:179–184.

DeVita P, Helseth J, Hortobagyi T (2007). Muscles do more positive than negative work in human locomotion. *J Exp Biol.* **210**:3361–3373.

Earls J (2014). *Born to Walk: Myofascial Efficiency and the Body in Movement.* Chichester: Lotus Publishing.

McCrory JL, Martin DF, Lowery RB, et al. (1999). Etiologic factors associated with Achilles tendinitis in runners. *Med Sci Sports Exerc.* **31**:1374–1381.

Maganaris CN, Narici MV, Maffulli N (2008). Biomechanics of the Achilles tendon. *Disabil Rehabil.* **30**:1542–1547.

Myers TW (2009) *Anatomy Trains: Myofascial Meridians for Manual and Movement Therapists.* Edinburgh: Churchill Livingstone.

Novacheck TF (1998). The biomechanics of running. Gait Posture. 7:77–95.

Sawicki GS, Ferris DP (2008). Mechanics and energetics of level walking with powered ankle exoskeletons. *J Exp Biol.* **211**:1402–1413.

Sawicki GS, Lewis CL, Ferris DP (2009). It pays to have a spring in your step. *Exerc Sport Sci Rev.* **37**:130–138.

Schleip R (2012). *Fascia: the Tensional Network of the Human Body: the Science and Clinical Applications in Manual and Movement Therapy.* Edinburgh: Churchill Livingstone/Elsevier.

Shin D, Finni T, Ahn S, et al. (2008). Effect of chronic unloading and rehabilitation on human Achilles tendon properties: a velocity-encoded phase-contrast MRI study. *J Appl Physiol (1985).* **105**:1179–1186.

Stecco C (2014). *Functional Atlas of the Human Fascial System.* Edinburgh: Elsevier Health Sciences.

Van Ginckel A, Thijs Y, Hesar NG, et al. (2009). Intrinsic gait-related risk factors for Achilles tendinopathy in novice runners: a prospective study. *Gait Posture.* **29**:387–391.

Wilson AM, Goodship AE (1994). Exercise-induced hyperthermia as a possible mechanism for tendon degeneration. *J Biomech.* **27**:899–905.

Zadpoor AA, Nikooyan AA (2011). The relationship between lower-extremity stress fractures and the ground reaction force: a systematic review. *Clin Biomech (Bristol, Avon).* **26**:23–28.

FURTHER READING

DeVita P, Janshen L, Rider P, et al (2008). Muscle work is biased toward energy generation over dissipation in non-level running. *J Biomech.* **41**:3354–3359.

CHAPTER 9

STRENGTH AND CONDITIONING PRINCIPLES

INTRODUCTION

This chapter presents the basic principles of resistance exercise prescription and provides guidance on exercise parameters. Specific strengthening exercises to help manage lower-limb tendinopathy can be found in the individual tendon chapters. Common misconceptions relating to strength training for endurance athletes are discussed and current research is reviewed at end of the chapter.

A lot of confusing information regarding exercise rehabilitation for tendinopathy is available. The most popular was, and perhaps still is, the Alfredson's protocol involving eccentric loading, which is documented widely in the sports injury literature. This chapter does not include any exercise protocols because they fail to cater for individual variables. They also do not promote the effective use of a therapist's clinical reasoning skills. Further reading on the current literature is provided by the review at the end of this chapter.

We have already detailed tendon structure from a macroscopic to a cellular level in Chapter 1, but it is useful to begin this chapter by revisiting the concept that a tendon is the non contractile element of the musculotendinous unit and not an isolated structure. This correlates with the kinetic chain theory, which highlights the need for groups of muscles to improve strength and function by appreciating the distribution of forces through contractile and non-contractile tissue. In practice, this means that we may start by isolating the desired musculotendinous unit to bias the stress on the correct tissues, and then ensure that more functional compound exercises are performed to ensure the correct neuromuscular adaptation. In addition, gait re-education and training planning are important factors to consider and review.

ANATOMICAL CONTINUITY REVIEW

The fibrous connective tissues that surround and divide the different organisational levels within skeletal muscle form part of the body's fascial network. Fascia consists of sheets of fibrocollagenous support tissue that contains bundles of collagen fibres arranged in different planes to provide resistance to forces from different directions. The differentiated layers of fascia within muscle include: the epimysium (the fibrous elastic tissue that surrounds each muscle); the perimysium (the tissue surrounding each bundle of single muscular fibres); and the endomysium (the layer of connective tissue that ensheathes each individual muscle fibre). These layers continue through the contractile region and into the structure that we label the tendon, thus becoming the epitenon and endotenon, respectively. The peritenon refers to the outer paratenon and its underlying epitenon. (Note: tenon not tendon. It is not a spelling error.) Described in another way, the fascia within muscle tissue continues and converges at the end of the muscle to form the tendon. They are one structure and not separate entities. Highlighting this tissue continuity is important when considering and justifying an adequate strength and conditioning programme to improve the musculotendinous tolerance to load.

Tendons have an adequate blood supply for their non-contractile nature, which results in a metabolism and vascularity much lower than the contractile region. For this reason, a tendon's acute response and adaptation to loading is slower than that of muscle tissue.

STRENGTH TRAINING FOR ENDURANCE ATHLETES

Tendinopathy is usually caused by overuse (or wrong use) from endurance-based activities. Persuading patients to begin a strength training programme is often met with some resistance (no pun intended). Endurance athletes are often concerned about weight gain from muscle hypertrophy, while less athletic patients aiming to lose or control weight have similar concerns about increased muscle mass.

While these concerns are understandable, they are not justified by the research, which clearly supports the benefits of strength training for endurance-based sports. Many athletes continue to avoid resistance training based on unfounded fears and incorrect advice. This chapter seeks to debunk these myths and provide a framework for safe, effective, research-informed loading programmes for tendinopathy management.

The review or design of a training programme should be performed with a working knowledge of the principles of training. We will look at each of these in turn and relate them to lower-limb tendinopathy.

RUNNING FEEDBACK TO INFORM STRENGTHENING

For running-based sports, running form and fitness drills should continue during off-season. Feedback from running drills can also inform a strengthening programme. For example, if an athlete's strength training programme has noticeably improved their hip flexor and quadriceps strength, they may report increased control when descending hills but feel lesser influence during hill climbing, which requires hip extension; therefore, more hip extension drills should be included in the strengthening programme.

THE PRINCIPLES OF TRAINING

Overload

Progressive adaptation within our musculotendinous units only occurs if we provide a stimulus that overloads the tissues beyond their normal capacity. This varies significantly between sedentary and active individuals, with the overload stimulus being minimal for sedentary patients whereas more active individuals require a more significant load. An individual's training history and starting point are the first factors to consider when designing a customised programme.

A history of previous activity is also important. Activities such as cycling and rowing do not use stretch-shortening in the same way as running and jumping activities, which repetitively use this efficiency mechanism. Loading on the lower limbs can be very different depending on the activity being carried out.

The key overload principle to remember is, if they are doing more than they routinely do, then they are overloading their system. This means that overload activities may range from simple walking to heavy resistance training. It is clear to see that protocol-type, one-size-fits-all programmes are to be avoided from the outset. This would include the Alfredson's protocol.

How to overload the lower-limb musculotendinous units

It is a fundamental principle that resistance training leads to adaptive tissue changes, first within contractile tissue, then within connective tissue, and finally within the bone matrix. This is commonly referred to as Davis's law of adaptive soft tissue remodelling. It is the corollary to Wolff's law of adaptive bone remodelling. Both laws highlight our body's ability to adapt to the stresses placed on it.

How much overload?

Studies have indicated that tendon stiffness increases with resistance training (Kubo et al., 2006a), with one study reporting a 19% increase in Achilles tendon stiffness after eight weeks of resistance training (Kubo, Kanehisa and Fukunaga, 2002). The intensity of the training stimulus needs to be high, at around 75–85% of one-repetition maximum (1RM), with lower loads of 20% 1RM showing no adaptation (Kubo et al., 2006b). Benchmarking the load based on the individual's 1RM is a key principle for an individualised programme.

How to safely test one-repetition maximum

Directly testing an individual's 1RM should be avoided for tendinopathy patients in most cases because the usual pain and dysfunction associated with tendinopathy would reduce the likelihood of a valid test result. Testing 1RM also involves considerable knowledge and skill from both the assessor and patient.

A 10-repetition maximum test is recommended, and guidelines exist for interpreting the results. **Table 9.1** can be used to interpret the results for a repetition range.

PERCENTAGE OF 1 REPETITION MAXIMUM (%1RM)	PREDICTED MAXIMUM NUMBER OF REPETITIONS ACHIEVED BEFORE FAILURE
100	1
95	2
93	3
90	4
87	5
85	6
83	7
80	8
77	9
75	10
70	11
67	12
65	15

TABLE 9.1 Interpreting the results of a 10-repetition maximum test

Increasing the repetition range reduces the risk of injury by lowering the required resistance; in addition, unilateral testing allows a further reduction in load, while using fixed machines with safety features should lead to safe testing procedures. Calculating the 1RM from a testing procedure involving >10 repetitions is increasingly less accurate. Once you have found the individual's 10RM (predicted 75% of 1RM), simply use the following calculation to predict the 1RM:

10RM weight ÷ 3 × 4 = 1RM (predicted)

A programme with a repetition range of 6–10 repetitions per set provides a training stimulus bias towards strength gains, which also correlates with the 75–85% of 1RM shown to produce the desired structural adaptation. **Table 9.2** shows that a lower repetition range (below six repetitions) can further bias the training outcome in favour of strength and power. This is only advisable if both athlete and coach are suitably skilled and qualified in executing the correct movement patterns.

REPETITION MAXIMUM CONTINUUM

	<2	3	4	5	6	7	8	9	10	11	12	13	14	15	16	17	18	19	>20
TRAINING GOAL	STRENGTH						STRENGTH								STRENGTH				
	POWER						POWER								POWER				
	HYPERTROPHY				HYPERTROPHY						HYPERTROPHY				HYPERTROPHY				
	MUSCULAR ENDURANCE						MUSCULAR ENDURANCE					MUSCULAR ENDURANCE							

TABLE 9.2

It is feasible to begin a training programme with a resistance <75% 1RM. This is a sensible option to learn a new movement pattern, but resistance should be increased as soon as possible to promote the correct adaptation. If an individual displays very low strength levels, 10RM testing will detect this and lead to a very low and safe loading start point. Therefore, RM testing, rather than specifying loads from protocols, is recommended.

Common misconceptions

Common barriers to heavy resistance training include concerns surrounding tendon damage from loading, a painful tendon, and the previously mentioned concern over muscle hypertrophy and weight gain for endurance athletes. Let us examine each of these in turn.

Tendon damage from loading

Understandably, being told that you have an overused or degenerative tendon, then being advised to load it with a heavy weight and perform resistance training can seem illogical for patients. Understanding some simple biomechanics helps to explain the approach and hopefully clarify the plan. When we walk, we momentarily load our lower-limb tendons with a peak force of multiple times our body weight; these forces increase significantly with running and jumping, two key risk factors for tendinopathy. For example, the ankle can take up to 13× our body weight during jumping activities, while patellofemoral joint compression can reach 9 times our body weight when descending stairs. (This correlates with task-specific pain reporting.) When we compare these forces to controlled heavy resistance training, we can appreciate how the added weight and controlled movements provide an overloading stimulus with minimal risk that serves to strengthen the musculotendinous unit and increase its capacity for future loading. Simply resting tendons leads to a poor outcome in most cases.

In some cases of acute tendinopathy from sudden unaccustomed activity, a short period of rest is advised if the initial stressor is not likely to be repeated.

A painful tendon

As previously discussed in the Chapter 3, tendon pain and structural tendon damage are not correlated. A patient may think that loading a sore tendon is counterintuitive when compared to the typical advice to rest the tendon. The patient should be advised that their painful symptoms, if typical, often acutely fluctuate from stiff and painful to potentially pain-free episodes during a typical day. Within this time, it is not possible for the tendon to experience such rapid changes in structure. Parenthetically, because activity typically reduces symptoms, direct, focused, and sustained loading of sore tendons can lead to a more rapid downregulation of pain compared to general ambulation.

Muscle hypertrophy

Historically, resistance and endurance training have been viewed as opposed training styles, polarised by their association with large, muscular strength athletes and slim, efficient endurance athletes. Despite nearly 30 years of research supporting the inclusion of resistance training for endurance athletes, many athletes continue to consciously avoid it. Indeed, endurance training for strength athletes has been shown to be detrimental to maximal strength performance, but the same is not true of the reverse. Significant endurance performance outcomes are reported with the addition of strength training. More specifically, increases in 1RM outcomes by up to 30% have been reported in athletes without any measurable changes in physical muscle size (Hickson, 1980; Hickson et al., 1988). These studies are supported by more recent research (Aagaard et al., 2011), and strength training for endurance athletes continues to be supported in the literature by coaches and academics (Bazyler et al., 2015).

The benefits to endurance performance occur in both untrained and trained athletes. Proposed mechanisms include conversion of fast-twitch type IIX fibres into more fatigue-resistant fast-twitch type IIA fibres with improvements in maximal voluntary contraction and rate of force development. In addition, improvements in neuromuscular recruitment and control, as well as increased musculotendinous stiffness, can improve the energy storage capabilities of tendons and enhance movement economy (Millet et al., 2002).

Consider in-season or out-of-season management

Managing tendinopathy during the competitive season is challenging. The main aim should be to manage pain and maintain function. If pain and function dramatically limit performance, then the continuation of competition needs to be reviewed with the individual and their management team. Balancing the benefit of participating and completing an event against the risk of significant time out because of an exacerbating condition needs to be considered.

A loading programme needs to consider the additional loading from training and competition with the flexibility to reduce the loading volume after intense training sessions and unaccustomed levels of activity. Because the tendinopathic pain response is delayed, using a morning pain diary to record the response to the training load provides useful data for modifying a training plan. Because of the poor correlation between pain and pathology, monitoring tendinopathy can be challenging. Even Doppler ultrasound (US) is of limited use. US tissue characterisation (USTC) is a promising method of monitoring structural integrity during a competitive season and during a rehabilitation programme, but its ability to predict a future symptomatic tendinopathy is limited. USTC is described in Chapter 16.

Progression

Training programmes must be progressed gradually by changing one of the four key variables: frequency; intensity; type; and time. Because the overall aim is to strengthen the musculotendinous unit, progression should focus mainly on intensity by increasing resistance, rather than the frequency or time spent training. A "2-2" method is recommended to guide progression: when two extra repetitions can be performed on two separate loading sessions outside of the initial repetition range, then a small amount of load can be added to reduce the repetition range back down to the initial 6–10 repetitions per set. Specifying this load is difficult, but I advise small (5%) increments of the current resistance, or close to this based on the equipment available.

Specificity

Using isolation, machine-based exercises to initially bias the load on specific musculotendinous units allows focusing on loading with minimal interference from balance, synergistic muscle action, and coordination. Specific isolation exercises are most suitable for isometric exercises and initial concentric/eccentric exercises. Specificity must also be considered when planning more compound exercises and functional movement training. For example, a runner may benefit more from performing the lunge than deadlifts, and running technique drills would be more specific than cross-training on a rowing machine A rehabilitation session should always aim to be as efficient as possible to make the most of the client's time and energy.

Reversibility

When beginning a rehabilitation programme, it is important to set an end point, ideally with smaller goals along the way. One of the many reasons for poor exercise adherence during rehabilitation is the absence of a clear goal and end point. Once adaptation has been achieved, reversibility can be limited by performing a once-weekly session to maintain the improvements gained from the high-volume training programme.

Variety

In theory, sticking to specific exercises and calculating loading volumes should result in the quickest physiological response. Too much continuity of bland exercises often leads to a lack of motivation that may also limit physiological adaptation if the exercises are not completed regularly. It is far better to have a less specific but varied programme that people engage and adhere to than a specific programme that people are more likely to get fed up with.

Plyometrics

Most athletes can benefit from plyometric training, but not all of them have the necessary physical strength to perform the techniques correctly and without risk of injury. Non-competitive patients do not need to perform plyometric training unless a need is identified. Plyometrics are not recommended for non-active patients and carry an increased risk of injury. Before performing plyometric exercises, the individual should be able to squat 1.5× their own body weight or perform 5 squats at 60% 1RM within a 5-second time frame. These tests are recommended to assess for suitable baseline strength before completing plyometric exercises. Younger and older athletes can benefit from plyometric training with some precautions, and this style of training often represents the final hurdle in the rehabilitation programme. There is some interesting research regarding tendons and plyometrics in the research review at the end of this chapter.

Exercise adherence

In relation to exercise, the word "adherence" refers to the maintenance of an exercise rehabilitation programme for a prolonged period. Even before adherence becomes an issue, some patients may not begin the programme in the first instance. There are a few common reasons for this and clinicians should try to avoid them.

Even the very best rehabilitation programmes are pointless if the patient does not perform the exercises correctly or chooses not to do them. It may not be surprising to know that the best reported method to ensure exercise completion and programme adherence is through active one-to-one guidance in a "personal trainer"-style session. This is often not an option for most patients, but partnering with a fitness professional is one option to be considered. These one-to-one sessions are achievable in certain settings where patients are residential, such as some military settings and professional sports clubs and teams. Here adherence can be enforced and more closely guided.

Adherence can also be improved with patient education. Helping the patient to understand their condition, the likely causes, and best treatment approach helps to include the patient in their own injury management. This may involve answering questions, providing support material in the form of advice leaflets and fact sheets, planning a programme with the patient, and setting agreed targets. This is often achieved over 2–3 sessions rather than one long appointment and should be pre-planned to avoid overloading the patient with information during their first appointment.

Monitoring progress improves motivation and adherence. The self-report assessment, Victorian Institute of Sport Assessment questionnaire, and morning pain diary are excellent tools for recording useful information that can be evaluated at regular intervals.

Regular one-to-one sessions, and regular contact and assessment, also provide further motivation.

RESEARCH REVIEW

Mechanical loading

A range of tendon loading programmes have reported adaptive stiffening of the tendon (Kubo et al., 2001; Kubo, Kanehisa and Fukunaga, 2002). The literature is more supportive of tendon material changes and less supportive of hypertrophic changes after a loading programme. Some loading programmes have reported superior adaptive tendon responses. Research suggests that the reasons for this are muscle contraction type, load intensity, and programme duration. Bohm, Mersmann and Arampatzis (2015) carried out a meta-analysis of each of these variables from published loading intervention programmes. Their meta-analysis included a total of 264 participants monitored during 37 different exercise interventions, reported across 27 different studies between 1970 and 2014. The subgroup analysis demonstrated that high loading intensities are more effective compared to low intensities. The type of contraction is less important, and may even be potentially unrelated to changes in tendon stiffness.

One potential mechanism can be explained by the influence of different loading intensities on tenocyte deformation, a key mechanism for adaptive changes, often described as mechanotransduction. The required stimulus is one of high load, sustained either isometrically or through slow dynamic loading and repeated over a 2–3-month period (Kubo et al., 2012; Bohm, Mersmann and Arampatzis, 2015). Changes in fluid excavation and gene expression have also been noted (Lavagnino et al., 2008). According to Bohm and collaborators (2014), the short duration of plyometric tendon loading may not serve up the adequate duration of cellular stimulus to facilitate tendon adaptation. Cell proliferation has been shown to increase following short, repetitive contractions and decrease under more sustained loading (Barkhausen et al., 2003). Plyometrics still have their place in rehabilitation programmes as a means of stimulating higher levels of neuromuscular adaptation. The lack of tendon response to plyometrics may be a contributing factor to the onset of tendinopathy following the repeated rapid loading typical of running and jumping activities. These activities may not produce a sufficiently progressive tendon adaptation while still allowing muscle adaptation to occur, thus creating an imbalance in muscle and tendon adaptation.

Isometric loading theory

A new treatment approach for tendinopathy, in the form of sustained isometric contractions, is gaining ground among clinicians.

How does isometric loading work?

Three mechanisms have been proposed:

1. Mechanotransduction: a sustained load mechanically stimulates tenocytes to synthesise the correct components of the extracellular matrix (e.g. collagenase and the correct type of proteoglycans)

2. Sustained isometric fatiguing stimulates descending pain inhibitory pathways: this occurs via the modulation of pressure pain thresholds. Pain reduction for patellar tendon pain has been reported to last for 45 minutes (Rio et al., 2015). Research reports more varied results for other tendon pathologies.

3. Reduced muscle inhibition: again, patellar tendon research only, but good clinical results have been reported.

4. Isometrics do not use and stretch the elastic properties of the tendon, but still provide a loading stimulus.

When compared to an eccentric loading programme, isometric loading provides the following key benefits: increased time under tension to maximise tendon adaptation; reduced delayed-onset muscle soreness; performance at an optimal joint range; and the ability to avoid joint positions that may cause tendon compression (Malliaras et al., 2013).

Alfredson's eccentric protocol

Alfredson's protocol describes the use of a "heavy load", but the programme is more akin to a high-volume, low-load programme in comparison to the usual athletic demands placed on the Achilles tendon and its surrounding structures. To reflect this, many authors have reported on a variety of recommend modifications to the programme. With this range of modifications, two key problems have arisen. First, a lack of programme standardisation has hindered the development of evidence for a modified programme. Second, because of this lack of new evidence for a modified programme, the well-documented effectiveness of Alfredson's standard protocol remains unchallenged by better methods.

The initial results of Alfredson's 12-week heel-drop exercise programme were very promising, curing approximately 90% of those with a mid-tendon pain and pathology (Alfredson et al., 1998). However, more recent results have reported much lower success rates of 60% for both athletic and non-athletic populations (Sayana and Maffulli, 2007; Rompe, Furia and Maffulli, 2008).

Despite the disparity in reported treatment success rates, eccentric exercise remains a popular conservative Achilles tendinopathy treatment technique and eccentric loading remains one of the few treatment regimens with an evidence base demonstrating positive results (Alfredson and Cook, 2007).

Eccentric efficacy

The efficacy of eccentric loading when compared with other treatments is difficult to evaluate given the inconsistencies, variations, and confounding treatment additions inherent of the various research studies (Grigg, Wearing and Smeathers, 2009). The most suitable client group for eccentric exercises appears to be middle-aged recreational athletes (Maffulli et al., 2008). The programme is less successful for sedentary or young, highly athletic patients (Sayana and Maffulli, 2007; Maffulli et al., 2008; Allison and Purdam 2009). Additionally, eccentric loading beyond a plantar grade ankle position is not recommended for Achilles tendon insertional pain because of tendon compression over the posterior calcaneus during dorsiflexion (Allison and Purdam, 2009).

How does eccentric training work?

The mechanisms by which eccentric exercises may help reduce pain are unclear. One possible mechanism is through the reduction in tendon thickness. Research has shown that eccentric loading reduces the thickness of the pathological Achilles tendon. One study reported a fourfold greater decrease in tendon thickness immediately post-exercise when compared with the concentric exercise protocol (Grigg, Wearing and Smeathers, 2009). The reduced thickness is likely the result of an extravasion of water in accordance with collagen realignment and stretching that produces lateral compressive forces between collagen fibrils and causes a reduction in the interfibrillar space, thus giving rise to a positive hydrostatic pressure that pushes the fluid out of the tendon (Hannafin and Arnoczky, 1994; Cheng and Screen, 2007). Collagen cross-linking also occurs as part of the normal collagen fibre realignment and remodelling process suggested to occur under eccentric loading (Rompe et al., 2007).

While it is tempting to speculate that eccentric exercise may generate greater strain and fluid flow within the tendon (Grigg, Wearing and Smeathers, 2009), many elements of the theory remain questionable and the important link to pain relief or increased function is not clear.

Many clinicians have suggested that eccentric muscle action always leads to greater muscle-tendon loading than concentric and isometric contraction. It is worth noting that this is an unsubstantiated theory. In fact, eccentric muscle action uses fewer motor units than concentric action when external load and speed are equal. Less electromyography activity and less oxygen consumption has also been measured during the eccentric phase of contraction (Henriksen et al., 2009; Malliaras et al., 2013).

Another proposed mechanism is via reduced neovascularisation. The increased force through the Achilles tendon during eccentric loading may cause an increased shear force between the tendon and the paratenon (Alfredson, 2005), leading to a reduction in neovascularisation commonly seen on colour Doppler sonography (Ohberg, Lorentzon and Alfredson, 2004). A reduction in pain may have a secondary benefit on the ability to increase the eccentric loading of the tendon.

CONCLUSION

The proposed benefits of the Alfredson's eccentric protocol may feasibly be achieved or improved with more tailored loading interventions that match individual variables and are thus more likely to be completed for the necessary 2–3 months.

This chapter has presented the basic strength and conditioning principles; these were supported by the conclusions of the recent systematic review and meta-analysis carried out by Bohm, Mersmann and Arampatzis (2015) and are linked to the cellular response to loading. Through the assimilation of this information, tailored exercise interventions can be prescribed that are based on sound, evidence-based principles and not default protocols. The creation of another protocol is not warranted, and the wider aim should be greater communication between the therapy and strength and conditioning professions. There is scope for widening the knowledge of strength and conditioning principles within the therapeutic professions.

REFERENCES

Aagaard P, Andersen L, Bennekou M, et al. (2011). Effects of resistance training on endurance capacity and muscle fiber composition in young top-level cyclists. *Scand J Med Sci Sports.* **21**:298–307.

Alfredson H (2005). The chronic painful Achilles and patellar tendon: research on basic biology and treatment. *Scand J Med Sci Sports.* **15**:252–259.

Alfredson H, Cook J (2007). A treatment algorithm for managing Achilles tendinopathy: new treatment options. *Br J Sports Med.* **41**:211–216.

Alfredson H, Pietilä T, Jonsson P, et al. (1998). Heavy-load eccentric calf muscle training for the treatment of chronic Achilles tendinosis. *Am J Sports Med.* **26**:360–366.

Allison GT, Purdam C (2009). Eccentric loading for Achilles tendinopathy: strengthening or stretching? *Br J Sports Med.* **43**:276–279.

Barkhausen T, van Griensven M, Zeichen J, et al. (2003). Modulation of cell functions of human tendon fibroblasts by different repetitive cyclic mechanical stress patterns. *Exp Toxicol Pathol.* **55**:153–158.

Bazyler CD, Abbott HA, Bellon CR, et al. (2015). Strength training for endurance athletes: theory to practice. *Strength Cond J.* **37**:1–12.

Bohm S, Mersmann F, Arampatzis A (2015). Human tendon adaptation in response to mechanical loading: a systematic review and meta-analysis of exercise intervention studies on healthy adults. *Sports Med Open.* **1**:1–18.

Bohm S, Mersmann F, Tettke M, et al. (2014). Human Achilles tendon plasticity in response to cyclic strain: effect of rate and duration. *J Exp Biol.* **217**:4010–4017.

Cheng VWT, Screen HRC (2007). The micro-structural strain response of tendon. *J Mater Sci.* **42**:8957–8965.

Grigg NL, Wearing SC, Smeathers JE (2009). Eccentric calf muscle exercise produces a greater acute reduction in Achilles tendon thickness than concentric exercise. *Br J Sports Med.* **43**:280–283.

Hannafin JA, Arnoczky SP (1994). Effect of cyclic and static tensile loading on water content and solute diffusion in canine flexor tendons: an in vitro study. *J Orthop Res.* **12**:350–356.

Henriksen M, Aaboe J, Bliddal H, et al. (2009). Biomechanical characteristics of the eccentric Achilles tendon exercise. *J Biomech.* **42**:2702–2707.

Hickson RC (1980). Interference of strength development by simultaneously training strength and endurance. *Eur J Appl Physiol Occup Physiol.* **45**:255–263.

Hickson RC, Dvorak BA, Gorostiaga EM, et al. (1988). Potential strength and endurance training to amplify endurance performance. *J Appl Physiol (1985).* **65**:2285–2290.

Kubo K, Kanehisa H, Fukunaga T (2002). Effects of resistance and stretching training programmes on the viscoelastic properties of human tendon structures in vivo. *J Physiol.* **538**:219–226.

Kubo K, Ikebukuro T, Maki A, et al. (2012). Time course of changes in the human Achilles tendon properties and metabolism during training and detraining in vivo. *Eur J Appl Physiol.* **112**:2679–2691.

Kubo K, Kanehisa H, Ito M, et al. (2001). Effects of isometric training on the elasticity of human tendon structures in vivo. *J Appl Physiol (1985).* **91**:26–32.

Kubo K, Komuro N, Ishiguro N, et al. (2006a). Effects of low-load resistance training with vascular occlusion on the mechanical properties of muscle and tendon. *J Appl Biomech.* **22**:112–119.

Kubo K, Yata H, Kanehisa H, et al. (2006b). Effects of isometric squat training on the tendon stiffness and jump performance. *Eur J Appl Physiol.* **96**:305–314.

Lavagnino M, Arnoczky SP, Kepich E, et al. (2008). A finite element model predicts the mechanotransduction response of tendon cells to cyclic tensile loading. *Biomech Model Mechanobiol.* **7**:405–416.

Maffulli N, Walley G, Sayana MK, et al. (2008). Eccentric calf muscle training in athletic patients with Achilles tendinopathy. *Disabil Rehabil.* **30**:1677–1684.

Malliaras P, Barton CJ, Reeves ND, et al. (2013). Achilles and patellar tendinopathy loading programmes: a systematic review comparing clinical outcomes and identifying potential mechanisms for effectiveness. *Sports Med.* **43**:267–286.

Millet GP, Jaouen B, Borrani F, et al. (2002). Effects of concurrent endurance and strength training on running economy and VO2 kinetics. *Med Sci Sports Exerc.* **34**:1351–1359.

Ohberg L, Lorentzon R, Alfredson H (2004). Eccentric training in patients with chronic Achilles tendinosis: normalised tendon structure and decreased thickness at follow up. *Br J Sports Med.* **38**:8–11.

Rio E, Kidgell D, Purdam C, et al. (2015). Isometric exercise induces analgesia and reduces inhibition in patellar tendinopathy. *Br J Sports Med.* **42**:1277–1283.

Rompe JD, Furia J, Maffulli N (2008). Eccentric loading compared with shock wave treatment for chronic insertional achilles tendinopathy. A randomized, controlled trial. *J Bone Joint Surg Am.* **90**:52–61.

Rompe JD, Nafe B, Furia JP, et al. (2007). Eccentric loading, shock-wave treatment, or a wait-and-see policy for tendinopathy of the main body of tendo Achillis. *Am J Sports Med.* **35**:374–383.

Sayana MK, Maffulli N (2007). Eccentric calf muscle training in non-athletic patients with Achilles tendinopathy. *J Sci Med Sport.* **10**:52–58.

CHAPTER 10

GAIT MANIPULATION

INTRODUCTION

Everyone has their own signature walk. Have you ever identified a friend from a distance simply by the way that they walk? People also have individual running styles, with a wide range of variations. Recent research has indicated that a runner's technique can be consciously altered to avoid, treat, or rehabilitate injury, and this alteration can be maintained following an initial period of retraining.

Gait manipulation or "re-education" is a strategic tool for the treatment of many lower-limb pathologies, including tendinopathy. This chapter identifies common gait patterns associated with increased injury risk and then offers evidence-based advice and guidance on gait alteration. You will find the content of this chapter highly valuable for your patients with running-related tendon problems. The basics of gait and some of the terms used in this chapter are covered in Chapter 8, which may serve as useful preparatory reading.

GAIT ANALYSIS

Gait analysis has become a popular term among rehabilitators, but what is it exactly? How is it achieved? And what can we do with the information?

Gait analysis is simply the process of visually assessing the movement patterns of walking or running, ideally identifying any factors that may inform a treatment plan (**Figure 10.1**). The current gold standard for assessing gait is three-dimensional motion analysis, but a wide range of less expensive options are available as 'apps' on tablets and smartphones. While gait analysis technology has become cheaper and more accessible, a large amount of information can still be recorded with simple visual assessment. A basic knowledge of which gait faults to look for and how to make changes to them is all that is required to get started and make helpful changes.

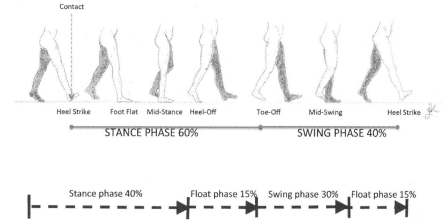

FIGURE 10.1   (a) A typical gait cycle featuring common terms for the different phases. (b) Running gait cycle showing the addition of the float (flight) phases.

Traditionally, gait analysis was most commonly used for research purposes. However, recent evidence supports its clinical efficacy and ability to inform treatment choices (Wren et al., 2011). Furthermore, any changes temporarily enforced on a gait pattern appear to have some lasting effect (Crowell et al., 2010; Allen, 2014).

Interestingly, because most gait patterns alter due to injury, the original and possibly causative gait pattern may not present itself during testing. There is still a void between gait analysis data and its clinical relevance, but gait analysis can serve as a useful assessment tool for those seeking to manipulate gait for rehabilitation purposes.

STEP RATE MANIPULATION

Step rate is one of the simplest measures of running form, and one of the quickest to influence. A slower step rate often leads to overstriding, which is one of the most common faults made by new and novice runners. Because of overstriding, the foot's initial contact occurs considerably anterior to the body's centre of mass (COM), most commonly as a heel strike pattern. The negative effects of this are an increased vertical displacement, an increased breaking force to the forward momentum of the runner and an increased leg adduction towards or across the midline (**Figure 10.2**). Therefore, overstriding increases lower-limb joint stress and has been suggested as a risk factor for knee pain (Heiderscheit et al., 2011), iliotibial band syndrome (Allen, 2014), gluteal tendinopathy (Grimaldi et al., 2015), and hamstring tendinopathy (Malliaras and Purdam, 2014). Then, it makes sense to attempt to consciously shorten the stride length in favour of an increased step rate to maintain a given speed. Put another way – take smaller, but faster steps. Let us explore this idea in more depth.

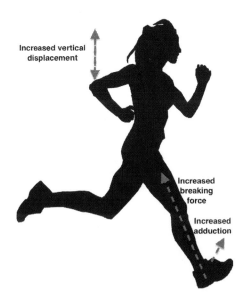

FIGURE 10.2   Diagram showing the directions of force associated with an overstriding gait pattern, including increased vertical displacement and increased breaking force. Increased leg adduction towards or across the midline is also a common feature of a longer stride pattern.

While there are a few other factors to consider, the fact remains that you can change the way people run and this change can be maintained following practice and repetition. We will now discuss the important elements of step rate manipulation.

What is the recommended step rate?

Running coaches often advocate a step rate (or cadence) between 175 and 200 steps/minute. If this is not achievable within a 10% increase from the existing step rate, then it will simply have to be a longer-term goal rather than a sudden change.

Here is why. Increasing the existing step rate by 10% appears to be the most beneficial for reducing lower-limb impact loading (Heiderscheit et al., 2011; Chumanov et al., 2012). Step rate increases above 10% are likely to prove challenging, both metabolically and cognitively (Cavanagh and Williams, 1982), thus countering any impact loading benefits. If a 10% step rate increase proves to be challenging or difficult to maintain, then a smaller step rate increase of just 5% has also proven beneficial (Allen, 2014).

The long-distance running community, consisting of marathon and ultra-distance runners (**Figure 10.3**), are advocates of a high step rate because the huge distances covered during training and competition require them to run in the most economical and injury-resistant way. The experience of these athletes and the pooled scientific study of their gait patterns have led to some useful extrapolations for novice runners.

FIGURE 10.3   Seasoned ultrarunner, running coach and physiotherapist Paul Coker trains and aims for a step rate of 180 steps per minute.

What are the benefits?

A reduced impact loading is achieved with each step, partly because of a lower vertical displacement of the body with each stride and partly because of a better total distribution of loading through an increase in steps; that is, less impact per step over a set distance. Key lower-limb muscles also demonstrate an increased anticipatory contraction at the end of the swing phase, and the increased total work done by the gluteus maximus and medius is indicative of an overall improvement of lower-limb function, with less eccentric work, reduced stance time, and an improved movement economy per step.

An increased step rate should also encourage a reduced anterior foot placement; this would reduce the braking force during the initial contact and weight acceptance phase. With an increased step rate, the foot should make contact closer to the COM under the body. This often encourages less heel strike and more of a mid-foot or forefoot strike pattern, which can be beneficial for lower-limb shock absorption (**Figure 10.4**). Interestingly, many of the biomechanical changes seen with step rate manipulation are like those seen with barefoot or minimalist running. (Minimalist running is discussed later in this chapter.)

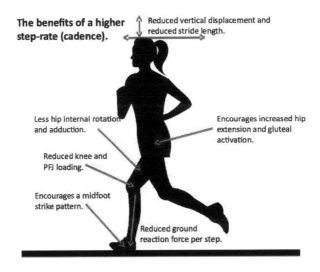

The benefits of a higher step-rate (cadence). Reduced vertical displacement and reduced stride length. Less hip internal rotation and adduction. Encourages increased hip extension and gluteal activation. Reduced knee and PFJ loading. Encourages a midfoot strike pattern. Reduced ground reaction force per step.

FIGURE 10.4   Summary of the key benefits of an increased step rate or cadence.

A 2011 study on the effects of step rate manipulation involving 45 healthy runners identified that the knee appears to benefit the most from step rate manipulation, with a 34% reduction in energy absorption following a 10% step rate increase (Heiderscheit et al., 2011). Energy absorption through the hip and ankle was less affected by a 10% increase, but it showed significant increases when the step rate was reduced below the preferred rate, indicating that a runner's choice to reduce their step rate and increase their stride length would ultimately be detrimental for joint loading. The study also reported that the increased step rate reduced the hip flexion moment and maximal hip adduction. This would be beneficial for gluteal and hamstring tendinopathy and promote hip extension as a preferred gait strategy as opposed to the body being pulled over a flexed hip with an anteriorly placed foot; this is commonly a feature of an overstriding pattern (Heiderscheit et al., 2011).

Reduced contact, increased spring
Successful gait manipulation leads to a reduced stance time per stride. This is beneficial because it lessens the time lower-limb muscles need to contract, and allows a better return of the stored elastic energy from the tendon.

Are there any negatives to step rate manipulation?

Yes! A conscious manipulation of step rate requires a change in running style and movement patterns. This involves an increased cognitive effort to maintain an altered step rate and avoid returning to the previous habitual step rate. This change may also affect running economy; increased oxygen consumption has been noted with a step rate change >10% (Cavanagh and Williams, 1982; Hamill, Derrick and Holt, 1995).

Increasing the number of steps required for a given distance may increase injury risk, through the cumulative loading cycle volume. Explained another way, this means that if you take more steps over a given distance, each step will have less impact but there will be more impacts over that set distance. This theory (Heiderscheit et al., 2011) has not been substantiated in practice; therefore, it appears that the benefits of reducing the magnitude of each loading cycle outweigh the potential detriment of increasing loading cycle volume. However, the runner should be careful not to unknowingly increase their pace because this would most likely shift the plantar centre of pressure of the foot forward and increase the demand on the gastrocnemius-soleus complex, as seen when moving from running to sprinting or from a rearfoot to a forefoot strike pattern.

THE INFLUENCE OF PAIN ON MOVEMENT

Pain alters our movement patterns via its influence on sensory input and motor output. During the acute stage of an injury, the nervous system alters movement patterns to reduce the threat of further insult to the injured tissues. This often provides a rapid benefit; however, once altered, these changes to movement patterns do not require a constant noxious stimulus to be maintained, and altered motor output is often sustained for an unnecessary length of time once the pathology becomes more chronic. A noxious stimulus can also produce a redistribution of activity both within and between muscles rather than a simple stimulation or inhibition of a whole contractile unit (Hodges, 2011). Put another way, if pain causes a limp, the limp will not always resolve with the pain. For many reasons, people's running styles are often not self-optimised for efficiency and performance.

Making changes

Any improvements in motor control require precision, rapid error correction, and repetition. The repetition of bad form does not induce the correct adaptation and fails to take advantage of cortical plasticity (Remple et al., 2001). The subjective reporting of pain from a tendinopathy pathology does not correlate with the more objective pathological signs. So, although pain does not denote the state of the pathology and encouraging patients to do their specific exercises in the presence of some pain is considered acceptable, we need to be aware that movement quality and motor control are significantly hindered by experiencing pain; any available pain-reducing methods, even if short-term ones, are highly beneficial during specific exercise times.

The influence of pain on gait

Runners with Achilles tendinopathy demonstrate a reduced anticipatory contraction of the gastrocnemius muscle before foot contact, followed by an increased contraction during stance and an increased stance time with reduced lower-limb extension at the terminal stance (Van Ginckel et al., 2009; Kim and Yu, 2015). As indicated by the reduced leg extension, this adaptation influences the whole gait cycle and the function of other muscles, such as the gluteal muscles, which show reduced activity in those with Achilles tendinopathy (Franettovich Smith et al., 2014). The general effect of pain on gait was identified by Hamill and collaborators (1999), who reported a reduced gait variation that may lead to a poor gait pattern less responsive to the running terrain.

Muscular preactivation, also known as anticipatory contraction, helps to stiffen the musculotendinous unit in anticipation of rapid loading, increasing the tolerance to tensional forces and reducing energy dissipation. Patients with lower-limb pathology appear to demonstrate reduced preactivation in the key muscles loaded during the stance phase and then appear to compensate for this with a prolonged contraction time. Both changes could be protective mechanisms that reduce the peak tensile and time-to-peak forces by using a longer and slower contraction at the cost of increasing the metabolic demand by reduced use of the tendons' elastic energy storage capacity. It is not clear whether these changes are the result of the tendinopathy or the potential cause of it. It may be a mix of both and may vary between individuals. The possible solutions to this issue are explained in the following sections.

Solutions

It is possible to benefit from motor control training when performed in the presence of pain, but only if the technique is not influenced by pain. Often, however, the pain has an influence on the movement and therefore negatively hinders motor learning during corrective exercise programmes.

In addition, exercise adherence is always reduced in the presence of pain and discomfort. For this reason, analgesic treatments partner well with corrective exercises and gait retraining methods. Furthermore, any methods that boost the sensory feedback from inhibited areas would also be beneficial.

Common analgesic therapy includes: prescribed analgesic medication; soft tissue treatment of the surrounding tissue and associated contractile tissue; kinesiology tape; needling methods; and extracorporeal shockwave therapy following an initial post-treatment settling period.

Methods used to increase sensory input might include: barefoot or minimalist footwear to heighten the sensory feedback from contact with the ground; kinesiology tape for cutaneous stimulation; real-time feedback on technique and foot position using simple visual/verbal coaching; real-time video; a mirror; or smart technology.

Mirror feedback

A simple method of providing real-time feedback to the patient to help them modify their gait pattern is with a full-length mirror placed in front of a treadmill. In a study involving 10 recreational runners requiring improved pelvic stability to reduce patellofemoral pain, Willy, Scholz and Davis (2012) used a combination of recorded video, a full-length mirror and scripted verbal cues[10] during a 2-week gait retraining programme involving 8 sessions, starting with a 15-minute duration and increasing to 30 minutes. Any errors in correcting conscious movement were corrected by the assessor. From session 4, the feedback was gradually reduced by reducing verbal cues and intermittently removing the mirror. Significant benefits were noted for dynamic pelvic and hip alignment, pain, and functional improvements after the two-week training period. These benefits were largely sustained after one and three months. The study did not perform any further follow-up assessment. This study did not have a control or comparison group, but a previous study by two of the authors (Willy and Davis, 2011) reported that an increase in hip muscle strength had no effect on abnormal hip mechanics during running. This indicates the importance of gait training in addition to specific strengthening programmes for runners.

Joint restrictions

Gait manipulation may also be limited by individual joint dysfunction. Most commonly, these present as reduced ankle dorsiflexion and reduced hip extension. To allow efficient performance from these joints, a combination of sufficient range of motion that is pain-free and performed with adequate motor control is required. Hip and ankle restrictions and solutions are described later in this chapter.

Footwear

Footwear influences gait and step rate, with minimalist footwear naturally promoting an increase in step rate and associated gait changes. Minimalist footwear is discussed later in this chapter.

Strength

Runners with lower-limb pathology often demonstrate poor muscle strength and motor control in specific muscle groups, such as the gastrocnemius, quadriceps, or gluteal muscles, and may present with generally poor lower-limb strength. Strength and conditioning is very important for runners and is covered in Chapter 9.

---

[10] The verbal cues used were: run with your knees apart with your knee caps pointing straight ahead; and squeeze your buttocks. Two common faults following the cues were: excessive widening of the base of support; and turning the feet out by externally rotating the legs.

HOW TO MEASURE STEP RATE

There are many ways to measure step rate. The simplest way is to count how many steps are taken by one leg in 1 minute at a preferred training pace and then simply double the figure to obtain the step rate for both legs. You could reduce the time to record your step rate and then simply multiply the result accordingly, allowing you to provide step rate data more quickly while running.

There are many smartphone apps that record cadence (step rate). If cadence can be monitored during a run, it is much more helpful than simply reviewing it after a run.

Once a desired step rate is determined, it can be calculated and programmed into a metronome to help inform the new running style; metronomes are also available to download onto smartphones. By practising on the treadmill, runners can increase their step rate and avoid the temptation to simply run faster. With practice, this new step rate is more easily transferred off the treadmill and without the metronome.

An alternative to a metronome is to listen to music with a suitable 'beats per minute' (bpm) rate, to provide a rhythm for the step rate. JogTunes (http://jogtunes.com/) is a helpful website that clearly indicates the bpm rate of many popular running tunes.

Running drills to improve step rate

Treadmill drill

The treadmill drill allows the step rate to be increased while ensuring that the same speed is maintained. In addition, the focus on step rate is not reduced by other environmental factors; this is particularly beneficial during initial gait retraining.

Intervals

Suddenly increasing the step rate and maintaining it over a typical training run is challenging both cognitively and metabolically. You should introduce increases in step rate over multiple training sessions and in short intervals during the same session. The intervals can then become longer until the new step rate can be maintained for a full training session. For new and novice runners, this interval session is most effective as a walk-run programme, using the correct step rate with each running interval.

Speed step intervals

With the interval method discussed here, some runners find it helpful to practise an enhanced step rate for short intervals to overcompensate and achieve a more moderate increase overall.

Downhill drills

Running down a slight gradient can help stimulate an increased step rate. Approach this method with caution because many novice runners demonstrate poor form when running downhill and more coaching may be required for the overall technique. The most common fault seen in novice runners going downhill is an exaggerated anterior foot placement and excessive braking forces.

FURTHER GAIT FAULTS TO LOOK FOR

Step rate manipulation is the most well-documented strategy that alters a range of biomechanical factors as part of an overall change in gait. The following are other identified running faults that have either been linked to tendinopathy or to a more general increase in the risk of injury.

Poor hip extension

Poor hip extension when running may be due to a variety of factors that might cause compensatory patterns, such as overstriding or increased lumbar lordosis. The most common cause of poor hip extension is increased muscle tension in the hip flexors, which reduces the available range of hip extension and reciprocally inhibits hip extensor muscle function.

Available hip extension can be checked with the modified Thomas test, with the patient's leg off the end of the couch so that it does not block available hip extension (**Figure 10.5**). Hip extension can also be tested with a standing single-leg hip extension (**Figure 10.6**). Several hip extension exercises are shown in Figures 10.7 and 10.8.

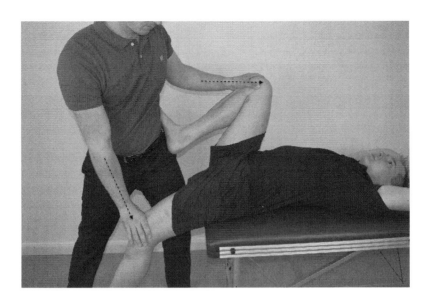

FIGURE 10.5   The modified Thomas test can be used to assess passive hip extension range.

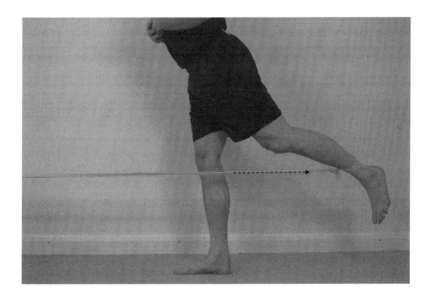

FIGURE 10.6   Standing single-leg active hip extension can indicate hip extension function. Excessive twisting of the pelvis and hyperextension of the lumbar spine are common compensations.

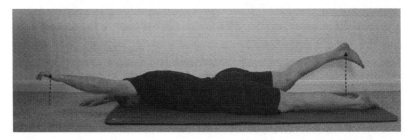

FIGURE 10.7 Selection of hip extension strengthening exercise options.

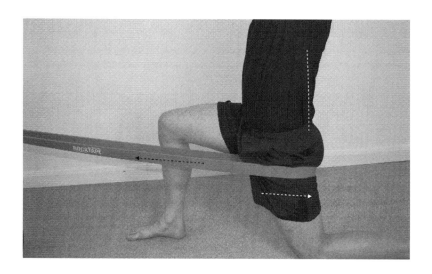

FIGURE 10.8   Example of a hip extension stretch, with the useful addition of a mobility band to encourage articular mobilisation in conjunction with soft tissue stretching.

Limited ankle dorsiflexion

Reduced ankle dorsiflexion has been identified in patellar and Achilles tendinopathy patients and has implications for the gait cycle and specifically hip extension. The ankle is required to dorsiflex at the terminal stance and dorsiflex further when barefoot, in minimalist shoes or when running uphill.

Available dorsiflexion can be checked with a goniometer or with the knee-to-wall test (**Figure 10.9**). A total ankle range of <60 degrees is considered restricted and a big toe-to-wall measurement of <10 cm during the knee-to-wall test is also an indicator of restriction. Several methods can be used to help improve dorsiflexion. These include: soft tissue treatment; joint mobilisation (**Figure 10.10**); and self-massage techniques (**Figure 10.11**).

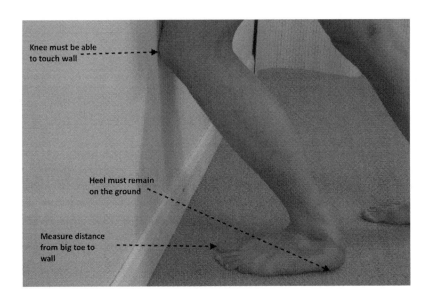

Knee must be able to touch wall

Heel must remain on the ground

Measure distance from big toe to wall

FIGURE 10.9   The knee-to-wall test is a simple measure of ankle dorsiflexion ability. The distance from the toes to the wall can be measured at the point of maximum dorsiflexion before the heel begins to lift off the floor.

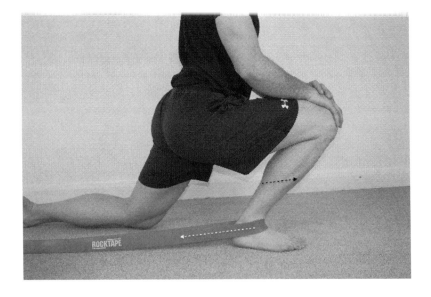

FIGURE 10.10   Self-administered ankle mobilisation and soleus stretch combination.

FIGURE 10.11   A roller can be used to reduce muscle tone in the plantar flexors.

Hip adduction

Excessive hip adduction is easily identified during gait analysis by observing hip stability in the frontal plane and identifying hip drop on the non-weight-bearing side (**Figure 10.12**). In addition, overstriding is often associated with increased hip adduction because the foot is placed further towards the midline as the base of support width reduces. Hip adduction can be consciously altered with the help of prompts and real-time feedback (Davis, 2005) and may reduce hip adduction if step rate increases successfully.

FIGURE 10.12   Diagram showing the contralateral hip drop, which may be bilateral or unilateral. This is a common gait assessment finding.

FOOTWEAR

Current research provides little clarity on foot biomechanics associated with lower-limb tendinopathies. Footwear guidance also remains confusing and dominated by contradicting professional opinions. The correct shoes are likely dependent on both the external environment and the individual's intrinsic variables, which also change. The challenge is to provide your patient with clear and helpful footwear advice that serves to positively influence their running and rehabilitation.

As a guide, we can breakdown the different types of footwear into categories and subcategories.

Cushioned

First, we have cushioned trainers, also referred to as shod when compared to barefoot and generally considered to be traditional running shoes. This is slightly confusing because cushioned running shoes became popular in the 1970s; before this time, running footwear was far less cushioned and rather more minimalist.

Cushioned trainer designs have been differentiated into several subcategories: neutral; stability; and motion control. Neutral shoes are simply designed to offer cushioning and do not influence stability, whereas stability shoes offer a degree of stability to help control pronation, and motion control shoes offer an enhanced level of stability and are often recommended for heavier runners with poor pronation control. Many of the theories and claims made regarding different types of trainers have been challenged by academics and running specialists. Despite the lack of clarity among experts, it is generally agreed that there is no such thing as a perfect running shoe; instead, there is likely to be a selection of suitable shoes. However, it is also possible to mistakenly purchase shoes that negatively influence running form and may increase the risk of injury. For several reasons, many runners have a selection of different shoes they switch between to add an element of variety and load distribution. This strategy is particularly common among regular runners.

Minimalist footwear

Minimalist shoes allow you to run with a more natural 'barefoot-style' gait pattern and are designed to promote a transition from a heavier cushioned shoe while still offering protection and promoting improvement in running form. Unfortunately, many injuries have been caused by a sudden switch to minimalist footwear because the successful use of such footwear requires gait changes and strength adaptations that affect the way you run, rather than constituting a simple shoe change.

The drop

You will often hear minimalist running shoes described in terms of drop, usually ranging from a 0- to an 8-mm drop. The drop relates to the degree of drop between the rearfoot and forefoot or from the heel to the toe. So, a completely flat shoe would be referred to as a zero-drop shoe and is as close to barefoot as you can get before removing your shoes altogether. A runner transitioning from a traditional cushioned shoe should begin with a minimalist shoe with a higher drop. Many minimalist runners can comfortably tolerate a 4-mm drop without the need to progress to a 0-mm drop.

From a tendinopathy rehabilitation perspective, minimalist running represents a tool for improving running form, which can be of significant benefit, as this chapter suggests.

Here are some guidelines on minimalist running drills for transitioning purposes and to aid form. I do not advocate my patients should become minimalist runners, but I do advocate improvements in form; minimalist running drills can be used as a tool to help achieve this. If they then find that minimalist running drills are helpful (and enjoyable), patients often end up gradually spending more time running in minimalist shoes.

Minimalist running guidelines

1. Choose a minimalist shoe with a drop of ≥4 mm to reduce the demands on the ankle and posterior calf musculature.
2. All minimalist running drills should be executed with a focus on good running form rather than speed or distance covered.
3. Runners must mid-foot or forefoot strike when running in minimalist footwear. Continuing to heel strike without a cushioned shoe is likely to cause heel pain.
4. Practise a fast step rate and avoid striding out in front of the body and bounding.
5. Begin with a 10-minute session that alternates 1 minute of walking with 1 minute of running. Monitor muscular soreness 24 hours after the session; if no muscular soreness occurs, then extend the session time. If muscular soreness occurs, simply maintain the session length and allow time for muscular adaptation.
6. Perform regular mobility sessions for ankle dorsiflexion and hip extension.
7. Supplement minimalist training sessions with suitable strength and conditioning exercises.

Therapists should be cautious not to suggest minimalist running as a panacea for all ailments; they should discourage a sudden unplanned, unmanaged, and uneducated switch to minimalist footwear.

ALTERED ANKLE AND FOOT BIOMECHANICS

There are differences in lower-limb joint forces between rearfoot and forefoot loading patterns and their associated gait patterns (Almeida, Davis and Lopes, 2015).

Fundamentally, a mid-foot (or forefoot) strike pattern decreases knee loading but increases foot and ankle loading; a heel strike pattern reduces foot and ankle loading but increases knee loading. As discussed in this chapter, the mid-foot strike pattern is the most desirable. Conscious changes to a strike pattern can be used to alter tendon loading, especially when rest and rehabilitation are not currently options.

CONCLUSION

There is reasonable evidence to suggest that gait modification can be an effective management tool for lower-limb injuries, including tendinopathies. There is no recognised "perfect" running style; any sudden changes to an existing technique are likely to increase the risk of injury rather than reduce it. This is perhaps evidenced by the historical increase in lower-limb injuries when many people switched to minimalist footwear without transitioning correctly.

Based on current knowledge of the running gait, existing injury and pain will negatively influence gait patterns even after the pain has stopped. Running gait changes identified following Achilles tendinopathy are the opposite to those we are aiming to achieve through gait re-education. While it is not clear whether these changes are causative, correlative, or a mix of both, it demonstrates that implementing gait changes in the presence of existing lower-limb pathology is more challenging and that the quality of movement retraining is an important factor for treatment success. Any deficits in joint range and motor control also need to be checked. Footwear choices are important, and minimalist footwear or barefoot are options that can be used to aid gait re-education.

The benefits of combining pain-reducing and sensory-increasing modalities with gait manipulation are also well supported. Strength training was only briefly mentioned in this chapter but should be combined with gait re-education for maximal benefit.

A gait assessment form can be found in Appendix 2.

GAIT RE-EDUCATION GUIDELINES

Here are some very simple guidelines to offer patients. They can also be discussed and implemented without any gait analysis. They are purposefully brief and simple to avoid overburdening patients with too many things to try and change at once.

Beginner

- Keep your torso upright.
- Aim for a foot strike below the body.
- Keep the knees facing forward.

Intermediate

- Use step rate drills between 175 and 200 steps per minute (spm).
- Aim for a mid-foot strike pattern for short intervals.
- Focus on hip extension.

Advanced

- Use rapid step rate drills >200 spm, level or downhill.
- Use barefoot or minimalist training drills.
- Use running form drills.

MORE RUNNING DRILLS

Butt kicks

Butt kicks or step overs help to speed up the legs and shorten the lever arm during the swing-through phase of gait (**Figure 10.13**). They are a training method used to help reduce ground contact time in combination with an increased step rate.

Technique

Flick the heels back towards the bum while jogging on the spot or moving forward. Spring off the forefoot with each push-off.

FIGURE 10.13   Butt kicks.

Calf jumps

This is a simple late-stage rehabilitation plyometric exercise to increase plantar flexor function (**Figure 10.14**).

Technique

Jump up and down flexing the ankles, knees, and hips but focus on pushing up with the ankles with maximal plantar flexion.

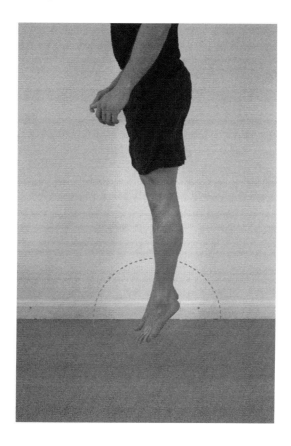

FIGURE 10.14   Calf jumps.

Kickbacks

This hip extension exercise helps to reinforce the correct lower-limb movement pattern (**Figure 10.15**).

Technique

Balance on one leg and then let your foot lightly contact the ground below your body before extending your hip and sliding your foot back, simulating a push-off phase. The foot does not have to slide over the ground, but this helps initially with fine motor control and sensory feedback.

FIGURE 10.15   Kick-backs.

Static forward lean jogging

A key component of good running form is a slight forward lean from the ankles, not the waist (**Figure 10.16**).

Technique

Using a thick resistance band around the waist allows a forward lean while jogging on the spot. This technique works well with a small trampoline.

FIGURE 10.16 Static forward lean jogging.

REFERENCES

Allen DJ (2014). Treatment of distal iliotibial band syndrome in a long distance runner with gait re-training emphasizing step rate manipulation. *Int J Sports Phys Ther.* **9**:222–231.

Almeida MO, Davis IS, Lopes AD (2015). Biomechanical differences of foot-strike patterns during running: a systematic review with meta-analysis. *J Orthop Sports Phys Ther.* **45**:738–755.

Cavanagh PR, Williams KR (1982). The effect of stride length variation on oxygen uptake during distance running. *Med Sci Sports Exerc.* **14**:30–35.

Chumanov ES, Wille CM, Michalski MP, et al. (2012). Changes in muscle activation patterns when running step rate is increased. *Gait Posture.* **36**:231–235.

Crowell HP, Milner CE, Hamill J, et al. (2010). Reducing impact loading during running with the use of real-time visual feedback. *J Orthop Sports Phys Ther.* **40**:206–213.

Davis IS (2005). Gait retraining in runners. *Orthop Pract.* **17**:8–13.

Franettovich Smith MM, Honeywill C, Wyndow N, et al. (2014). Neuromotor control of gluteal muscles in runners with Achilles tendinopathy. *Med Sci Sports Exerc.* **46**:594–599.

Grimaldi A, Mellor R, Hodges P, et al. (2015). Gluteal tendinopathy: a review of mechanisms, assessment and management. *Sports Med.* **45**:1107–1119.

Hamill J, Derrick TR, Holt KG (1995). Shock attenuation and stride frequency during running. *Hum Mov Sci.* **14**:45–60.

Hamill J, van Emmerik RE, Heiderscheit BC, et al. (1999). A dynamical systems approach to lower extremity running injuries. *Clin Biomech (Bristol, Avon).* **14**:297–308.

Heiderscheit BC, Chumanov ES, Michalski MP, et al. (2011). Effects of step rate manipulation on joint mechanics during running. *Med Sci Sports Exerc.* **43**:296–302.

Hodges PW (2011). Pain and motor control: from the laboratory to rehabilitation. *J Electromyogr Kinesiol.* **21**:220–228.

Kim S, Yu J (2015). Changes of gait parameters and lower-limb dynamics in recreational runners with Achilles tendinopathy. *J Sports Sci Med.* **14**:284–289.

Malliaras P, Purdam C (2014). Proximal hamstring tendinopathy assessment and management. *Sport Health.* **32**:21–30.

Remple MS, Bruneau RM, VandenBerg PM, et al. (2001). Sensitivity of cortical movement representations to motor experience: evidence that skill learning but not strength training induces cortical reorganization. *Behav Brain Res.* **123**:133–141.

Van Ginckel A, Thijs Y, Hesar NG, et al. (2009). Intrinsic gait-related risk factors for Achilles tendinopathy in novice runners: a prospective study. *Gait Posture.* **29**:387–391.

Willy RW, Davis IS (2011). The effect of a hip-strengthening program on mechanics during running and during a single-leg squat. *J Orthop Sports Phys Ther.* **41**:625–632.

Willy RW, Scholz JP, Davis IS (2012). Mirror gait retraining for the treatment of patellofemoral pain in female runners. *Clin Biomech (Bristol, Avon).* **27**:1045–1051.

Wren TA, Gorton GE 3rd, Ounpuu S, et al. (2011). Efficacy of clinical gait analysis: a systematic review. *Gait Posture.* **34**:149–153.

FURTHER READING

Clement DB, Taunton JE, Smart GW (1984). Achilles tendinitis and peritendinitis: etiology and treatment. *Am J Sports Med.* **12**:179–184.

Cowan SM, Bennell KL, Hodges PW (2002). Therapeutic patellar taping changes the timing of vasti muscle activation in people with patellofemoral pain syndrome. *Clin J Sport Med.* **12**:339–347.

Hodges PW, Moseley GL (2003). Pain and motor control of the lumbopelvic region: effect and possible mechanisms. *J Electromyogr Kinesiol.* **13**:361–370.

CHAPTER 11

MASSAGE FOR TENDON PAIN

INTRODUCTION

Massage is an ancient treatment and a natural reaction to pain (e.g. rubbing a sore elbow). Massage has been accepted in the clinical setting without question, the evidence of its effectiveness being principally anecdotal and largely undocumented.

The significance of therapeutic touch and the value of simple "hands-on" treatment for tendinopathy have become overshadowed by our changing approach to the pathology and treatment. Increasingly sophisticated equipment is being used for assessment and treatment and specific exercise protocols often negate the patient's chief concern – pain.

Pain hinders the management of tendinopathy because patients are often reluctant to perform loading exercises when in pain, even following patient education. There are many ways to reduce pain from musculoskeletal conditions and while massage has received some bad press from academia for its overall lack of evidence, one thing research supports is massage as a tool for pain reduction for musculoskeletal conditions, although not specifically tendon-related pain (Cherkin et al., 2003; Frey Law et al., 2008; Sherman et al., 2009).

There is evidence to support the use of direct deep transverse friction massage (DTFM) on tendons to reduce pain (Joseph et al., 2012), but this needs to be approached with caution against the backdrop of the tendinopathy continuum pathology model. In my opinion, DTFM might aggravate reactive tendons and cause an unhelpful increase in protein production. However, DTFM often leads to a period of analgesia and a reduction in the size of any tendon thickening; thus, some therapists continue to use this treatment method. Based on current information, I recommend DTFM as a treatment option only for refractory degenerative tendinopathies, so please avoid the temptation to directly rub sore acute tendons.

Massage has multiple alternative names that describe the style of the massage, the teaching school from which it originated, and the philosophy on which it is based.

You may know, practise, or have heard of some of the following: sports massage; soft tissue release; myofascial release; fascial manipulation; trigger point release; transverse friction; and instrument-assisted.

In terms of tendinopathy management, you need to experiment to find which massage method(s) help to reduce your patients' pain and appreciate that these may be different between individuals.

An important point to reiterate before we look at massage options, is the poor pain-to-pathology correlation. Massage treatment is solely for pain relief and the reduced pain should encourage improved exercise adherence and load management, but it is not a cure.

EFFECTS OF MASSAGE

The effects of massage are well known but fundamentally unproven. There are many debatable points that could form a lengthy discussion. To keep things brief, it is unlikely that massage increases blood flow, and even if so, not in a way significant to benefit a tendon. It is most likely that the benefits of direct massage of a tendon are through desensitisation from a short period of hyperstimulation. Direct tendon massage may irritate the pathology in the acute stages, so most of the techniques in this chapter target regional musculature. The benefits of massage are most likely to occur from an initial pain gating; this is followed by descending inhibition influencing the "volume" of the noxious input and a more global relaxation of muscular tone.

Massage causes movement of the underlying tissue and fascia, which may improve the slide and glide between different layers and influence fluid flow and hydration between the tissues. Research has also shown alterations in the following hormones: cortisol, serotonin, and dopamine (Field et al., 2005); and oxytocin (Morhenn, Beavin and Zak, 2012). This hormonal mix helps regulate many processes within the body, including immunity, pain perception, and injury recovery. There is undoubtedly a placebo effect, and the building of rapport and trust with the patient that are vital to any successful management programme.

The following techniques are some of the recommended massage treatments for the lower limbs.

TESTING

Before performing a treatment, it is very useful to pre-test a painful movement and then retest it after a massage treatment. This also allows you to determine how long the benefits of massage last and when further treatment ceases to improve the outcome. As a result, you should then be able to select the most effective massage options for each individual patient.

ACHILLES TENDON-RELATED TECHNIQUES

Calf massage and focal pressure

Aims

Provide a moderate-to-firm massage stimulus over the gastrocnemius-soleus complex to reduce the pain from the Achilles region.

Position

Your patient should be prone with their feet off the end of the couch to allow relaxed dorsiflexion (**Figure 11.1**).

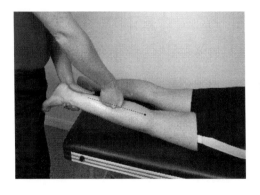 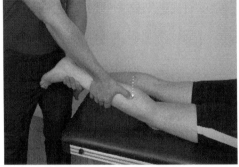

FIGURE 11.1   Calf massage and focal pressure.

Action

Begin with a dynamic massage using your preferred techniques before directing sustained pressure onto any specific tender points for a short period of time.

Note

Working above the tendon often reduces the pain, tension, and discomfort from the tendon region; you do not need to massage the tendon directly.

Flossing for the calf region

Aims

Improve pain-free range and reduce the sensation of muscle tension.

Position

Apply the compression (floss) band around the lower limb from above the ankle with moderate pressure and a 50/50 overlap (**Figure 11.2**).

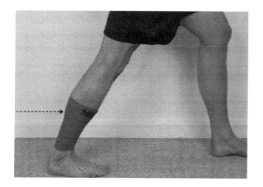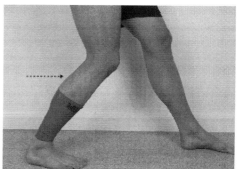

FIGURE 11.2   Flossing for the calf region.

Action

With the compression band in place, ask your patient to complete 10 full-range dorsiflexion stretches while standing.

Tips

Stretch with the knee straight and bent to target the gastrocnemius and soleus fibres.

Note

Flossing is like a pin-and-stretch massage technique. It is quick and easy to do and often yields great results.

Rolling the calf

Aims

Provide a self-massage option for individuals and groups.

Position

Long sitting, with one leg resting on the roller in a relaxed state (**Figure 11.3**).

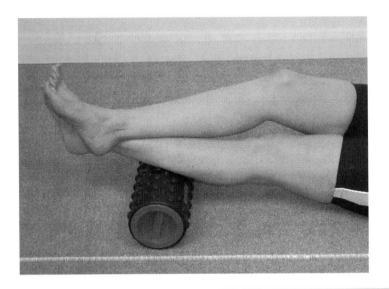

FIGURE 11.3   Rolling the calf.

Action

Ask your patient to lift their torso up using the arms and allow the leg to roll up and down over the roller.

Tips

Instruct your patient to apply moderate pressure; the exercise should not be painful, but some discomfort is acceptable. Tell your patient to angle the leg to target the medial and lateral sides of the calf.

Plantar fascia roll

Aims

Self-massage the plantar fascia region using a small, firm ball. This often reduces posterior tension and sensitivity through the plantar and Achilles region

Position

Seated, ball under foot (**Figure 11.4**).

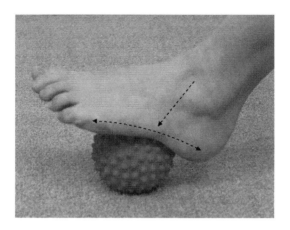

FIGURE 11.4   Plantar fascia roll.

Action

Very slow rolling with moderate pressure.

Tips

Experiment with different ball sizes and textures.

PATELLAR-RELATED TECHNIQUES

Quad massage and focal pressure

Aims

Apply a moderate-to-firm massage stimulus over the quadriceps muscle group, with the option of using sustained pressure over a specific region of the lateral thigh (**Figure 11.5**).

Position

Patient long sitting or with their knee bent.

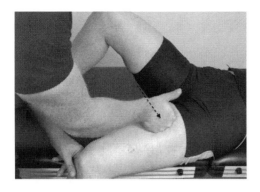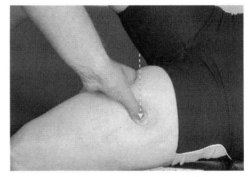

FIGURE 11.5   Quad massage and focal pressure.

Action

Begin with a dynamic massage using your preferred techniques before directing sustained pressure onto a specific tender point commonly located on the mid-thigh, slightly lateral from the centre.

Tips

Once the tender spot has been located, apply a tolerable pressure with your elbow or a massage tool to save your thumbs from fatigue.

Rolling the quads

Aims

Provide a self-massage option for individuals and groups (**Figure 11.6**).

Position

Lying on the floor with one thigh on the roller and the other leg out to the side to stabilise the body.

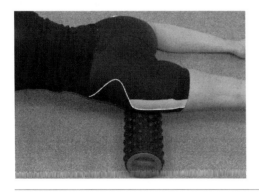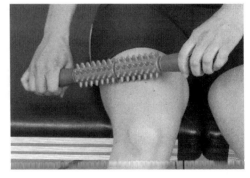

FIGURE 11.6   Quad roller and massage stick.

Action

Roll forward and back so the roller stays between the knee and hip.

Tips

If this technique is difficult, try the stick option as shown in **Figure 11.6.**

Flossing the knee

Aims

Improve the pain-free range and reduce the sensation of muscle tension (**Figure 11.7**).

Position

Apply the compression (floss) band around the knee joint with moderate pressure and a 50/50 overlap.

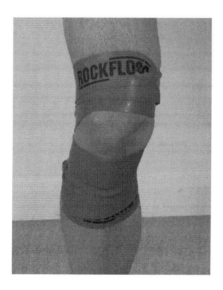

FIGURE 11.7   Flossing the knee joint.

Action

With the compression band in place, ask your patient to complete 10 squats within a pain-free range.

Tips

This technique can be used to control pain during specific loading programmes.

Note

Flossing is like a pin-and-stretch massage technique. It is quick and easy to do and often yields great results.

HAMSTRING-RELATED TECHNIQUES

Hamstring massage with pin-and-stretch
Aims
Apply a moderate-to-firm massage stimulus over the hamstring muscle group with the option of using sustained pressure over a specific region of the muscle while extending the knee to mobilise the underlying tissue.

Position
Patient lying face down with the legs straight or the knees bent (**Figure 11.8**).

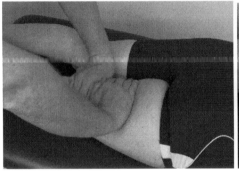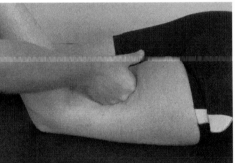

FIGURE 11.8   Hamstring massage and pin and stretch.

Action
Begin with a dynamic massage using your preferred techniques before applying sustained pressure over a specific area of the posterior thigh, followed by a passive straightening of the knee (pin-and-stretch).

Hamstring roller
Aims
Provide a self-massage option for individuals and groups.

Position

Sitting on the floor with one leg resting on the roller behind the knee (**Figure 11.9**).

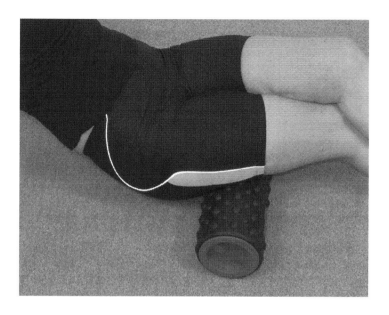

FIGURE 11.9   Hamstring roller.

Action

Instruct your patient to roll forward and backwards, so that the roller stays between their knee and hip.

GLUTEAL-RELATED TECHNIQUES

Gluteal massage techniques

Gluteal tendinopathy often leads to some associated focal muscular tender points, which commonly desensitise after sustained pressure treatments.

Aim

Provide sustained pressure to desensitise focal regions and reduce pain with movement.

Position

Lying and standing, as shown in **Figure 11.10.**

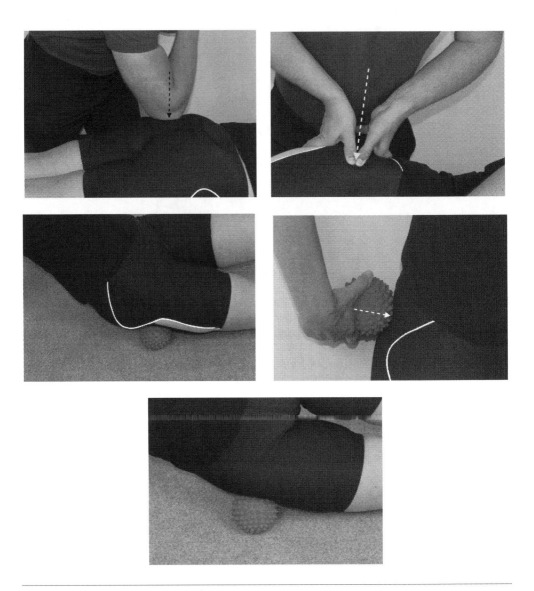

FIGURE 11.10   Gluteal massage techniques.

Action

Apply light to moderate pressure for a sustained period until the region is reported to be less tender.

Tips

Try these techniques with guidance first, then consider suggesting them as home management tasks.

Rolling the iliotibial band

For most people, rolling the iliotibial band (ITB) (**Figure 11.11**) is very painful. This is unnecessary and the therapeutic benefits of rolling the lateral thigh are disputed. Rolling the quadriceps and hamstring group may prove helpful as an alternative. These two muscle groups connect laterally at the lateral intermuscular septum of the thigh, whose superficial fibres are continuous with the ITB. In addition, reducing the tone of the ITB tensioners, gluteus maximus, and tensor fasciae latae with the ball methods described previously, is likely to reduce the tension through the ITB.

FIGURE 11.11   Iliotibial roll.

MYOFASCIAL ANATOMY

This chapter forms a small, but important part of successful tendinopathy management and treatment. The techniques described predominantly focus on the adjoining muscle groups for each tendon. To expand on this idea of myofascial continuity, many therapists have reported the benefits of performing soft tissue work along the length of the myofascial continuities rather than maintaining the massage near the tendon. An example of this for gluteal tendinopathy would be to massage the lateral line of tissue or to massage the whole back line for an Achilles or hamstring tendon problem.

CONCLUSION

Massage is one of the oldest treatment modalities with a proven anecdotal track record. More recent evidence has disputed many of its historic claims, but its ability to reduce pain from a variety of causes is well documented. Based on what we currently know, massage can confidently be used as an analgesic tool for tendinopathy-related pain; a positive outcome from massage can hopefully improve patient rapport and exercise adherence.

REFERENCES

Cherkin DC, Sherman KJ, Deyo RA, et al. (2003). A review of the evidence for the effectiveness, safety, and cost of acupuncture, massage therapy, and spinal manipulation for back pain. *Ann Intern Med.* **138**:898–906.

Joseph MF, Taft K, Moskwa M, et al. (2012). Deep friction massage to treat tendinopathy: a systematic review of a classic treatment in the face of a new paradigm of understanding. *J Sport Rehabil.* **21**:343–353.

Field T, Hernandez-Reif M, Diego M, et al. (2005). Cortisol decreases and serotonin and dopamine increase following massage therapy. *Int J Neurosci.* **115**.1397–1413.

Frey Law LA, Evans S, Knudtson J, et al. (2008). Massage reduces pain perception and hyperalgesia in experimental muscle pain: a randomized, controlled trial. *J Pain.* **9**:714–721.

Morhenn V, Beavin LE, Zak PJ (2012). Massage increases oxytocin and reduces adrenocorticotropin hormone in humans. *Altern Ther Health Med.* **18**:11–18.

Sherman KJ, Cherkin DC, Hawkes RJ, et al. (2009). Randomized trial of therapeutic massage for chronic neck pain. *Clin J Pain.* **25**:233–238.

CHAPTER 12
TAPING TENDONS

INTRODUCTION

The popularity of kinesiology tape has increased dramatically over the last decade. Despite having been invented in the 1970s by Dr Kenzo Kase, a Japanese chiropractor, kinesiology tape rose to prominence following the Beijing Olympics in 2008, and it is increasingly seen on athletes at all levels of competition (**Figure 12.1**). However, despite this rise in popularity, there is still significant debate about the clinical efficacy of kinesiology tape.

FIGURE 12.1   Runner with kinesiology tape applied to their knee for pain relief.

The literature remains divided on the efficacy of kinesiology tape. High-quality evidence is lacking, and while systematic reviews exist, they are divided in their conclusions. This is likely because few high-quality reviews exist; therefore, summarising the evidence is troublesome, and many studies lack sufficient power to draw robust conclusions. Kalron and Bar-Sela (2013) found that there was "moderate evidence" for pain reduction, while Lim and Tay (2015) found that kinesiology taping was "superior to minimal intervention for pain relief" for those with more than four weeks of pain, and was effective at reducing pain when used as an adjunct to exercise and other conventional therapies. Clinically, this supports the way most practitioners would use kinesiology tape; that is, as an adjunct to their existing treatment modalities.

Firth et al. (2010) compared the effects of kinesiology taping on a group with Achilles tendinopathy and a group without. There were little differences between the two groups and the authors did not report any significant change in pain reporting. In contrast to this result, a single case report of the treatment of Achilles tendinopathy with kinesiology taping has also been well cited and reported significant improvement in pain reporting and other measures, including the Victorian Institute of Sports Assessment-Achilles (VISA-A) questionnaire, following repeated application (Lee and Yoo, 2012). Another tendinopathy study measured maximal grip strength and force sense when tape was applied to the forearm to treat medial elbow tendinopathy. The results showed no significant difference in maximal grip strength but reported a significant increase in force sense for both standard kinesiology tape and placebo tape (Chang et al., 2013). Understandably, both tapes would have provided a sensory input to the skin; therefore, both influenced force sense. Unfortunately, this study did not measure pain reporting, but the increased force sense adds to a general theme of increased reactivity of contractile tissue. Other studies involving different regions of the body reported increased muscle preactivation (Griebert et al., 2016), peak force (Fratocchi et al., 2013), time-to-peak force (Wong, Cheung and Lee, 2012), endurance (Álvarez-Álvarez et al., 2014), and electromyography activity (Huang et al., 2011). Aside from pain reduction, any additional influence on muscle function in the presence of pain inhibition would be highly beneficial for rehabilitation purposes.

OUTCOME MEASURES

I recommend testing a simple outcome measure before applying the tape and again immediately after the tape has been applied, to determine if the application has proved beneficial at reducing pain and improving movement.

PREPARATION

Kinesiology tape only sticks to clean and dry skin; body hair may also hinder adhesion and needs to be trimmed.

CONTRAINDICATIONS

Most kinesiology tapes are hypoallergenic and are unlikely to irritate the skin if applied correctly. There are no published case reports of any serious adverse effects from kinesiology taping, but taping should not take place in the presence of the following conditions:

- broken skin;
- active infection;
- areas treated with radiation;
- history of kidney and heart failure.

REDUCING THE RISK OF SKIN REACTION

Ask your patient if they have ever had any skin reactions to common substances or tapes. If they have or you are concerned about their skin reacting to the tape, use a test patch or patches over the area you would like to tape. The test patches should be 1–2-cm squares (see **Figure 12.2**) and you should instruct your patient to remove them if the skin becomes itchy or irritated. If no adverse reactions have occurred after 3 hours, then apply the tape over the area for 1 day (12 hours or less) before removing it, and then reapply the tape the next day for a longer period. This gradual approach allows the careful introduction of taping techniques for individuals with sensitive skin and avoids unnecessary skin irritation.

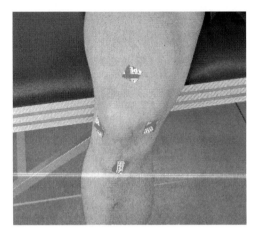

FIGURE 12.2   Test patches can be used to assess skin reactivity if the patient reports previous sensitivity to other tapes or as a general precaution.

There are generally no set rules for tape application, but I recommend following the guidelines (golden rules) in the next section for all taping techniques.

The golden rules (as taught by RockTape UK)
Apply the following guidelines when taping a patient:

1. Round the ends of the tape before application.
2. Apply each end of the tape with no stretch.
3. The tape can overlap, but each end of the tape should always be stuck to the skin.
4. Avoid handling the adhesive side of the tape.
5. After application, rub over the tape to ensure it has adhered to the skin.

ACHILLES TENDINOPATHY TECHNIQUES

Patient position

The ankle should be fully dorsiflexed and the knee extended. This is best achieved with the foot off the end of a couch, as shown in **Figure 12.3**.

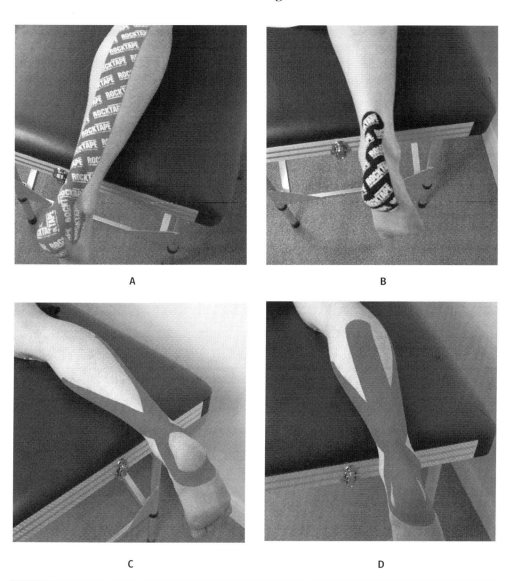

FIGURE 12.3 Achilles tendon taping options. (a) Standard application. (b) Short application. (c) Achilles wrap. (d) Combination application.

Application

Apply one piece of tape from the plantar surface of the heel up over the Achilles tendon and up over the back of the calf region. Finish at any point below the back of the knee; do not cross the knee joint line because this can irritate the sensitive skin behind the knee joint. The second piece of tape should be placed across the painful region of the heel.

Tape stretch

Avoid overstretching the tape. Apply the tape with minimal stretch or add a moderate tape stretch over the tendon region.

Tip

Tape glue can help the tape adhere to sweaty feet, but make sure the skin is clean and dry.

Alternative 1

A short version of this application (**Figure 12.3b**); it provides a more discrete application that can often be worn under the patient's sock.

Tip

Leaving a sock on while showering helps the tape to stick on a little longer because it stops it from getting rubbed off under the foot.

Alternative 2

This stirrup style application (**Figure 12.3c**) is preferred by athletes, who report an increased feeling of support when compared to the linear technique. It uses twice as much tape, is a little fiddly to apply, and may not last as long as the other applications. However, for athletic events or heavy training sessions, it is often the preferred option. This application can also be combined with the single vertical strip (**Figure 12.3d**).

KNEE TECHNIQUES

Patient position

The application of kinesiology tape to the knee is best carried out with the knee flexed to approximately 90 degrees while sitting on a chair or treatment couch.

Application

Start the first piece of tape from the top of the shin, just below the tibial tuberosity. Stretch the tape moderately over the patellar tendon and then reduce the tape stretch over and above the patella. You can finish the tape just above the knee (**Figure 12.4a**) or continue up the thigh (**Figure 12.4b**). A second strip is placed with moderate stretch across the painful region on the tendon.

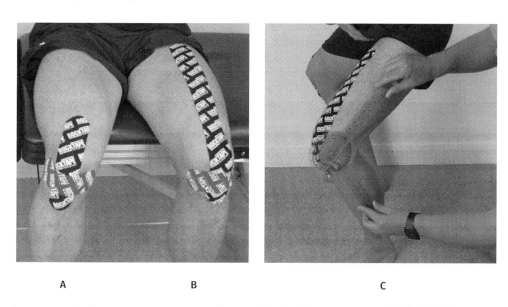

A   B   C

FIGURE 12.4   Knee taping applications. (a) Standard application. (b) Extended quadriceps coverage. (c) Measuring improvements during a squat using a goniometer.

Tape stretch

Check that you have not overstretched the tape by asking your patient to perform a full-knee bend. The tape should not limit the range of movement. If it does, remove it, and apply new tape with less tension.

Tip

A good pre-and post-taping test is to measure the pain-free range during a squat (**Figure 12.4c**).

GLUTEAL TECHNIQUES

Patient position

This technique should not require the removal of underwear, but tape application is best done after explaining the application technique and with suitable privacy. The tape is applied while side-lying, with the patient pulling their underwear high over the lateral hip (**Figure 12.5a**).

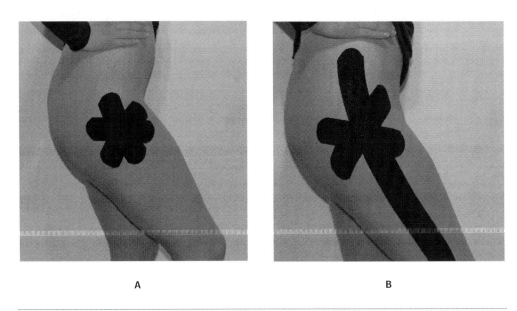

A   B

FIGURE 12.5   Hip taping application options. (a) Lateral hip decompression star. (b) Lateral hip decompression and iliotibial band taping combined.

Application

Have three strips of tape cut and ready to apply over the lateral hip. The centre of the tape strips should be positioned over the most painful region.

Tape stretch

Apply the tape strips with a moderate-to-firm stretch.

Alternative

Many runners have reported the benefits of lateral thigh taping for iliotibial band-related issues. You could use this as an alternative or combine the two as shown in **Figure 12.5b**.

Tip

In addition to reducing pain, gluteal taping has been shown to improve gluteal muscle activation. Test and retest your patient's gait pattern to see if it has any influnce on pelvic stability. This may be visual or reported by your patient.

HAMSTRING TECHNIQUES

Because of where the pain is located, direct taping can be problematic for a variety of reasons including: traction of regional body hair causing discomfort; the tape rubbing off when seated; and general application difficulties. Hamstring taping is popular for more musclular hamstring injuries, especially amoung athletes.

Here is a general technique for hamstring pain. I do not usually use it for upper hamstring tendinopathy (**Figure 12.6**).

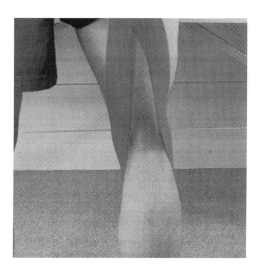

FIGURE 12.6   Hamstring taping option, typically more suitable for hamstring strains than hamstring origin pain.

Patient position

Standing and bent forward from the hips to stretch the hamstrings. The upper body should be rested on a couch or chair. Ask your patient to hold their shorts up at the back of their leg.

Application

Measure two strips of tape from, or just below, the ischial tuberosity down to the posterior medial and posterior lateral sides of the knee. Apply each strip of tape from top to bottom with minimum-to-moderate tape stretch.

Tape stretch

You may find that increased tape stretch provides more sensory feedback and stimulation. However, too much tape stretch can cause skin irritation, so make sure you choose the correct amount.

Tip

Hamstring tape applications work well for training and sport but are less comfortable when sitting around and resting. For this reason, I suggest applying the tape for shorter time periods.

CONCLUSION

Taping for tendon-related pain and dysfunction can be used with the aim of reducing pain and potentially improving muscle function. Taping will not cure a tendinopathy, but it will probably help to improve the management and treatment experience for the patient.

REFERENCES

Álvarez-Álvarez S, José FG, Rodríguez-Fernández AL, et al. (2014). Effects of Kinesio® Tape in low back muscle fatigue: randomized, controlled, doubled-blinded clinical trial on healthy subjects. *J Back Musculoskelet Rehabil.* **27**:203–212.

Chang HY, Cheng SC, Lin CC, et al. (2013). The effectiveness of kinesio taping for athletes with medial elbow epicondylar tendinopathy. *Int J Sports Med.* **34**:1003–1006.

Firth BL, Dingley P, Davies ER, et al. (2010). The effect of kinesiotape on function, pain, and motoneuronal excitability in healthy people and people with Achilles tendinopathy. *Clin J Sport Med.* **20**:416–421.

Fratocchi G, Di Mattia F, Rossi R, et al. (2013). Influence of Kinesio Taping applied over biceps brachii on isokinetic elbow peak torque. A placebo controlled study in a population of young healthy subjects. *J Sci Med Sport.* **16**:245–249.

Griebert MC, Needle AR, McConnell J, et al. (2016). Lower-leg Kinesio tape reduces rate of loading in participants with medial tibial stress syndrome. *Phys Ther Sport.* **18**:62–67.

Huang CY, Hsieh TH, Lu SC, et al. (2011). Effect of the Kinesio tape to muscle activity and vertical jump performance in healthy inactive people. *Biomed Eng Online.* **10**:70.

Kalron A, Bar-Sela S (2013). A systematic review of the effectiveness of Kinesio Taping: fact or fashion? *Eur J Phys Rehabil Med.* **49**:699–709.

Lee JH, Yoo WG (2012). Treatment of chronic Achilles tendon pain by Kinesio taping in an amateur badminton player. *Phys Ther Sport.* **13**:115–119.

Lim EC, Tay MG (2015). Kinesio taping in musculoskeletal pain and disability that lasts for more than 4 weeks: is it time to peel off the tape and throw it out with the sweat? A systematic review with meta-analysis focused on pain and also methods of tape application. *Br J Sports Med.* **49**:1558–1566.

Wong OM, Cheung RT, Li RC (2012). Isokinetic knee function in healthy subjects with and without Kinesio taping. *Phys Ther Sport.* **13**:255–258.

Chapter 13

EXTRACORPOREAL SHOCKWAVE THERAPY

INTRODUCTION

Following the general shift in thinking from an inflammatory tendinitis to a degenerative tendinopathy, treatments aimed at tissue stimulation and regeneration are being increasingly trialled. Perhaps the most popular of these is extracorporeal shockwave therapy (ESWT), which is undergoing increasing clinical adoption and academic scrutiny (**Figure 13.1**).

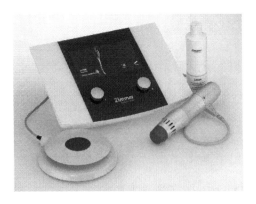

FIGURE 13.1   A (Zimmer) shock wave machine.

WHAT IS EXTRACORPOREAL SHOCKWAVE THERAPY?

Extracorporeal shockwave therapy (ESWT) is a non-invasive treatment where high-frequency acoustic shock waves pass through the skin and the underlying tissues, creating a pressure disturbance that influences the surrounding tissues.

Shock waves are an acoustically driven transfer of energy; they have been described as controlled explosions. A sonic boom from an aircraft breaking the sound barrier is another well-known example of a shock wave, as is a thunderclap.

The 1970s witnessed the first widespread medical use of shock waves for the breakdown of kidney stones, a process known as lithotripsy. Lithotripsy is still used today, and the medical community continues to experiment with the use of shock waves to target bone and soft tissue pathologies. Its use in the management of tendinopathy began shortly after its reported success on plantar fascia pain, which shares many of the pathological features of tendinopathy.

Extracorporeal refers to the treatment being applied from outside the body (hence being non-invasive); it is typically delivered as a focused shock wave or a radial shock wave (non-focused). The focused shock wave is generated using one of three methods depending on the treatment tool being used: spark discharge; piezoelectric; electromagnetic. Radial shock wave tools use a pneumatic production method to produce a wave characteristically different to a true shock wave (**Figure 13.2**).

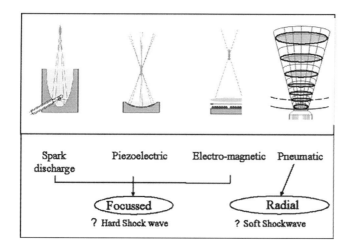

FIGURE 13.2   Extracorporeal shock wave therapy production methods for focused and radial generators.

Radial shock wave

Radial shock wave is not actually a form of shock wave. Radial shock wave has caused some confusion among researchers and clinicians because it does not deliver a focused shock wave or in fact a shock wave at all. A radial shock wave machine generates its shock, or more correctly "wave", by using compressed air to fire a projectile against the applicator to produce a shock and initiate a radial pressure wave (RPW). The pressure is maximal at source and then dissipates away from the applicator. When the distance between the source and target tissue is doubled, only one-fourth of the energy hits the target tissue (McClure and Dorfmüller, 2003). Some radial shock wave machines come with "focused" applicators, but due to the same initial shock, these commonly produce a more focused pressure wave. RPW is sometimes called radial pulse or ballistic therapy. Using terms such as low-energy shock wave or soft shock wave to describe RPW is not correct and adds further confusion. To avoid such confusion, this chapter refers to focused shock wave therapy as just ESWT and radial shock wave therapy as RPW.

The availability of ESWT/RPW machines and the volume of therapists offering this treatment has been steadily increasing considering the increasing amount of supportive research and lower equipment costs. However, this makes little sense. Most machines are RPW machines, and many clinics offering shock wave therapy are offering RPW therapy but basing treatment efficacy on ESWT research. The two types of machine are very different and cannot be considered equal or indeed similar. The key differences are described here (**Figure 13.3**).

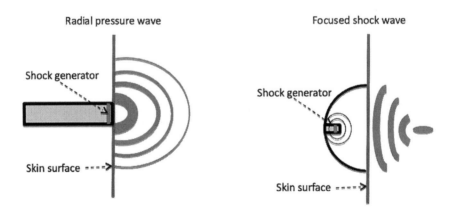

FIGURE 13.3   A focused shock wave versus a radial pressure wave.

A focused shock wave machine generates a shock wave within the applicator, which is focused using the fluid inside the applicator. This maximises the shock wave distal to the applicator and within the targeted tissue, without causing unnecessary side effects to the surrounding tissue. This is particularly important when using a higher-energy output to break up kidney stones while preserving the kidney itself. The precision of the focusing is very important for lithotripsy; real-time ultrasound scanning is used to help calculate the correct setting. Musculoskeletal conditions use much lower energy outputs, so simpler depth calculations can be used. The characteristics of focused and radial shock waves are shown in **Figure 13.4.**

The radial waves from radial generators are up to 100 times lower in amplitude and have a rise time and pulse duration that is up to 1000 times longer compared with a true focused shock wave.

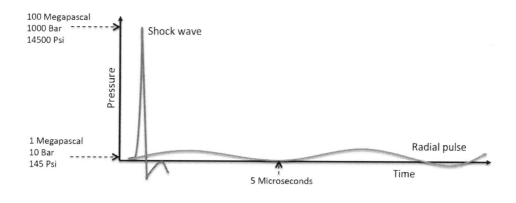

FIGURE 13.4   Graph showing the different characteristics of focused shock wave and radial pressure wave.

A true shock wave is produced when the projectile reaches a speed that is comparable or higher to the speed of sound in tissue, which is around 1500 m/s. The projectile in radial machines has only been documented to reach speeds of around 20 m/s (McClure and Dorfmüller, 2003).

While the characteristics of focused and radial waves vary significantly, the differences seen in the clinical setting remain uncertain. I found only one study that compared the difference between the two for the treatment of plantar fasciitis; both ESWT and RPW correlated, with positive outcomes slightly favouring ESWT (Lohrer et al., 2010). In addition, most research to date has been completed using solely ESWT.

Although the wave characteristics are very different, it is unclear whether this has any influence on the outcome because the mechanisms by which a shock wave can help reduce pain associated with tendinopathy remain inconclusive. The characteristics of ESWT are shown in **Figure 13.5.**

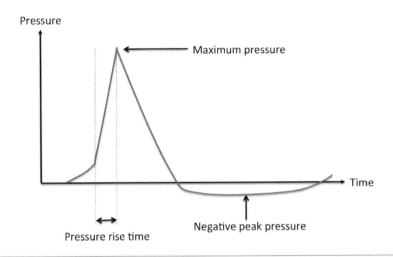

FIGURE 13.5   The typical features of a shock wave.

The concentrated shock wave energy per unit area is measured as the energy flux density (EFD) in millijoules (mJ) per millimetre squared (mm2). There is no consensus as to the definition for high- or low-energy ESWT. Energy levels >0.4 mJ/mm2 have been shown or suggested to have detrimental effects on soft tissues. For guidance purposes, suggested treatment doses are detailed later in this chapter; they are informed by limited evidence and are not evidence-based recommendations. The principal energy divisions for ESWT in medical practice are shown in **Figure 13.6.**

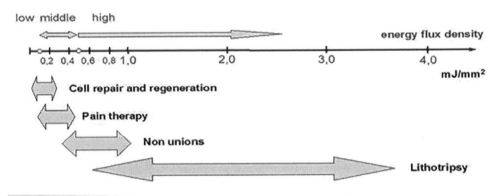

FIGURE 13.6   The principal energy divisions for extracorporeal shock wave therapy in medical practice. Reproduced with kind permission from Professor Tim Watson.

PROPOSED MECHANISMS OF ACTION

In vitro animal studies consistently show the effects of ESWT on tendon tissue, but the results from human trials are less consistent. An increasing body of evidence supports the use of ESWT for soft tissue pathologies, including tendinopathies, and although a small amount of published research disagrees, the efficacy of ESWT in the management of tendinopathy continues to grow. Despite the well-documented treatment outcomes, the mechanisms of action remain uncertain. One suggestion is that it aggravates a chronic tendon and restarts a repair sequence. Patients report varied discomfort during the procedure, but they often experience transient pain relief after an initial period of post-treatment discomfort.

Cavitation

One of the key mechanisms by which a shock wave can help reduce pain associated with tendinopathy regularly discussed in the literature is the double cavitation effect of focused shock wave. Cavitation refers to the air cavities or bubbles generated around gas or solid particles within the extracellular matrix. Examples of cavitation include the bubbles around a propeller rotating in water or the ultrasonic cleaning baths used to clean medical tools. During ESWT, cavitation is initially caused when the wave becomes negative after the positive pressure spike and pressure turns to tension causing the negative pressure environment needed for cavitation to occur. Secondary cavitation is caused by the next positive pressure spike, when the wave hits and collapses the preformed cavities. This results in an accelerated water jet faster than those seen with natural cavitation collapse. Essentially, the shock wave is creating and destroying cavities in rapid succession. The full impact of this process is unknown, but an increase in cell membrane permeability is commonly cited as a positive cellular response.

Pain relief

Hyperstimulation analgesia, whereby the overstimulation of nociceptors leads to a diminished transmission to the brainstem, is the most popular theory for ESWT-derived pain reduction. In addition, substance P production and gene-related peptide expression are two of the more contested pain relief mechanisms (Bosch et al., 2009)

Tissue regeneration

ESWT has been shown to increase collagen synthesis (Vetrano et al., 2011), matrix turnover (Bosch et al., 2009), and vascularisation (Wang et al., 2003), as well as decreasing the expression of substances associated with tendinopathy (matrix metallo-proteinases and interleukins) in human and animal studies (Han et al., 2009).

Destruction of calcifications

ESWT has been shown to break down calcifications in rotator cuff tendons via the same mechanism used to break down kidney stones (Bannuru et al., 2014).

EXTRACORPOREAL SHOCKWAVE THERAPY FOR ACHILLES TENDONS

Some patients report a poor outcome from the use of ESWT. Post-treatment ruptures have been reported in a minority of cases, although a previous tendon condition was the likely cause of the rupture rather than ESWT. Some animal studies have shown that excessive EFDs cause damage in rabbit (Rompe et al., 1998) and turkey tendons (Maier et al., 2001).

ESWT may be more beneficial for more focal pathology, but less so for the more diffuse or insertional pathology; however, at present it is considered for all Achilles tendinopathies.

When compared to other modalities, research has shown that ESWT is superior to a "wait-and-see" approach (Rompe et al., 2007). It also appears to match the efficacy of eccentric loading, potentially beating it with lower reported pain outcomes (Rompe, Furia and Maffulli, 2008).

EXTRACORPOREAL SHOCKWAVE THERAPY FOR PATELLAR TENDONS

A literature review published in the *British Journal of Sports Medicine* in 2008 reviewed the effectiveness of ESWT for patellar tendinopathy using 7 articles all published after 2000 with a combined total of 283 patients. While the studies varied in the quality of their methodology, ESWT appeared to be an effective treatment for patellar tendinopathy with no serious side effects reported (van Leeuwen, Zwerver and van den Akker-Scheek, 2009).

EXTRACORPOREAL SHOCKWAVE THERAPY FOR HAMSTRING TENDONS

There is a low volume of research on the use of ESWT for hamstring tendinopathy, but it has been reported as a safe and effective treatment for chronic hamstring tendinopathy (Cacchio et al., 2011).

EXTRACORPOREAL SHOCKWAVE THERAPY FOR LATERAL HIP PAIN

Although two studies have reported positive outcomes for lateral hip pain treated with shock wave therapy (Furia, Rompe and Maffulli, 2009; Rompe et al., 2009), further review of the methodology showed that it was radial shock wave and not focused shock wave therapy.

CAN EXTRACORPOREAL SHOCKWAVE THERAPY BE USED ON REACTIVE TENDONS?

ESWT should not be used on acute (reactive) tendons. The outcome is often poor and the suggested tissue aggravation mechanisms are likely to exacerbate a fresh pathology. This is largely based on expert opinion and anecdotal evidence from colleagues, but it is partially supported by recent studies showing "no effect" in acute patellar (Zwerver et al., 2011) and plantar fascia pathology (Rompe et al., 2010).

SHOULD THE PATIENT CONTINUE TO EXERCISE WHILE RECEIVING EXTRACORPOREAL SHOCKWAVE THERAPY?

A well-managed loading programme should be used in combination with ESWT to maximise any soft tissue adaptation that may occur. The initial catabolic tissue response to ESWT, before a healing response is initiated, suggests that an initially restricted exercise programme may be sensible, especially one that avoids ballistic loading. This logical plan may be challenged by the reduction in pain and the individual's motivation to exercise more as a result. As previously discussed, pain is a poor indicator of pathology.

HOW LONG WILL IT TAKE?

Any potential tissue repair takes a period of six weeks or more following treatment, even though pain may reduce in a much shorter time frame. These time frames are an important factor to discuss with your patient.

HOW CAN THE PAIN RESPONSE BE DESCRIBED?

Understandably, patients often focus on the pain generated from their tendon. Inform your patient of the potential discomfort during and after the procedure and that any pain reduction (although positive) does not denote resolution of tendon pathology; the tendinopathy is still there, but the symptoms have reduced.

IS EXTRACORPOREAL SHOCKWAVE THERAPY SAFE?

ESWT is considered a safe treatment following the exclusion of any contraindications. Good treatment head-to-skin coupling reduces the chance of skin irritation.

IS EXTRACORPOREAL SHOCKWAVE THERAPY LIKE ULTRASOUND?

A therapeutic ultrasound (US) wave has a biphasic pattern and a peak pressure averaging 1000 times less that of a uniphasic shock wave, 0.5 bar for therapeutic ultrasound versus up to 500 bar for ESWT. For reference, a car tyre is usually inflated to just over 2 bar.

CLINICAL GUIDELINES

Treatment doses: EFD parameters
Up to 0.08 mJ/mm2 (low-energy).

Shock number
1000–2000 shocks per session.

Number of treatment sessions
3–5 sessions, allowing time for symptoms to settle between each session.

Coupling

Hair removal and the use of standard US coupling gel are recommended. Poor coupling can lead to skin irritation and pain during treatment. Coupling is a simple but important part of effective shock/pulse therapy.

FURTHER GUIDANCE ON EXTRACORPOREAL SHOCKWAVE THERAPY

Safety considerations for extracorporeal shockwave therapy: contraindications, dangers, and precautions (information adapted with permission from Professor Tim Watson's Electrotherapy.org website.)

While not intended to constitute a definitive list, there are several areas/pathologies where concern has been expressed regarding the use of shockwave therapy; until further clarification has been obtained, some of the key issues have been identified here. This list is compiled from the best (currently) available evidence and expert advice/opinion. It may be that this is an overconservative approach; however, as with many "new" or "emerging" therapies, it is normal to err on the side of caution in the initial stages of clinical application:

- Lung tissue appears to be damaged unequivocally and treatment should be avoided.

- The epiphysis has been considered; while some experiments demonstrated a detrimental outcome, others did not. While clarification is being obtained, it makes sense to avoid treating the epiphyseal regions.

- Patients with haemophilia or who are on anticoagulant therapy are best not treated with shock wave therapy given that some visible tissue damage (skin petechiae and disruption of the microvasculature) has been noted in several studies.

- Malignancy remains on the contraindications list, although, as with other modalities, some experimental work is ongoing whereby shock wave therapies are being employed to try and minimise the growth and spread of malignant tissue. Given the present unknowns, it is best to avoid such areas.

- Metal implants appear to be OK regarding bone-based treatments, but implanted cardiac stents and implanted heart valves have not been fully evaluated.

However, if one is already avoiding the lungs, then they should also not be exposed to shock wave therapy.

- Infection in the local area should be treated very cautiously given the so far unknown effect of the therapy in this situation.

- Joint replacements, interestingly, show mixed results. Some have used the therapy experimentally to help with the removal of prostheses, making extraction easier. Given this, it would seem wise to avoid cemented implants. On the other hand, several researchers have used shock wave therapy to stimulate bone growth around an already loose prosthesis (osseous ingrowth). It would seem prudent to avoid the area given the possible loosening effect, which, unless desired, would certainly constitute a detrimental outcome.

CONCLUSION

There is a general misunderstanding regarding the use of shock wave therapy for tendinopathy. The research evidence that informs its use is promising and the treatment method appears safe; however, the treatment most clinicians are offering is often radial wave therapy (RWT) and not (focused) ESWT. The wave characteristics of RWT are very different to those of ESWT and most of the research is based on ESWT rather than RWT; it is not logical to expect the same results. This misunderstanding may be commercially driven; RWT devices are cheaper and easier to use than focused devices.

ESWT/RWT comparative research and specific RWT research is being completed and will soon begin to inform practice. For now, RWT often masquerades as true ESWT and is less effective.

ESWT seems most effective for more chronic tendinopathies (disrepair or degenerative phases) and as part of a general management strategy.

REFERENCES

Bannuru RR, Flavin NE, Vaysbrot E, et al. (2014). High-energy extracorporeal shock-wave therapy for treating chronic calcific tendinitis of the shoulder: a systematic review. *Ann Intern Med.* **160**: 542–549.

Bosch G, de Mos M, van Binsbergen R, et al. (2009). The effect of focused extracorporeal shock wave therapy on collagen matrix and gene expression in normal tendons and ligaments. *Equine Vet J.* **41**: 335–341.

Cacchio A, Rompe JD, Furia JP, et al. (2011). Shockwave therapy for the treatment of chronic proximal hamstring tendinopathy in professional athletes. *Am J Sports Med.* **39**: 146–153.

Furia JP, Rompe JD, Maffulli N (2009). Low-energy extracorporeal shock wave therapy as a treatment for greater trochanteric pain syndrome. *Am J Sports Med.* **37**: 1806–1813.

Han SH, Lee JW, Guyton GP, et al. (2009). J. Leonard Goldner Award 2008. Effect of extracorporeal shock wave therapy on cultured tenocytes. *Foot Ankle Int.* **30**: 93–98.

Lohrer H, Nauck T, Dorn-Lange NV, et al. (2010). Comparison of radial versus focused extracorporeal shock waves in plantar fasciitis using functional measures. *Foot Ankle Int.* **31**: 1–9.

McClure S, Dorfmüller C (2003). Extracorporeal shock wave therapy: theory and equipment. *Clin Tech Equine Pract.* **2**: 348–357.

Maier M, Saisu T, Beckmann J, et al. (2001). Impaired tensile strength after shock-wave application in an animal model of tendon calcification. *Ultrasound Med Biol.* **27**: 665–671.

Rompe JD, Furia J, Maffulli N (2008). Eccentric loading compared with shock wave treatment for chronic insertional achilles tendinopathy. A randomized, controlled trial. *J Bone Joint Surg Am.* **90**: 52–61.

Rompe JD, Cacchio A, Weil L Jr, et al. (2010). Plantar fascia-specific stretching versus radial shock-wave therapy as initial treatment of plantar fasciopathy. *J Bone Joint Surg Am.* **92**: 2514–2522.

Rompe JD, Kirkpatrick CJ, Küllmer K, et al. (1998). Dose-related effects of shock waves on rabbit tendo Achillis. A sonographic and histological study. *J Bone Joint Surg Br.* **80**: 546–552.

Rompe JD, Nafe B, Furia JP, et al. (2007). Eccentric loading, shock-wave treatment, or a wait-and-see policy for tendinopathy of the main body of tendo Achillis: a randomized controlled trial. *Am J Sports Med.* **35**: 374–383.

Rompe JD, Segal NA, Cacchio A, et al. (2009). Home training, local corticosteroid injection, or radial shock wave therapy for greater trochanter pain syndrome. *Am J Sports Med.* **37**: 1981–1990.

van Leeuwen MT, Zwerver J, van den Akker-Scheek I (2009). Extracorporeal shockwave therapy for patellar tendinopathy: a review of the literature. *Br J Sports Med.* **43**: 163–168.

Vetrano M, d'Alessandro F, Torrisi MR, et al. (2011). Extracorporeal shock wave therapy promotes cell proliferation and collagen synthesis of primary cultured human tenocytes. *Knee Surg Sports Traumatol Arthrosc.* **19**: 2159–2168.

Wang CJ, Wang FS, Yang KD, et al. (2003). Shock wave therapy induces neovascularization at the tendon-bone junction. A study in rabbits. *J Orthop Res.* **21**: 984–989.

Watson T (1995–2017). Electrotherapy on the web. Accessed 11 December 2017 from www.electrotherapy.org/.

Zwerver J, Hartgens F, Verhagen E, et al. (2011). No effect of extracorporeal shockwave therapy on patellar tendinopathy in jumping athletes during the competitive season: a randomized clinical trial. *Am J Sports Med.* **39**: 1191–1199.

FURTHER READING

Raabe O, Shell K, Goessl A, et al. (2013). Effect of extracorporeal shock wave on proliferation and differentiation of equine adipose tissue-derived mesenchymal stem cells in vitro. *Am J Stem Cells.* **2**: 62–73.

Speed C (2015). Shockwave therapies for sports injuries. *SportEX Med J.* 10–12.

van der Worp H, van den Akker-Scheek I, van Schie H, et al. (2013). ESWT for tendinopathy: technology and clinical implications. *Knee Surg Sports Traumatol Arthrosc.* **21**: 1451–1458.

CHAPTER 14

AN INTRODUCTION TO REGENERATIVE BIOMEDICINE

INTRODUCTION

Following the general shift in thinking from an inflammatory tendinitis to more degenerative tendinopathy, medical treatments aimed at stimulating an immune response have been increasingly adopted. When grouped together, these often-injectable forms of treatment are used to alter the natural pathological processes in favour of regenerating a stalled healing response. The most important of these substances are described in this chapter separately; the conclusion to the chapter brings together some of the features they share and discusses the mechanisms that lead to reduced symptoms and altered pathology.

PLATELET-RICH PLASMA

Platelet-rich plasma (PRP) is a concentrate of platelet-rich plasma protein derived from whole blood; it has up to eight times the concentration of platelets compared to whole blood. PRP is most commonly prepared by centrifugation of whole blood; it is then extracted from the separated blood layers and injected into tendons. PRP is also available in a gel formulation for surgical applications. PRP was originally used in surgery to assist wound healing; its use in the treatment of musculoskeletal injury has rapidly increased in recent years, despite a paucity of robust studies. PRP is currently not listed as a drug and is not banned by the main sporting regulatory bodies. There is little regulation for its use; no official administration or dosage guidelines currently exist.

PRP has a greater concentration of growth factors than whole blood; these growth factors have been used to encourage brisk tissue healing (Bachl et al., 2009). The key growth factors are shown in **Table 14.1** (adapted from Engebretsen et al., 2010).

GROWTH FACTOR	EFFECT(S)
PLATELET-DERIVED GROWTH FACTOR	Angiogenesis; macrophage activation; fibroblasts (proliferation, chemotaxis, collagen synthesis). Enhances proliferation of bone cells.
TRANSFORMING GROWTH FACTOR-B	Fibroblast proliferation; synthesis of type I collagen and fibronectin. Induces bone matrix deposition and inhibits bone resorption.
PLATELET-DERIVED EPIDERMAL GROWTH FACTOR	Stimulates epidermal regeneration; promotes wound healing by stimulating the proliferation of keratinocytes and dermal fibroblasts. Enhances the production and effects of other growth factors.
VASCULAR ENDOTHELIAL GROWTH FACTOR	Vascularisation (by stimulating vascular endothelial cells).
INSULIN-LIKE GROWTH FACTOR 1	Chemotactic for fibroblasts. Stimulates protein synthesis. Enhances bone formation.
PLATELET FACTOR 4	Stimulates initial influx of neutrophils into wounds. Chemoattractant for fibroblasts.
EPIDERMAL GROWTH FACTOR	Cellular proliferation and differentiation.

TABLE 14.1   Growth factors and their physiological roles

In the case of tendons, PRP is injected under ultrasound guidance to ensure it reaches the exact location. It has been suggested that irritation from needle insertion and removal may provide a significant tissue response, especially if a peppering technique is used (Filardo et al., 2010).

Activation of PRP is required to release the growth factors. When injecting tendons, the collagen and surrounding environment biologically activates PRP without any additional intervention (Fufa et al., 2008).

Many studies have reported a reduction in pain following PRP injection (Kon et al., 2009; Filardo et al., 2011). The lack of controls and additional treatments (typically exercise interventions) included in the research do not make it possible to specify the causal outcome of PRP in isolation.

In vitro studies have demonstrated an increase in collagen production, tenocyte proliferation (de Mos et al., 2008), and angiogenic stimulation (Kajikawa et al., 2008). The usefulness of these biological responses must be weighed against the continuum theory outlined in Chapter 3. The changes reported match those seen with the onset and development of tendinopathy, thus PRP may aggravate or be neutralised by a reactive tendinopathy. There is ground to suggest that it is best used in more recalcitrant tendinopathy that has reached a degenerative state, to potentially reinstate a more active healing environment.

Most in vivo studies involving tendons have been on animals; most studies involving humans have been simple case studies (Engebretsen et al., 2010). Mechanisms of action have been suggested, but it is not clear whether the clinical benefits reported are a direct result of these mechanisms or other factors not yet understood.

Summary

The popularity of PRP has accelerated faster than the science underpinning its use. Popularity has been partially driven by a small amount of promising research and by the lower cost of PRP compared to surgery. PRP is part of a new group of biomedical options for chronic tendinopathy. Based on what we know, there is little rationale for injecting PRP into a reactive tendon. However, tendons that have failed to respond to more conservative treatments, and have become degenerative, may benefit from a PRP injection. PRP is considered safe if delivered by a medical professional under sterile conditions and without an added activation (thrombin, calcium chloride) or analgesic ingredient.

NITRIC OXIDE AND GLYCERYL TRINITRATE

Glyceryl trinitrate (GTN) patches are being used as an off-label treatment for tendinopathy. GTN is converted to nitric oxide (NO) in tissues and causes changes at the cellular level. GTN patches are most commonly used for angina (sprays are also popular) to trigger a rapid vasodilatory response. For tendon treatment, the patches are cut and placed over the painful area, where it has been suggested they influence the contents of the extracellular matrix (ECM), rather than having a purely vasodilatory effect.

NO is a free radical in a soluble gas form under standard conditions; it is biosynthesised by several NO synthase enzymes. Naturally occurring NO acts as a messenger molecule in normal physiological processes, but is toxic if artificially administered in large doses (Murrell, 2007).

NO is important for collagen synthesis (Xia et al., 2006). It is a key facilitator of the gene expression associated with tissue healing that has been shown to improve the structure of the ECM. Many histological studies have been performed on cultured human cells. Human study groups have reported reduced pain and increased strength following NO intervention in combination with more traditional, exercise-based treatment (Paoloni and Murrell, 2007, Paoloni et al., 2004, 2009).

NO may provide a regenerative stimulus to tendinopathic tissue. Because of changes noted in vitro, treatment with NO may prove beneficial in a degenerative tendon; however, it may also unhelpfully add to the hypercellularity seen in more acutely reactive tendons.

GTN patches need to be prescribed appropriately. This may be difficult because their application over tendons is not a typical prescription.

STEM CELL THERAPY

It has been suggested that injecting high concentrations of bone marrow-derived mesenchymal stem cells into a tendinopathic tendon will speed up the healing process, reduce scar tissue accumulation, and reduce the risk of re-injury. While the mechanisms remain uncertain, one equine study reported positive results, with reduced comparative re-injury rates and improved elasticity of the superficial digital flexor tendon (Smith, 2013), which is similar to the human Achilles tendon. No adverse effects were noted.

SCLEROSING INJECTIONS

Sclerosing injections have increasingly been used to treat chronic tendon conditions. Polidocanol is the most common sclerosant (injectable irritant) used for varicose veins (Mimura et al., 2009) because of its safety profile and analgesic properties.

Polidocanol has been reported to reduce pain and neovascularisation. The rationale is that reduced neovascularisation causes a reduction in pain. This causal link between neovessel generation and pain remains speculative and unlikely.

A systematic review of the efficacy of sclerosing injections by Wilde and collaborators (2011) highlighted the uncertainty surrounding the recommendations of using sclerosing injections.

LARGE-VOLUME INJECTIONS

These are also referred to as saline injections or bulking injections. Large-volume injections have predominantly been used for mid-substance Achilles tendinopathy; they consist of a saline solution with an added anti-inflammatory agent to calm the tendon and stop it from reacting to the mechanical stress caused by the large-volume injection.

The proposed mechanism of action is mechanical stretching of pathological tissue, which ruptures the neovessels and their associated nerve supply. High-volume injections offer a short-term analgesic option for refractory tendinopathy in the Achilles tendon (Humphrey et al., 2010).

APROTININ

Aprotinin is a broad-spectrum proteinase inhibitor, including matrix metalloproteinases (MMPs). MMPs are collagenases found within our tissues; they breakdown collagen as part of a natural regenerative cycle in the absence of pathology. Tendinopathic tissue shows an increased number of MMPs, which play an active role in the pathology, may delay recovery, and thus lead to chronicity (Magra and Maffulli, 2005). Aprotinin has been used and researched as an MMP inhibitor. The premise is that a reduction in MMPs helps support tissue healing.

Aprotinin is typically used for the prevention of blood loss and tissue healing during and post-surgery. Much higher doses are required for surgery in comparison to its use in tendon pathology. There is also a risk of anaphylaxis, which has lessened the popularity of aprotinin among other available injectables.

In a case review of 430 patients receiving a total of 997 aprotinin injections, 64% of patients thought the injections were helpful while 36% reported neither a positive nor negative influence on their tendinopathy symptoms. The highest success rate for mid-substance Achilles tendinopathy was 84% of patients improving versus 69% improvement for patellar tendinopathy (Orchard et al., 2008a).

From the 430 cases reviewed by Orchard and collaborators (2008a), there were 13 probable allergic reactions and 7 patients were treated within 30 minutes of aprotinin administration with adrenaline injections, which successfully reversed the allergic reaction. Although the concentration of aprotinin used to treat tendinopathy is much lower at 4.2–8.5 mg compared to 980 mg for surgical use, repeated injections increase the likelihood of an allergic reaction (Orchard et al., 2008b).

It is not clear whether the low concentration of aprotinin injected into tendons is enough to significantly inhibit MMPs, or if another mechanism is at play. If aprotinin inhibits collagenases as suggested, then it would be superior to less active substances (e.g. PRP). Aprotinin should be considered as a second-line option when treating chronic tendinopathies, rather than a first-line treatment.

CONCLUSION

Several of the substances discussed in this chapter have been shown to increase cellularity in cultured cells; this has been used to justify their description as regenerative treatment options. When we consider this against the backdrop of the continuum theory described in Chapter 3, it is plausible to suggest that such substances may trigger a healing response in the degenerative phase and, potentially, in the disrepair phase. The overzealous use of regenerative treatments in the reactive phase of tendinopathy may exacerbate the problem, have no effect, or even hinder other more suitable treatment options.

Substance delivery (via injection) may also offer a significant tissue stimulus, especially if multiple injections are used in a peppering fashion. We should not ignore that this may be part of, or even the complete, mechanism through which neovessel generation and pain can be reduced.

The physical volume of the injected substance, expansion of the ECM, and disruption of neovessel formation have been suggested as the main mechanisms of action of large-volume injections, despite the addition of an anti-inflammatory agent that may also contribute to pain control. Although other injectables are not administered in such high volumes, their administration still mechanically influences the intratendinous environment.

There is also the question of what the injected substance is doing; for example, if the injected substance irritates the tissue in addition to other suggested responses, then it is possible that any substance capable of sclerosing would also be suitable. Higher-risk treatments such as aprotinin could then be avoided in favour of ones with a lower risk of allergic reactions.

Treatments such as GTN patches and aprotinin are considered off-label options; this means that they were developed and are used primarily for other conditions, and their use specifically for tendinopathy is not recommended by the drug manufacturer. This often creates problems with prescription and administration.

Stem cell treatment for tendinopathy may, or may not, prove a useful intervention. There is simply no current human tendon evidence to review.

Of all the substances reviewed, aprotinin appears to be the most active one, which may also account for it carrying the highest allergy risk.

The efficacy of regenerative biomedicine is, at best, moderate for degenerative tendinopathy. Regenerative treatments are best introduced after more conservative treatment methods have been used and before surgery. They must be used in conjunction with loading and other treatment approaches that treat the person in a more holistic fashion, not just the tendon.

REFERENCES

Bachl N, Derman W, Engebretsen L, et al. (2009). Therapeutic use of growth factors in the musculoskeletal system in sports-related injuries. *J Sports Med Phys Fitness.* **49**:346–357.

de Mos M, van der Windt AE, Jahr H, et al. (2008). Can platelet-rich plasma enhance tendon repair? A cell culture study. *Am J Sports Med.* **36**:1171–1178.

Engebretsen L, Steffen K, Alsousou J, et al. (2010). IOC consensus paper on the use of platelet-rich plasma in sports medicine. *Br J Sports Med.* **44**:1072–1081.

Filardo G, Kon E, Buda R, et al. (2011). Platelet-rich plasma intra-articular knee injections for the treatment of degenerative cartilage lesions and osteoarthritis. *Knee Surg Sports Traumatol Arthrosc.* **19**:528–535.

Filardo G, Kon E, Della Villa S, et al. (2010). Use of platelet-rich plasma for the treatment of refractory jumper's knee. *Int Orthop.* **34**:909–915.

Fufa D, Shealy B, Jacobson M, et al. (2008). Activation of platelet-rich plasma using soluble type I collagen. *J Oral Maxillofac Surg.* **66**:684–690.

Humphrey J, Chan O, Crisp T, et al. (2010). The short-term effects of high volume image guided injections in resistant non-insertional Achilles tendinopathy. *J Sci Med Sport.* **13**:295–298.

Kajikawa Y, Morihara T, Sakamoto H, et al. (2008). Platelet-rich plasma enhances the initial mobilization of circulation-derived cells for tendon healing. *J Cell Physiol.* **215**:837–845.

Kon E, Filardo G, Delcogliano M, et al. (2009). Platelet-rich plasma: new clinical application: a pilot study for treatment of jumper's knee. *Injury.* **40**:598–603.

Magra M, Maffulli N (2005). Matrix metalloproteases: a role in overuse tendinopathies. *Br J Sports Med.* **39**:789–791.

Mimura H, Fujiwara H, Hiraki T, et al. (2009). Polidocanol sclerotherapy for painful venous malformations: evaluation of safety and efficacy in pain relief. *Eur Radiol.* **19**:2474–2480.

Murrell GA (2007). Using nitric oxide to treat tendinopathy. *Br J Sports Med.* **41**:227–231.

Orchard J, Massey A, Brown R, et al. (2008a). Successful management of tendinopathy with injections of the MMP-inhibitor aprotinin. *Clin Orthop Relat Res.* **466**:1625–1632.

Orchard J, Massey A, Rimmer J, et al. (2008b). Delay of 6 weeks between aprotinin injections for tendinopathy reduces risk of allergic reaction. *J Sci Med Sport.* **11**:473–480.

Paoloni JA, Murrell GA (2007). Three-year followup study of topical glyceryl trinitrate treatment of chronic noninsertional Achilles tendinopathy. *Foot Ankle Int.* **28**:1064–1068.

Paoloni JA, Appleyard RC, Nelson J, et al. (2004). Topical glyceryl trinitrate treatment of chronic noninsertional Achilles tendinopathy. A randomized, double-blind, placebo-controlled trial. *J Bone Joint Surg Am.* **86-A**:916–922.

Paoloni JA, Murrell GA, Burch RM, et al. (2009). Randomised, double-blind, placebo-controlled clinical trial of a new topical glyceryl trinitrate patch for chronic lateral epicondylosis. *Br J Sports Med.* **43**:299–302.

Smith RKW (2013). Stem cell therapy for tendinopathy: lessons from a large animal model. *Br J Sports Med.* **47**:e2.

Wilde B, Havill A, Priestley L, et al. (2011). The efficacy of sclerosing injections in the treatment of painful tendinopathy. *Phys Ther Rev.* **16**: 244–260.

Xia W, Szomor Z, Wang Y, et al. (2006). Nitric oxide enhances collagen synthesis in cultured human tendon cells. *J Orthop Res.* **24**:159–172.

FURTHER READING

Everts PA, Devilee RJ, Brown Mahoney C, et al. (2006). Platelet gel and fibrin sealant reduce allogeneic blood transfusions in total knee arthroplasty. *Acta Anaesthesiol Scand.* **50**:593–599.

Nguyen RT, Borg-Stein J, McInnis K (2011). Applications of platelet-rich plasma in musculoskeletal and sports medicine: an evidence-based approach. *PM R.* **3**:226–250.

CHAPTER 15

MISCELLANEOUS TREATMENT OPTIONS FOR TENDINOPATHY

INTRODUCTION

This chapter describes several additional treatment options available to patients.

ANKLE NIGHT-TIME SPLINTS

Night-time splints are commonly prescribed for patients with plantar fasciitis and occasionally for patients with Achilles tendinopathy. They can only be used for mid-portion Achilles tendinopathy and are not recommended for insertional pain. de Vos and collaborators (2007) randomly assigned patients with Achilles tendinopathy to complete a heavy-load eccentric training programme with or without the use of a night splint; after 12 weeks, 63% of patients in the group who completed the training programme without wearing a night-time splint were satisfied, compared with 48% in the night-time splint group. There were no significant differences in pain or other outcome measures.

ACUPUNCTURE

Acupuncture has received increasing acceptance in Western medicine as a valid treatment for a variety of musculoskeletal conditions, including back pain and osteoarthritis. A small number of published studies exist that directly pertain to its use in the management of tendinopathy. Acupuncture is commonly used for pain reduction; a few studies reported short-term analgesia for tendinopathy (Green et al., 2002; Pfefer and Cooper, 2009). Acupuncture has also been shown to cause vasodilation (Carlsson, 2002), which may assist in tendon healing, though vasodilation should not be confused with neovascularisation. A study in 2010 demonstrated that heat and acupuncture treatments increased Achilles tendon blood volume and oxygen saturation; the acupuncture group sustained the increase for 30 minutes post-treatment, while the heat-treated group rapidly returned to baseline (Kubo et al., 2010). Acupuncture has also been shown to stimulate fibroplasia; when collagen fibrils are wound around the needle, a signalling pathway induces the matrix to increase fibroblast migration and collagen proliferation (Neal and Longbottom, 2012). In the concluding comments of Chapter 14, I suggested that the mechanical stimulus produced by the injection may provide a stimulus regardless of the substance being injected. If this were to be the case, then any injection-based treatment showing a positive outcome would indirectly support the use of acupuncture.

ULTRASOUND

Therapeutic ultrasound (US) has not been shown to be a beneficial treatment for tendinopathy. It does not provide any greater benefits compared to placebo or advice on pain reduction. When added to an exercise programme, US did not influence the outcome (Desmeules et al., 2015). The documented in vitro effects of US on cellularity and protein production (Doan et al., 1999) could also be detrimental to tendons in the reactive and disrepair phases. While US may be considered an option for a degenerative tendinopathy, the overall poor cohort results and the availability of more active treatments place it low on the list of possible treatment options.

LASER

Low-level laser therapy has been used therapeutically for over 40 years; the low-powered laser is thought to influence cellular homeostasis and promote healing and analgesia. Treatment success is very intensity-dependent and further research is needed to clarify optimal administration for a variety of conditions. There is evidence supporting its use in the management of tendinopathy (Tumilty et al., 2010), as well as evidence that does not support its use (Stergioulas et al., 2008).

IBUPROFEN

Ibuprofen is a non-steroidal anti-inflammatory drug (NSAID). NSAIDs were previously prescribed for tendon pain when the condition was considered inflammatory. Regardless of the shift in thinking, NSAIDs continue to be used, with mixed results. Ibuprofen appears to inhibit aggrecan expression (Riley et al., 2001). Aggrecans are the large proteoglycans associated with tendinopathy. When compared to other NSAIDs, ibuprofen appears unique in not having a detrimental effect on tendon repair (Ferry et al., 2007).

TUMOUR NECROSIS FACTOR ALPHA INHIBITORS

Tumour necrosis factor alpha (TNFα) can bind to tendon cells and may affect structural change and pain (Hosaka et al., 2004). TNFα expression was greater in inflamed equine tendons (Hosaka et al., 2005). There are many other less direct links between TNFα and tendinopathy. Many of the methods for inhibiting TNFα are expensive and have notable side effects (Fallon et al., 2008). Instead, the antibiotic doxycycline has been shown to inhibit TNFα and various MMPs; it also inhibits connective tissue breakdown (Golub et al 1991; Olmarker and Larsson 1998).

GREEN TEA AND FISH OIL

These non-pharmacological substances contain polyphenols and catechins that inhibit TNFα. Their efficacy has not been researched or tested, but it may suggest the influence of dietary intake on tendinopathy.

THE POLYPILL

In their 2008 report on the 'polypill', Fallon and collaborators (2008) described the following dosage combinations:

- ibuprofen 400 mg three times daily;

- doxycycline 100 mg once daily;
- green tea and/or fish oil (omega 3), no recommended higher or lower intake limits.

This should be continued for 14–28 days with optimal results expected by week 3.

APITHERAPY

Apitherapy involves the use of honey and other bee-derived substances. Some researchers have investigated the suggested antinociceptive and anti-inflammatory properties of bee venom in vivo! Yes, patients have been intentionally stung with bee stings to see if it helped a variety of complaints. The outcomes were poor in most cases and the risk of anaphylaxis is considerable. I do not support the use of bee venom to treat tendons.

REFERENCES

Carlsson C (2002). Acupuncture mechanisms for clinically relevant long-term effects: reconsideration and a hypothesis. *Acupunct Med*. **20**:82–99.

de Vos RJ, Weir A, Visser RJ, et al. (2007). The additional value of a night splint to eccentric exercises in chronic midportion Achilles tendinopathy: a randomised controlled trial. *Br J Sports Med*. **41**:e5.

Desmeules F, Boudreault J, Roy JS, et al. (2015). The efficacy of therapeutic ultrasound for rotator cuff tendinopathy: a systematic review and meta-analysis. *Phys Ther Sport*. **16**:276–284.

Doan N, Reher P, Meghji S, et al. (1999). In vitro effects of therapeutic ultrasound on cell proliferation, protein synthesis, and cytokine production by human fibroblasts, osteoblasts, and monocytes. *J Oral Maxillofac Surg*. **57**:409–419.

Fallon K, Purdam C, Cook J, et al. (2008). A "polypill" for acute tendon pain in athletes with tendinopathy? *J Sci Med Sport*. **11**:235–238.

Ferry ST, Dahners LE, Afshari HM, et al. (2007). The effects of common anti-inflammatory drugs on the healing rat patellar tendon. *Am J Sports Med*. **35**:1326–1333.

Golub LM, Ramamurthy NS, McNamara TF, et al. (1991). Tetracyclines inhibit connective tissue breakdown: new therapeutic implications for an old family of drugs. *Crit Rev Oral Biol Med*. **2**:297–321.

Green S, Buchbinder R, Barnsley L, et al. (2002). Acupuncture for lateral elbow pain. *Cochrane Database Syst Rev.* **(1)**:CD003527.

Hosaka Y, Kirisawa R, Ueda H, et al. (2005). Differences in tumor necrosis factor (TNF)alpha and TNF Receptor-1-mediated intracellular signaling factors in normal, inflamed and scar-formed horse tendons. *J Vet Med Sci.* **67**:985–991.

Hosaka Y, Sakamoto Y, Kirisawa R, et al. (2004). Distribution of TNF receptors and TNF receptor-associated intracellular signaling factors on equine tendinocytes in vitro. *Jpn J Vet Res.* **52**:135–144.

Kubo K, Yajima H, Takayama M, et al. (2010). Effects of acupuncture and heating on blood volume and oxygen saturation of human Achilles tendon in vivo. *Eur J Appl Physiol.* **109**:545–550.

Neal BS, Longbottom J (2012). Is there a role for acupuncture in the treatment of tendinopathy? *Acupunct Med.* **30**:346–349.

Olmarker K, Larsson K (1998). Tumor necrosis factor alpha and nucleus-pulposus-induced nerve root injury. *Spine (Phila Pa 1976).* **23**:2538–2544.

Pfefer MT, Cooper SR, Uhl NL (2009). Chiropractic management of tendinopathy: a literature synthesis. *J Manipulative Physiol Ther.* **32**:41–52.

Riley GP, Cox M, Harrall RL, et al. (2001). Inhibition of tendon cell proliferation and matrix glycosaminoglycan synthesis by non-steroidal anti-inflammatory drugs in vitro. *J Hand Surg Br.* **26**:224–228.

Stergioulas A, Stergioula M, Aarskog R, et al. (2008). Effects of low-level laser therapy and eccentric exercises in the treatment of recreational athletes with chronic achilles tendinopathy. *Am J Sports Med.* **36**:881–887.

Tumilty S, Munn J, McDonough S, et al. (2010). Low level laser treatment of tendinopathy: a systematic review with meta-analysis. *Photomed Laser Surg.* **28**:3–16.

Chapter 16

IMAGING TENDONS

INTRODUCTION

Plain radiographs and tenography are of little use when imaging tendons. They have been superseded by magnetic resonance imaging (MRI), ultrasound (US), and US tissue characterisation (USTC).

ULTRASOUND SCANNING

Advances in US scanning technology have resulted in increased image resolution coupled with reduced equipment costs. Colour Doppler imaging can be used to differentiate between fluid and synovium in inflammatory conditions and to detect neovessel growth within the tendon (**Figure 16.1**). When using colour Doppler for a reactive tendon, some collagen fibre separation may be observed, but no neovessels. A tendon in a state of disrepair often presents with neovessels; a fully degenerative tendon might show hypoechoic regions of degeneration.

There is a poor correlation between structural changes detected by US and current or future tendinopathy symptoms. According to the available data on elite volleyball players, abnormal US imaging may be present in 50% of competing volleyball players, with half of this group remaining asymptomatic and half becoming symptomatic during the competitive season (Laforgia et al., 1992; Lian et al., 1996).

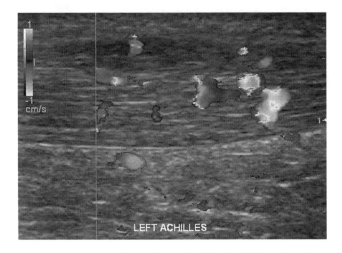

FIGURE 16.1   This colour Doppler image (red and orange areas) demonstrates neovascularisation in the ventral aspect of the tendon.

MAGNETIC RESONANCE IMAGING

Normal tendon structure shows low signal intensity on MRI. The degenerative region of the tendon shows an increased signal intensity, which presents as a white area on the scan (**Figure 16.2**).

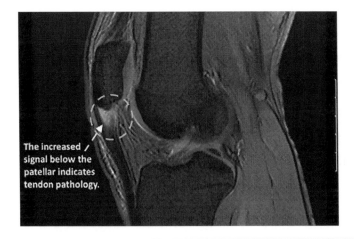

FIGURE 16.2   MRI showing an increased signal presenting as a white area just below the apex of the patella.

Both MRI and US provide a suitably sensitive method of imaging tendons. The wider use of US is due to the lower cost, accessibility, and ease of use. US is also used to guide injection procedures. MRI provides a wider view of the surrounding soft and bony anatomy, which can aid differential diagnosis (Campbell and Grainger, 2001).

ANISOTROPY

Anisotropy may be the cause of hypoechoic regions. Anisotropy is the property of being directionally dependent, that is, different properties in different directions. It is a method-dependent effect that produces hypoechoic regions because of the angulation of the probe. Essentially, it is a false positive due to operator error. **Figure 16.3** is an example of an US scan of the same tendon showing a different appearance because of the probe angle.

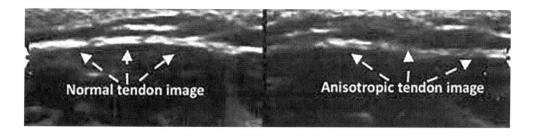

FIGURE 16.3   Transverse section of biceps tendon in the bicipital groove. On the left the tendon appears bright, but on the right a small change in the angle of the probe makes the tendon appear dark.

ULTRASOUND TISSUE CHARACTERISATION

USTC uses standard greyscale US in association with a tracker that images every 0.2 mm. It then reconstructs these images in the sagittal and frontal plane to produce a three-dimensional view to assess the structural integrity of the tendon. Research supports the use of UTC as a valid and reliable method of monitoring a tendon's response to load (Docking et al., 2012; Docking, Rosengarten and Cook, 2016).

Once the apparatus is held in position by the examiner, the probe then moves automatically over the tendon. Pixel brightness or echo types are then displayed in one of four colours on the monitor (**Figure 16.4**):

- green: good correlation and intact matrix;
- blue: <10% change in structure, indicating discontinuity or waving tendon bundles;
- red: >10% change in structure, generated by interfering echoes from mainly fibrillar components;
- black: no correlation, generated mainly by cellular components and amorphous tissue.

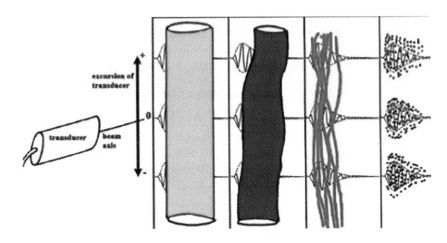

FIGURE 16.4   Colour coding used to identify structural changes detected during ultrasound tissue characterisation (Antflick and Myers, 2014). Green: good correlation and intact matrix; blue: <10% change in structure; red: >10% change in structure; black: no correlation.

The four different echo types help to provide objective markers of the structural changes and integrity along the length of the tendon, from the muscle junction to the calcaneal insertion. USTC specifically helps to monitor the change in pathology in response to load management strategies. The percentage values for healthy Achilles or patellar tendons are typically 80% green, 15% blue, and 5% red and black.

USTC can be used to monitor tendon recovery after surgery and for tendon management during the competitive season, when load demands remain high.

USTC is in its infancy; the equipment needed is expensive and not widely available. It is currently being used to research tendon response to injections and other treatment modalities including extracorporeal shock wave therapy (Antflick and Myers, 2014).

INDICATIONS FOR IMAGING

Imaging is mainly indicated to confirm a diagnosis or exclude other pathologies. Research has shown that lesions may exist in apparently healthy tendons (Cook et al., 1998); detection of these lesions does not predict the future development of symptomatic pathology (Khan et al., 1997). This highlights the importance of not relying on imaging independent of clinical assessment and to avoid imaging tendons too early or too frequently.

In many cases tendon pathology is diagnosed and managed without the use of imaging modalities.

REFERENCES

Antflick J, Myers C (2014). Management of tendinopathies with ultrasound tissue characterisation. *Sportex Med. 61:26–30.*

Campbell RS, Grainger AJ (2001). Current concepts in imaging of tendinopathy. Clin Radiol. **56**:253–267.

Cook JL, Khan KM, Harcourt PR, et al. (1998). Patellar tendon ultrasonography in asymptomatic active athletes reveals hypoechoic regions: a study of 320 tendons. Victorian Institute of Sport Tendon Study Group. *Clin J Sport Med.* **8**:73–77.

Docking SI, Rosengarten SD, Cook J (2016). Achilles tendon structure improves on UTC imaging over a 5-month pre-season in elite Australian football players. *Scand J Med Sci Sports.* **26**:557–563.

Docking SI, Daffy J, van Schie HT, et al. (2012). Tendon structure changes after maximal exercise in the Thoroughbred horse: use of ultrasound tissue characterisation to detect in vivo tendon response. *Vet J.* **194**:338–342.

Khan KM, Cook JL, Kiss ZS, et al. (1997). Patellar tendon ultrasonography and jumper's knee in female basketball players: a longitudinal study. *Clin J Sport Med.* **7**:199–206.

Laforgia R, Capocasala N, Saracino N, et al. (1992). Studio clinico-ecografico del ginocchio del saltatore (jumpers knee) e del tendine achilleo nella pallavolo. [Italian]. *Eur J Sports Traumatol Rel Research.* **14**:127–138.

Lian O, Holen KJ, Engebretsen L, et al. (1996). Relationship between symptoms of jumper's knee and the ultrasound characteristics of the patellar tendon among high level male volleyball players. *Scand J Med Sci Sports.* **6**:291–296.

APPENDIX 1

ASSESSMENT AND REHABILITATION GUIDELINES

ACHILLES TENDINOPATHY

SUBJECTIVE

RISK FACTORS	Previous injury; age >30; gender; menopause; strength deficits; flexibility deficits; obesity; carrying a loaded rucksack; rheumatoid arthritis; diabetes, fluoroquinolone antibiotics.
PAIN BEHAVIOUR	Morning stiffness and pain; diffuse or focal; mid-substance or insertional; chronic or acute; sudden pain/sensation; pain increase with recent loading; visa-a, if time allows.
LOADING HISTORY	Increase or rapid fluctuations; frequency; intensity; type (shoes/sport/surface); time.

CONSIDER

- Any indication of a partial or full rupture?
- Are morning stiffness and pain present?
- Is pain insertional or mid-substance?
- What stage is it? Reactive, disrepair, degenerative?

OBJECTIVE

OBSERVATION	Posture; muscle bulk; tendon thickening.
LOADING	Single-leg heel raise performed slowly; progress to single-leg hops, if appropriate.
LOWER-LIMB FUNCTION	Squat × 3; one-leg squat × 3, right & left; gait analysis (walking).
JOINT TESTING	Dorsi & plantar flexion range?
EXAMINATION	Plantar fascia to gastrocnemius; pain location; muscle tone/bulk/trigger points.
SPECIAL TESTS	Simmonds–Thompson; posterior impingement; plantaris (medial, more superior); sural nerve (lateral) flexor hallucis longus; tibialis posterior; accessory soleus (medial); foot posture.

OBJECTIVE	
GAIT ANALYSIS	Change in running style towards a forefoot strike pattern; recent switch to minimalist footwear; bounding with large vertical displacement.

ANALYSIS
• Stage: reactive, disrepair or degenerative?
• Has the loading or training history identified any contributing factors?
• Are there any strength or functional deficits?
• Which risk factors were identified?

Note: This guide only includes most of the key risk factors, signs, and symptoms, and should be used alongside your usual assessment procedures.

Note: The stages are not protocols and should be interpreted for patients on an individual basis. Stages 1 and 2 may be implemented together in a disrepair or degenerative tendon.

STAGE 1 (PAIN REDUCTION)

TIME FRAME	Up to four weeks.
FREQUENCY	Daily – determined by pain reduction and daily activities.
AIMS	Settle the tendon by reducing elastic loading; maintain regular load; reduce pain and sensitivity.
EDUCATION	Highly important for adherence and regime success.
EXERCISES	Isometric contractions of the calf musculature using a moderate and tolerable load for 30–60 seconds, 1–3 repetitions. Two to three times per day, depending on the duration of pain reduction after each exercise. Do the exercise when doing normal daily tasks, such as brushing teeth, making a drink, or while on the phone. Exercise should offer rapid and sustained pain relief.
ADJUNCTIVE TREATMENTS	Analgesic options can be used. Avoid interventions that stimulate the tendon during the initial reactive phase.

STAGE 2 (INCREASING STRENGTH)

TIME FRAME	From four to six weeks and performed in conjunction with the pain reduction exercises.
FREQUENCY	Twice-weekly for beginners and in-season; 3–4 weekly for strength-trained individuals; 4+ for highly active individuals.
AIMS	Increase the maximal capacity of the plantar flexor muscles and stimulate structural changes within the musculotendinous unit.
EXERCISES	3–4 Sets of 6–10 Repetitions Performed At A Slow Pace To Avoid Stimulating The Elastic Energy Storage Capacity Of The Tendon. A Range Of Motion That Avoids Excessive Dorsiflexion Should Be Taught. Allow Rest Period Of Approximately 1 Minute Between Sets.

TIPS:

- Add load, not repetitions or sets. Aim for 75–85% of 1 repetition maximum (1RM).
- Hold a wall or handrail to avoid challenging balance.

STAGE 3 (FUNCTIONAL STRENGTH)	
TIME FRAME	Based on symptomatic and functional assessment following stages 1 and 2.
FREQUENCY	Every other day.
AIMS	Continue to apply sustained loads to the tendon with the addition of more functional training. Reintroduce running with specific form training 2–3 times per week.
EXERCISES	Progress the exercises by gradually increasing the load.

TIPS:

- Increase the range of motion.
- Increase the resistance.
- Do not progress too rapidly.
- Monitor and manage the total training volume.

STAGE 4 (DEVELOP SPEED)	
TIME FRAME	Based on symptomatic and functional assessment following stages 1, 2, and 3.
FREQUENCY	Every 2–3 days. Keep strength training on the non-speed training days.
AIMS	Introduce functional speed; begin stressing the stretch/shorten capability of the tendon.
EXERCISES	Use exercises akin to the individual's sporting function. Ensure that the range of motion does not stress the enthesis by controlling any risk of excessive dorsiflexion.

- Begin with short sessions using a low load.
- Partial weight-bearing is an option.

STAGE 5 (ATHLETIC FUNCTION)	
TIME FRAME	Based on symptomatic and functional assessment following stages 1, 2, 3, and 4.
FREQUENCY	Athletic function days incorporated into a weekly programme containing strength and speed exercise days. The week should consist of a small cycle of **high, medium, and low loading days.**
AIMS	Combine the development of strength and speed into usable athletic function in preparation for full training.
EXERCISES	Advanced running form drills; propulsion activities; acceleration/deceleration; eccentric, concentric turnarounds; speed/agility/quickness (SAQ)-style training drills.

ADVICE AND MONITORING:

- Pain during activity does not correlate well with clinical outcome or pathology.
- Careful monitoring of morning pain and stiffness using a diary should be used to ascertain the appropriate speed of programme progression.
- Remember the cellular response to loading usually takes around >24 hours.
- Consider the programme's start and end points.
- This is a guide, not a protocol: consider activities of daily living (ADLs) and adapt the programme accordingly.
- Recovery speed can fluctuate.
- Cycle high, low, and medium days.

PATELLAR TENDINOPATHY

SUBJECTIVE	
RISK FACTORS	Jumping or running activities; previous patellar tendon anterior cruciate ligament graft; age >30; menopause; strength deficits; flexibility deficits; obesity; increased weight-bearing; leg length discrepancy; rheumatoid arthritis; diabetes, fluoroquinolone antibiotics.
PAIN BEHAVIOUR	Stiffness and pain in the morning or after prolonged sitting; focal pain below the patellar apex; complete VISA-P if time allows.
LOADING HISTORY	Jumping activities; increase or rapid fluctuations in frequency; intensity; type (shoes/sport/surface); time.

CONSIDER
· Do the symptoms indicate patellofemoral pain or patellar tendinopathy?
· Are stiffness and pain present?
· What recent changes has your patient made to their exercise regime?
· What stage is it? Reactive, disrepair, degenerative?

OBJECTIVE	
OBSERVATION	Posture; quadriceps muscle bulk.
LOADING	Squats; single-leg squats; step down; single-leg hop; repeat three times if asymptomatic; perform a single or double-leg decline or standard squat, recording pain-free range and board decline setting.
JOINT TESTING	Ankle dorsi to plantar flexion range; hip joint range.
EXAMINATION	Tibial tuberosity to rectus femoris origin; pain location over the patellar apex; muscle tone/bulk/trigger points; quadriceps and hamstring flexibility; leg length discrepancy; foot posture.
SPECIAL TESTS	Knee extensions to test the infrapatellar fat pad; patellar glide to test for reduced patellofemoral pain during resisted flexion.

OBJECTIVE	
GAIT ANALYSIS (RUNNING)	Overstriding; slow step rate; large vertical displacement; excessive heel strike pattern.

ANALYSIS
· Which stage: reactive, disrepair, or degenerative?
· Does the loading and training history identify any contributing factors?
· Were there any strength or functional deficits?
· Which risk factors were identified?

Note: This guide only includes most of the key risk factors, signs, and symptoms, and should be used alongside your usual assessment procedures.

Note: The stages are not protocols and should be interpreted for patients on an individual basis. Stages 1 and 2 may be implemented together in a disrepair or degenerative tendon.

STAGE 1 (PAIN REDUCTION)	
TIME FRAME	Up to four weeks.
FREQUENCY	Daily – determined by pain reduction and daily activities.
AIMS	Settle the tendon by reducing elastic loading; maintain regular load; reduce pain and sensitivity.
EDUCATION	Highly important for adherence and regime success.
EXERCISES	Ski squat with knees above 60 degrees for 30–60 seconds and repeat if tolerated; attempt one-leg static squat, adding decline 15–25 degrees or using a leg extension or leg press machine if available; exercise start point is determined by personal ability and athletic level.
	Two to three times per day depending on the length of pain reduction following each exercise.
	The exercises should not challenge balance; the focus should be on consistent tendon loading.
	This exercise should offer rapid and sustained pain relief.
ADJUNCTIVE TREATMENTS	Analgesic options can be used; avoid interventions that stimulate the tendon during the initial reactive phase.

STAGE 2 (INCREASING STRENGTH)	
TIME FRAME	From four to six weeks and performed in conjunction with the pain reduction exercises.
FREQUENCY	Two sessions per week for beginners and in-season; 3–4 sessions per week for strength-trained individuals.
AIMS	Increase strength and endurance capacity of the whole musculotendinous unit.
	Improve tendon structure and stiffness.
EXERCISES	Squat-based exercises to 60-degree knee flexion; 3–4 sets of 6–10 repetitions performed at a slow pace to avoid any stimulus of the elastic energy storage capacity of the tendon. Rest for approximately 2 minutes between sets.

TIPS:

- Add load not repetitions or sets.
- Use a resistance 75–85% of 1RM.

STAGE 3 (FUNCTIONAL STRENGTH)	
TIME FRAME	Based on symptomatic and functional assessment following stages 1 and 2.
FREQUENCY	Every other day.
AIMS	Continue to apply sustained loads to the tendon with the addition of more functional postures. Improve landing mechanics and gait re-education. Progress the retraining of motor pattern deficits. Reintroduce running with specific form training; 2–3 times per week; short sessions, avoid running downhill.
EXERCISES	Include a larger variety of squat and lunge variations

TIPS:

- Encourage balance and stability of the whole body when supported by the lower limb.
- Increase the resistance while continuing to focus on endurance.

STAGE 4 (DEVELOP SPEED)	
TIME FRAME	Based on symptomatic and functional assessment following stages 1, 2, and 3.
FREQUENCY	Every 2–3 days. Keep strength training on the non-speed training days.
AIMS	Introduce functional speed and begin stressing the rapid loading capability of the tendon.
EXERCISES	Jump squat; split squat; power cleans.

- Begin with just body weight or a barbell.
- Practise repetitive movement patterns first.

STAGE 5 (ATHLETIC FUNCTION)	
TIME FRAME	Based on symptomatic and functional assessment following stages 1, 2, 3, and 4.
FREQUENCY	Athletic function days will be incorporated into a weekly programme containing the strength and speed exercise days. The week should consist of a small cycle of **high, medium, and low loading days.**
AIMS	Combine the development of strength and speed into usable athletic function in preparation for full training.
EXERCISES	Running form drills; jumping activities; acceleration/ deceleration; eccentric, concentric turnarounds; SAQ-style training drills.

ADVICE AND MONITORING:

- Pain during activity does not correlate well with clinical outcome or pathology.
- Careful monitoring of pain and stiffness using a diary should be used to ascertain the appropriate speed of programme progression.
- Remember the cellular response to loading usually takes around >24 hours.
- Consider the programme's start and end points.
- This is a guide, not a recipe: consider ADLs and adapt the programme accordingly.
- Recovery speed can fluctuate.
- Cycle high, low, and medium days.
- Reassess running form regularly to avoid technique regression.

HAMSTRING TENDINOPATHY

SUBJECTIVE	
RISK FACTORS	Previous hamstring muscle or tendon injury; middle-to-long-distance running; hill running; deep squatting; lunging activities; poor hamstring strength or flexibility; obesity; rheumatoid arthritis; diabetes; menopause; fluoroquinolone antibiotics.
PAIN BEHAVIOUR	Gradual onset of deep buttock pain. Possible posterior thigh referral. Increases with prolonged sitting and hip flexion under load; pain may increase with uphill running. Referred pain of sciatic distribution. VISA-H if time allows.
LOADING HISTORY	Introduction of hill running; repetitive deep squats or lunging; sustained hip flexion positions.

CONSIDER
· Tendinopathy or muscle strain? Based on pain location, onset, and behaviour.
· Is there buttock pain with prolonged sitting, with or without sciatic distribution?
· What stage is it? Reactive, disrepair, degenerative?
· Are there any contributing risk factors?

OBJECTIVE	
OBSERVATION	Anterior pelvic tilt.
LOADING	Maximum voluntary contraction test; single-leg, long lever bridge test.
LOWER-LIMB FUNCTION	Squat; deadlift; straight leg deadlift.
JOINT TESTING	lumbar spine; hip and sacroiliac joint (SIJ) extension.
EXAMINATION	Hamstring muscle and proximal attachment; pain location; muscle tone/bulk/trigger points; piriformis muscle.

OBJECTIVE	
SPECIAL TESTS	Modified slump; hamstring stretch; h-test; laslett's sij test; prone hip extension.
GAIT ANALYSIS	Overstriding; poor hip extension.

ANALYSIS
· Stage: reactive, disrepair, or degenerative?
· Is there sciatic nerve involvement?
· Does the loading or training history identify any contributing factors?
· Were strength and functional deficits identified?
· What risk factors are evident?

Note: This guide only includes most of the key risk factors, signs, and symptoms, and should be used alongside your usual assessment procedures.

Note: The stages are not protocols and should be interpreted for patients on an individual basis. Stages 1 and 2 may be implemented together in a disrepair or degenerative tendon.

STAGE 1 (PAIN REDUCTION)	
TIME FRAME	Immediately; ongoing during the subsequent stages.
AVOID	Prolonged sitting on a hard surface; sitting or squatting with the knees above the hips; overstriding when walking or running; hill walking.
AIMS	Reduce symptoms and risk factors.
ISOMETRIC EXERCISES	Prone leg curl hold; long lever bridge holds; static straight leg deadlifts. Two to three times per day depending on the duration of pain reduction following each exercise. Isometric exercises should offer rapid and sustained pain relief.
GAIT RE-EDUCATION	Identify and modify any gait-related causes.
JOINT RESTRICTIONS	Improve hip extension range and power.
ADJUNCTIVE TREATMENTS	Analgesic options can be used; avoid interventions that stimulate the tendon during the initial reactive phase.

STAGE 2 (INCREASING STRENGTH)	
TIME FRAME	From four to six weeks and performed in conjunction with the pain reduction exercises.
FREQUENCY	Two sessions per week for beginners and in-season; 3–4 sessions per week for strength-trained individuals.
AIMS	Increase hamstring strength; flexibility if required. Improve hip extension muscle patterning. Improve tendon structure and stiffness.
EXERCISES	Long lever bridge; straight leg deadlift (half-range); gluteal hip extension exercises. Rest for approximately 2 minutes between sets.

TIPS:

- Increase the load not the repetitions or sets.
- Use a resistance 75–85% of 1RM.
- Avoid excessive hip flexion

STAGE 3 (FUNCTIONAL STRENGTH)	
TIME FRAME	Based on symptomatic and functional assessment following stages 1 and 2.
FREQUENCY	Replace approximately half the exercises from phase 2 with more functional phase 3 exercises.
AIMS	Continue to apply sustained loads to the tendon with the addition of more functional movement patterns. Progress the retraining of motor pattern deficits. Reintroduce running with specific form training; 2–3 times per week; short sessions; avoid running up hill.
EXERCISES	Include a larger variety of squat and lunge variations.

STAGE 4 (DEVELOP SPEED)	
TIME FRAME	Based on symptomatic and functional assessment following stages 1, 2, and 3.
FREQUENCY	Every 2–3 days. Keep strength training on the non-speed training days.
AIMS	Introduce functional speed and begin stressing the rapid loading capability of the hamstring.
EXERCISES	Sprint drills; kicking drills; weight training – power cleans.

TIPS:

- When weight training, use just body weight or a barbell.
- Begin sprint and kicking drills at a submaximal pace.

STAGE 5 (MAINTENANCE PROGRAMME)	
TIME FRAME	Based on symptomatic and functional assessment following stages 1, 2, 3, and 4.
FREQUENCY	Specific exercises from the previous stages should form part of a short maintenance session to be performed 2–3 times per week.
AIMS	Maintain strength and flexibility gains; maintain positive changes to running form.
EXERCISES	Specific strength training exercises; functional exercises; gait assessment and feedback.

ADVICE AND MONITORING

- Pain during activity does not correlate well with the clinical outcome or pathology.
- Careful monitoring of pain and stiffness using a diary should be used to ascertain the appropriate speed of programme progression.
- Remember the cellular response to loading usually takes around >24 hours.
- Consider the programme's start and end points.
- This is a guide, not a recipe: consider ADLs and adapt the programme accordingly.
- Recovery speed can fluctuate.
- Cycle high, low, and medium days.
- Reassess running form regularly to avoid technique regression.

GLUTEAL TENDINOPATHY

SUBJECTIVE

RISK FACTORS	Age >40; female/male = 4:1; menopause; low activity levels; seated exercise habits; endurance running; hip adduction stance; poor lower-limb muscle strength; trendelenburg sign; coxa vara; hip osteoarthritis; obesity; fluoroquinolones antibiotics.
PAIN BEHAVIOUR	Lateral hip pain with possible lateral thigh referral. Pain may increase with: adducted hip in standing; sitting cross-legged; sleeping side-lying; standing from a seat; stairs ascent and descent. Running and walking can be painful in severe cases. VISA-G, if time allows.
LOADING HISTORY	Changes in training, recently beginning a running programme.

CONSIDER

- Can your patient flex forward to tie their shoelaces? No indicates hip osteoarthritis.
- Are gluteal weakness and hip instability present?
- What stage on the continuum: reactive, disrepair, degenerative?
- Are there any risk factors that can be easily modified?

OBJECTIVE

OBSERVATION	Habitual postures, such as standing in hip adduction, sitting cross-legged, Trendelenburg gait.
LOWER-LIMB FUNCTION	Side-lying hip abduction; one-leg squat; gait analysis (walking).
JOINT TESTING	FABER (Flexion, ABduction and External Rotation; differentiating test for osteoarthritis).
EXAMINATION	Tensor fasciae latae to posterior gluteal muscles; pain location; muscle tone/bulk/trigger points.
SPECIAL TESTS	30-Second single-leg stance test; resisted derotation test; modified trendelenburg part 1 and 2.

OBJECTIVE	
GAIT ANALYSIS (WALKING AND RUNNING)	Overstriding; slow step rate; heavy heel strike; poor hip extension; high vertical displacement; trendelenburg gait.

ANALYSIS
· Osteoarthritis or gluteal tendinopathy or both?
· Which stage: reactive, disrepair, or degenerative?
· Were there any identifiable training errors?
· Were any deficits identified in hip and lower-limb stability?
· Were any risk factors identified?

Note: This guide only includes most of the key risk factors, signs, and symptoms, and should be used alongside your usual assessment procedures.

Note: The stages are not protocols and should be interpreted for patients on an individual basis. Stages 1 and 2 may be implemented together in a disrepair or degenerative tendon.

STAGE 1 (PAIN REDUCTION)

TIME FRAME	Immediately; ongoing during the subsequent stages.
AVOID	Hanging on the hip – standing habitually on an adducted leg; sitting with legs crossed; overstriding when walking or running; sitting in low chairs.
AIMS	Reduce symptoms and risk factors.
ISOMETRIC EXERCISES	Abductor wall push; double-abductor hold; side-lying isometric hip adduction; 1–4 sets of 30–60 seconds performed 2–3 times per day depending on the duration of pain reduction following each exercise. Isometric exercises should offer rapid and sustained pain relief. Improve hip stability, specifically hip abductors, to reduce hip drop during walking, running, and single-limb tasks.
GAIT RE-EDUCATION	Identify and modify any gait-related causes. These may include: overstriding, slow step rate; heavy heel strike; poor hip extension; high vertical displacement; trendelenburg gait.
ADJUNCTIVE TREATMENTS	Analgesic options can be used. Avoid interventions that stimulate the tendon during the initial reactive phase.

STAGE 2 (INCREASING STRENGTH)

TIME FRAME	From four to six weeks and performed in conjunction with stage 2.
FREQUENCY	Two sessions per week for beginners and in-season; 3–4 sessions per week for strength-trained individuals.
AIMS	Improve hip stability, specifically hip abductors, to reduce hip drop during walking, running, and single-limb tasks.
EXERCISES	Clam; side-lying hip abduction; band walk; kneeling hip stability. Rest for approximately 1 minute between sets.

- Increase the load not the repetitions or sets.
- If possible, use a resistance 75–85% of 1RM, which should allow 6–10 repetitions for the initial set.
- Performing inner-range muscle action may aid the shortening of elongated muscles.

STAGE 3 (FUNCTIONAL STRENGTH)	
TIME FRAME	Based on symptomatic and functional assessment following stages 1 and 2.
FREQUENCY	Continue to perform exercises from stages 1 and 2, with the addition of 1 or 2 modified functional exercises.
AIMS	The addition of more functional movement patterns, modified to stimulate the hip abductors through a functional range. Progress the retraining of motor pattern deficits. Reintroduce walking or running, with specific form training focusing on reduced leg adduction and reduced stride length; 2–3 times per week; short sessions; avoid hills and off-camber surfaces.
EXERCISES	Squat and deadlift activities with added abductor resistance using a band around the knees.

STAGE 4 (ADVANCED REHABILITATION)	
TIME FRAME	Based on symptomatic and functional assessment following stages 1, 2, and 3.
FREQUENCY	3–5 Times per week in addition to chosen exercises and techniques from the previous stages.
AIMS	Instil corrected movement patterns using a combination of analgesia, risk factor avoidance, strengthening, gait re-education and education.
EXERCISES	One-leg squat and deadlift if your patient has a suitable fitness level. Use the previous exercises alongside gait re-education with real-time (mirror) and post-training feedback.

- Short, high-quality and regular training sessions provide the best results.

ADVICE AND MONITORING

- Pain during activity does not correlate well with clinical outcome or pathology.
- Careful monitoring of morning pain and stiffness using a diary should be used to ascertain the appropriate speed of programme progression.
- Remember the cellular response to loading usually takes around >24 hours.
- Consider the programme's start and end points.
- This is a guide, not a recipe: consider ADLs and adapt the programme accordingly.
- Recovery speed can fluctuate.
- Reassess walking and running technique regularly to avoid technique regression.

Appendix 2

GAIT ASSESSMENT FORM

GAIT ASSESSMENT FORM

Assessment surface: Treadmill/road/track/trail

Assessment method: Video/visual

Shoe type: None/minimalist/cushioned

Pain during assessment   Yes – Location?   No

STEP RATE	<175	175–200	>200
FOOT STRIKE PATTERN	Heel	Mid-foot	Forefoot
INITIAL FOOT CONTACT	Clearly anterior to the body's centre of mass (COM)	Under or slightly anterior to COM	Under COM
PRONATION	Overpronating	Neutral	Underpronating
VERTICAL DISPLACEMENT (USE HEAD AS A REFERENCE POINT)	Large amount of displacement. Bouncy bounding style of running	Small amount of displacement	Minimal displacement
PELVIC STABILITY	Large amount of contralateral drop	Small amount of drop equal on both sides	Irregular unilateral drop
HIP INTERNAL ROTATION (KNEE REFERENCE POINT)	Noticeable internal rotation	Minimal to zero internal rotation	Unilateral internal rotation
MIDLINE CROSSOVER	Crossover	Minimal crossover	No crossover
HIP EXTENSION	None	Normal	Spinal extension compensation

Notes:

Plan:

Index

Seminars Talks & Workshops

For information on hosting or attending seminars, talks & workshops visit

www.PhysioBooks.com

PhysioBooks

Could you write for us?

www.PhysioBooks.com

Made in United States
Troutdale, OR
12/26/2023

16426116R00186